THE HISTORY OF THE
CORPS OF ROYAL MILITARY POLICE

THE HISTORY OF
THE CORPS OF ROYAL
MILITARY POLICE

BY

MAJOR S. F. CROZIER, M.B.E.

The Gloucestershire Regiment
(R.M.P. and Provost Service 1940-1946)

The Naval & Military Press Ltd

Published by

The Naval & Military Press Ltd
Unit 10 Ridgewood Industrial Park,
Uckfield, East Sussex,
TN22 5QE England

Tel: +44 (0) 1825 749494
Fax: +44 (0) 1825 765701

www.naval-military-press.com
www.military-genealogy.com

Printed and bound by CPI Group (UK) Ltd, Croydon, CR0 4YY

*In reprinting in facsimile from the original, any imperfections are inevitably reproduced
and the quality may fall short of modern type and cartographic standards.*

FOREWORD

BY

GENERAL SIR MILES DEMPSEY, K.C.B., K.B.E., D.S.O., M.C.

THERE can be few Corps or Regimental Histories of the Second World War which cover so wide a field as this book does.

There was certainly no campaign in which the Military Police was not strongly represented, and very few actions in which the Order of Battle did not include at least some members of the C.M.P.

The Military Policeman became so well-known a figure on every road to the battlefield that his presence was taken for granted. Few soldiers as they hurried over a bridge which was a regular target for enemy aircraft or artillery, gave much thought to the man whose duty it was to be there for hours on end directing the traffic and ensuring its rapid passage.

There were many other activities—this book describes them well —but that is the memory of the C.M.P. which I shall always carry with me: the man on point-duty within the battle area: the man who did so much to ensure the orderly deployment of the army for battle.

There was nothing spectacular about this work, and it gave to those who did it few opportunities of earning decorations for gallantry in action.

The Corps' reward came later when, on the 28th November, 1946, His Majesty authorized the prefix "Royal" to be added to its title.

General
COLONEL COMMANDANT
CORPS OF ROYAL MILITARY POLICE

January, 1951.

"REDCAPS".
A painting by Gilbert Holiday in the Sergeants' Mess, R.M.P. Depot

CONTENTS

ILLUSTRATIONS

MAPS

AUTHOR'S PREFACE

THIS history is the work of many contributors. Some of them produced manuscript for inclusion on which they had evidently spent much time and trouble. I fear they may think that the shortened form in which their contribution appears—and sometimes, indeed, its absence—is but a thankless return for their readiness to supply information for which appeals were made when the history was being prepared. There are about 100,000 words in this book; the material from which they have been reduced must amount to well over 1,000,000 words. With a few exceptions, therefore, only about one-tenth of all the material contributed could be used.

The purist who reads these pages will find ground for complaint. Some portions are written in the military phraseology of the professional officer, others in the language of the N.C.O., but this history is designed for soldiers, not purists, and it seemed to me that to reduce it to a common flatness would be to remove some of its essential military character.

Many readers, no doubt, will think that their own particular theatre of war ought to have had more prominence. I would ask them to remember that the readers who served in other theatres are probably thinking the same thing and that this history is designed to be a record of the progress of the R.M.P. throughout the world.

Here and there are gaps. For more than two years the Provost Marshal's office and myself tried to find former provost officers or N.C.Os. who had the requisite knowledge. Usually we succeeded, but occasionally we failed to find the right man or, if we found him, he would not write. Unfortunately, except in a few cases, little was available in the way of written records.

The chapter dealing with the history of the early Provost Marshals and the development of the Provost Service is compiled mainly from the research of Brigadier H. Bullock and Major A. V. Lovell-Knight. The chief contributors of information for latter parts of the book are Brigadier Bassett F. G. Wilson and Brigadier J. N. Cheney, former Provost Marshals of the B.L.A. and the British Army of the Rhine; Colonel H. V. McNally, Deputy Provost Marshal, the War Office; Lieutenant-Colonel F. H. Elliott, Deputy Provost Marshal, Special Investigation Branch; and many other officers, N.C.Os. and civilians.

Although this history is published under my name it is to these officers and to Major-General I. D. Erskine, Colonel P. Godfrey-Faussett, and the staff of the War Office, who gave so much of their time to this work, that the gratitude of the Corps is due for making possible the first complete history of what is probably the oldest police force in the world.

I must record a special word of thanks to Brigadier Bassett Wilson, my Provost Marshal in North-West Europe, who revised and improved the final draft of this history with that meticulous care and attention to detail for which he was well known to all who served under him.

S. F. Crozier.

The War Office, S.W.1.

NOTE BY PROVOST MARSHAL.—The history contains a number of tributes to individuals and to Wings and Branches of the Corps. Major Crozier is not responsible for these tributes, which come from Provost Marshals and other senior Provost officers, whose contributions to the history are acknowledged in the author's Preface.

INTRODUCTION

THERE can be few people in Great Britain—or, indeed, in Europe—who have not, at one time or another, seen a pair of British soldiers with red caps on their heads and M.P. brassards on their arms. To the civilian these are military police; to the soldier they are N.C.Os. of the Corps of Royal Military Police, or "Redcaps"; but the student of military history knows they are the descendants and representatives of one of the oldest military offices under the Crown, that of the Provost Marshal.

Although the earliest record of a Provost Marshal by name is dated 1511, it is possible that the office was in existence in the twelfth and thirteenth centuries. Indeed, as long as the King relied upon an army raised by the barons it is probable that he had an officer appointed to enforce a uniform standard of discipline in the army.

It is not clear whether the Provost Marshal's department or that of the Chaplains was the first to be established under the Norman kings, but certain it is that hundreds of years before the King had an army of his own these two officers had been appointed to ensure the discipline, order and spiritual welfare of the feudal levies.

It is interesting to note that the King still exercises his right to possess a Provost Marshal, and that officer was until recently appointed directly by him.

The relationship between the Chaplain and the Provost Marshal was in former times much closer than it is today, for in those days the Provost Marshal enforced discipline by means of a halter and the most convenient tree and thus the attendance of a chaplain to console the condemned in his last moments was necessary.

In the Second World War one of the problems which faced the War Office was how to find men who would make efficient Provost Marshal's, deputies and assistants. They had to be men who could combine firmness with tact and discretion, who would know when to be ruthless or when to turn a blind eye, who would not be tempted by the wide authority granted them by their appointment. This was no new problem. In 1662 Francis Markham wrote: "The Gentleman which should be elected to this place of Provost Marshal, would be a man of great judgment and experience in all martial discipline, well seen in the laws and ordinances of the camp, and such a one as knew well the use, benefit and necessity of all things belonging either to food or raiment. He should be a lover of justice, impartial in his dealings, and free from the transportation of passions: he should have an ear that could contemptuously beat back, not furiously drink in, slander and railing language: he should have an eye that could gaze on all objects without winking; and a heart full of discreet compassion, but not touched with foolish or melting pity. In brief he ought to be only the Law's servant." Of the assistants of the Provost Marshal in former times little has been written, but we may take it that they were, like Military Policemen today, men of large statue and of discretion. It is not known whether in former times there were special agents of the Provost Marshal who performed the duties now carried out by the detectives of the Special Investigation Branch, R.M.P., but Markham wrote that it was the duty of the Provost Marshal to "discover the lurking subtleties of treacherous spies, and by learning the true interpretation of men's words, looks, manners, forms and habits of apparel, to be able to turn the insides of their heart outwards, and to pull out that little devil of malicious deceit, though he lie hid in never so dark a corner; and truly a better service cannot be done, nor is there any Art sooner learned if a man will apply his knowledge but seriously thereto."

Not a bad definition of the art of the detective.

It may be appropriate here to mention that by one of those typical oddities of British law the military police officer or N.C.O. had, until well into the Second World War, only the powers of arrest conferred by his rank when on duty at home stations. He could not therefore arrest any offender of superior rank. Abroad, however, Section 74 of the Army Act gave the Provost Marshal and his assistants the power of arrest over all persons subject to military law. This unsatisfactory position was rectified during the Second World War by a Defence Regulation which amended Section 45 of the Army Act to allow N.C.Os. of the Military Police to arrest any N.C.O. or warrant officer, and provost officers to arrest officers of any rank. These changes were, in 1948, incorporated as an amendment to the Army Act.

The Military Police N.C.O. has never had any power to arrest on his own authority an officer, except, of course for his common law obligation, which also applies to every other citizen, to arrest any person whom he sees committing a felony. It is, however, necessary that in war time N.C.Os. should, for reasons of security, have the power of arrest over officers. It was therefore the custom in some theatres to provide each policeman with a warrant card in which he was specifically empowered by the Commander-in-Chief to detain officers in certain named circumstances.

In the last war the Military Police underwent a huge expansion. Its duties, hitherto largely confined to the maintenance of discipline in rear areas, were to include the organization and running of a linked system of traffic control and information posts, covering the whole theatre of operations, including the forward areas, assault beaches, and the control of minefields ; the handling of prisoners of war and refugees, investigation of complicated and serious crime, and the organization and planning of a police network throughout the various theatres of operations.

The new commitments brought new problems: not the least of these was the difficulty of choosing the right type of men to fill vacancies for provost officers. So many men, mostly ex-policemen, had what has been called elsewhere in this history the "policeman's complex"; these men were first-class policemen when it was necessary to deal with unruly troops or investigate crime, but by the very nature of their training, which requires caution and consideration before taking action and a rigid view of the necessity for the enforcement of law, were not always the right type of men to undertake operational duties where dash and initiative and little professional police knowledge were required.

On the other hand, many soldiers who made first-class military policemen in forward areas when engaged on operational duties were of little value when it came to doing the unpopular job of maintaining discipline.

From these two types emerged the new "Redcaps"—the men who marked the way through the minefields of El Alamein, directed traffic on D Day on the beaches of Normandy, and who, by patient investigation, saved the country thousands of pounds in recovering W.D. property.

The military police have today become known as the friends of the soldier rather than as the stern enforcers of a ruthless rule of discipline, but it has not been easy for them to achieve that popularity. A military policeman of any rank is always confronted with the difficulty that if he does his job without fear or favour he will inevitably make enemies of those who wish to see the law loosely enforced or only enforced against certain sections of the military community, but, on the other hand, if he occasionally turns his blind eye to a trifling offence he is likely to earn a reproof from those who are ever ready to find a policeman at fault.

A retiring Commissioner of the Metropolitan Police once said to his successor: "You are coming to a funny place; you will be blamed if you do your duty and you will be blamed if you don't." The position of the Military Police in the Army until very recent times could not have been described more aptly.

The Corps owes a special debt of gratitude to a group of officers who did much to raise its prestige. Among them are Major-General Sir Percy Laurie, who founded the Vulnerable Points Wing of the

C.M.P. and brought his experience as Assistant Commissioner of the Metropolitan Police to the service of the Corps; Major-General J. Seymour Mellor, Provost Marshal during the critical period when the invasion of Europe was being planned and executed; Brigadier Bassett Wilson, who prepared the provost plans for the greatest invasion in history and whose devotion to the Corps and knowledge of his job gained him a unique reputation in the history of the military police; Brigadier J. N. Cheney, whose technical knowledge and enthusiasm for police work were an inspiration to those who served under him; and Brigadier Mark Sykes, under whose infectious energy and leadership the Depot was so efficiently organized in the early years of the war.

Although Major-General I. D. Erskine, Provost Marshal until December, 1948, did not take up his post until the end of the war in Europe, it was due to his determined efforts (which had all the more weight because he was not a professional policeman) that the Corps was distinguished by the grant of the prefix "Royal," was raised to No. 18 in the order of precedence, and that all lance-corporals now receive the pay of their appointment.

It is also by his efforts that the office of Provost Marshal is now, for the first time, vested with authority over the provost service in all parts of the world.

Although, in this history, individuals, units and incidents are in a number of cases identified, for the most part the events described and persons mentioned should be taken as typical rather than selective, as characteristic rather than pre-eminent.

This introduction should therefore end with a tribute to those officers and other ranks, unnamed in this book, whose skill, integrity, and determination did so much to raise the prestige of the Corps.

CHAPTER I

THE PROVOST SERVICE, 1511-1939

IN the port of Plymouth in May, 1511, there mustered an expedition against the Moors of Barbary under command of Lord Darcie, the King's Captain-General. Among his subordinate officers was a Provost Marshal, Henry Guylford, "a lusty young man, and well beloved of the King."

He was a busy official and had plenty of work from the moment the expedition arrived in port, for the soldiers, we are told, "fell to drinking hote wynes and were scarce masters of them selfes. Some ran to the stewes, some broke hegges, and spoyled orchardes and wyneyardes and orynges before they were ripe, and did many other outragious dedes; wherefore the chefe of the tourne of Caleys came to complaine to the lord Darcie in hys shippe, whiche sent forth his Provost Marshal which scarcelie with payne refrayned the yomen archers, they were so hote and wilfull, yet by commaundement and policie, they were all brought on borde their shippes."

This Guylford was not the first Provost Marshal, but he is the first of whom any personal record has been found. Later he attended Henry VIII at the Field of the Cloth of Gold, but no one has recorded what happened to him after that, and history contains no further mention of a Provost Marshal until 1547, when Sir William Patten and Sir William Cecil, Provost Marshals, were judges of a military court accompanying the expedition into Scotland.

The Provost Marshal was also active in England at this time and Sir William Patten refers in his journal to the setting up of a gallows by the Provost Marshal, Sir James Wylford, in the market-place in Newcastle, in 1547, for the hanging of a soldier for quarrel-ling and fighting. After the arrival in Scotland of the expedition, the garrisons of Douglas and Thornton were handed over to the Provost Marshal when they surrendered.

Two years later Sir Anthony Kingston was appointed Provost Marshal to deal with the West Country rebels. His grim humour was in keeping with the nature of his work. A story is told of a miller, who, having been out with the rebels, feared reprisals and persuaded a servant to take his place and name. This man was arrested by the Provost Marshal. "Are you the miller?" asked Kingston.

"If you please, yes," was the reply.

"Up with him!" said the Provost to his assistants. "He is a busy knave, hang him up!"

The unfortunate man protested in vain that he was no miller, but an honest servant.

"Then thou art a double false knave," said the Provost Marshal, "to be false in two tales; therefore hang him up!"

The Mayor of Bodmin's name was joined with Arundell's in the rebels' articles. But, unlike the miller, he did not fear reprisals, relying upon the influence of friends and a bold face. Kingston visited Bodmin and sent the Mayor a notice that he would dine with him—adding that he had a man to hang, too, and a stout gallows should be made ready. The dinner was eaten and the gallows afterwards inspected.

"Think you," said Kingston, "is it stout enough?"

"Yes, sir," replied the Mayor, "it is, of a surety."

"Well, then," replied the Provost, "get you up, for it is for you!"

The Mayor protested.

"Sir," said Kingston, "there is no remedy. You have been a busy rebel, and this is appointed for your reward." And so, "without respite or stay," the Mayor was hanged.

The ruthless Kingston was succeeded by a man of milder temperament, Barnaby Googe, who was appointed Provost Marshal in Ireland in 1582. He was only paid £40 a year, exclusive of rations, perquisites and free quarters, but, in keeping with the custom of the times, he had other perquisites such as charge of the Marshal's gaol, worth some £20 a year, and the custody of hostages; usually the sons of Irish chieftains, surrendered as a surety for their fathers' good behaviour. From them he hoped to secure about £100 a year, but he was disappointed, for, as he himself records, he drew not a penny. Poor Barnaby also complained that the Queen had, contrary to all precedent, failed to provide him with any regular soldiers to accompany him, and that he therefore had to employ local unpaid yokels for his protection.

"These," he reported, "are commonly more given to extortion than the Englishman is. Neither can I," he continues, "since they serve without pay, use whatever means I can, restrain them of their evil demeanour: besides, serving altogether with such kind of companions, I am always in danger to have my throat cut amongst them." As a result of these complaints, he seems to have been allowed at least a dozen horsemen.

Finally, thoroughly disillusioned, Barnaby applied in 1585 to be allowed to dispose of the patent of his office to a "gentleman of good discretion," having five and twenty horsemen from Connaught under his command. The "gentleman of good discretion" offered Barnaby £100 for the office.

The year of the Armada was a busy one for the Provost Marshal, Captain Crisp. The Queen's orders, issued to the Lord-Lieutenants of the counties in 1588, contained instructions not unlike those issued to the police in England in 1940 when invasion was expected: ". . . and because in such doubtful times it falleth out commonly that divers false rumours are given forth and spread abroad, which do distract the minds of the people and breed confusion, it is thought very requisite that a care should be had thereof, and that the authors of such rumours and tales should be diligently and speedily punished."

Crisp and subordinate Provost Marshals appointed in each county were charged with the duty of punishing the rumour-mongers.

The names of some of the county Provost Marshals are known. In Hertfordshire it was Humphrey Coningesby and in East Kent Thomas Nevinson of Eastry, gent., "a person of good discretion and ability."

It is not inappropriate here to refer to the duties of the Provost Marshal in these times. Although the Provost Marshal's chief duty was, of course, to maintain discipline amongst the troops, he had arbitrary powers over civilians as well.

Henry VIII is said to have been the first person to lay down specific duties for his Provost Marshal. These rules, contained in the Articles of War, bear a remarkable resemblance to the duties of a provost officer in the field today. These are the orders which Henry VIII gave to his Provost Marshal:

1. Having received from the High Marshal a State of the Army, and having been told by that officer where the Army was to encamp, he was to lay out the boundaries and divisions of the camp.

2. He was to appoint a market-place in the camp, to mark streets, and to settle a place for the Lieutenant-General, giving him the place of honour in the Field.

3. He was strictly to enforce the rule that no tent was to be pitched within 20 feet of what we should now call the perimeter of the camp.

4. He should post all sentries himself and give them their orders and the watchword; and inspect them two or three times in a night.

5. In action, he was to serve "in his owne person with the foot-men, in the rank of Sergeant-Major" (equivalent to Major today).

6. He should give "straighte commaundment that after the watche be set, and the watchpiece shotten-off, there be no manner of noise in the Camp, but that all men be quiet."

To assist him he had a company of tipstaves, to keep good order, prevent brawling and fighting and to arrest offenders who were punished at his discretion.

A reference to the grimmer side of the Provost Marshal's duties is contained in "A Pathway to Military Practice," by Barnaby Rich, published in 1587:

"The Provost Marshal is to have charge of the Marshalsea; he must be provided of fetters, gyves, handlocks and all manner of irons for the safe keepings of such prisoners as shall be committed to his keeping. He is to see due execution of all malefactors having received sentence of death, and to apprehend the authors of any disorders."

A detailed description of the Provost Marshal and his activities is given by Francis Markham in his "Five Decades of Epistles of Warre," published in 1662.

Military manuals written in more recent times casually dismiss the Provost Marshal in a few lines. Not so Markham. His reflections upon the duties of the officer and the character of the holder show such insight into the qualities needed by a Provost Marshal that his description deserves repetition in these pages.

". . . The office upon which I touch in this place is that of the Provost Marshal, which howsoever the General (through his greatness and priority of place) hath power to confirm and appoint, yet commonly the Gentleman which is designated thereunto, is always nominated and recommended by the Lord Marshal of the Field, being his under officer, and one unto whom is delivered the charge and keeping of all Delinquents and criminal offenders whatsoever. This office I have seen in mine experience to carry a double and two-fold estimation. . . . Judging of the good or evil thereof according to the worthiness or unworthiness of the party which held it, the honest, wise and understanding men swaying it with Reputation and Renown. The foolish, base, and contemptible person ordering it with a regard of as much or more Imputation. But all this is fault in Election, not in place: for it is certain, the office in itself is both worthy, necessary, and good, a calling fit for a gentleman of blood and quality, and a degree wherein a man may express any virtue to the life, both with applause and admiration.

"It is also of great profit and advancement (which infers merit) and there is knit into it a singular trust, which must ever allow of much Faith and Wisdom. . . .

"For the nature of his office, he is first the greatest and principal gaoler of the Army, having power to detain and keep prisoner whosoever shall be committed unto him by lawful authority, and though some contemptuously have called him the Hangman, or Executioner of the Army, yet it is not so, but as our Sheriff's of Counties are bound to find slaves for such needful uses: so he by his place is obliged to find men and other implements for all such occasions, and to that end hath allowance for many attendants to dispatch any execution how suddenly soever commanded, and to that end it is not lawful for the under Provosts to go at any time without halters, withs, or strangling cords of match, ever about them.

"The Provost Marshal hath the charge of all manner of tortures, as gyves, shackles, bolts, chains, belbowes, manacles, whips and the like and may by his ministers use them, either in the case of judgment or commandment from a Martial Court or otherwise upon unruliness at his own discretion: he is by his officers to see all places of Execution prepared and furnished with engines fitting to the judgment, whether it be gallows, gibets, scaffolds, pillories, stocks, or strappadoes, or any other engine which is set up for terror and affright to such as behold it.

"This officer hath the guard and keeping of all such prisoners as are taken in the wars, till they be either ransomed, exchanged or by the General otherwise disposed: and in this case the nobler his usage is, the greater will the praise be of his humanity and virtue. If any drums or trumpets shall happen to come from the Enemy, they are by the Provost Marshal to be entertained, accommodated and provided, unless it shall please the Lord Marshal himself otherwise to dispose of them. And that all these duties beforesaid may with more efficiency and luster be performed, he shall have his Quarter in the Strongest and most securest part of all the Army: and in all marches he is also to have the place of greatest safety, for the assurance of his prisoners.

"Moreover, it is the office of the Provost Marshal, by the authority of the Lord Marshal, to guard with a good convoy of men, both to the camp and in the camp, and from the camp, all manner of victuallers, viandors, merchants and others which bring any provisions to the camp, and as soon as they are entered, he shall rate and set price (in a reasonable and indifferent manner) upon all their goods, and secure them from the insolence of the soldier, providing that no man take anything from them without payment: he also looks to the proportions of the true weights and measures, and reconciles any difference in buying and selling, for which labour he hath of the Providors or Merchants, the hides and tongues of all manner of cattle that are killed, and every week sixpence apiece in money numbered for their stalls, which sixpence a week he is accountable for unto the Lord Marshal, for to him that fee is belonging.

"It is likewise the office of the Provost Marshal, to see that the Market Place of the Camp be once in two days swept and kept sweet and clean, that all garbage and filthiness be burned and consumed, that no man do the office of nature but in places convenient, and that in the whole camp or Garrison there may not be anything which may turn to a general nuisance.

"The Provost Marshal must have an especial care to the keeping of the Peace, and to apprehend the least occasion which may tend to breach of the same, he must prevent all Mutinies, Quarrels, and disorders, and that no uncivil discussion may have strength to out-face or withstand the power of his command: he shall ever have about him a guard of Under-Provosts and servants, who with short truncheons in their hands, according unto Military Form, shall enforce obedience to any lawful commandment which proceedeth from him, and having taken them in their actual transgressions, to commit them to prison, or the bolts, as the nature or evil example of the crime deserveth: for it is a duty expected at this officer's hands to be a ready suppressor of vice and disorder, and to be a maintenance and advancer of all those which have any semblance or likeness with an honest, sober and civil inclination.

". . . whence it behoveth him to have a ready and quick judging eye between the good and the bad, so that he may in an early hour restrain all immoderate and unlawful gain, and rather compel the cut-throat to kill himself with envy, than to consume others with the rust and cankour of his unsatisfied covetousness.

"To conclude, the last duty of the Provost Marshal is (after the watch is set at night) to survey the Army, and see if it remains calm and still, and that no disorderly noises or tumults keep any part of it awake and not silent; and in this survey, if he encounter with any immoderate fires or superfluous candle-lights he shall cause them to be put out and extinguished; or if he hear in Sutler's cabins or other harbour any drunkards, tobacco-takers, or other unruly persons, whose noise is both offensive to the camp and giveth to others an evil example, he shall presently suppress them, and make them depart, or else upon grosser disorder, commit them for besides the undecency and unfitness of the action, such clamours and noises are more than hurtful in a camp, specially being anything near where the Sentinel standeth: for it is an interruption and hindrance through which he cannot possibly discharge his duty. . . ."

Although the Provost Marshal held his appointment from the King, he was nevertheless a subordinate officer of the Earl Marshal. This is made clear in correspondence between the Privy Council and the Earl Marshal of England, then the Earl of Essex, in 1598 when the Privy Council wrote to the Earl Marshal informing him that the Queen had ordered the appointment of a Provost Marshal to take office in London.

". . . Here upon we have proceeded thus far by her Majesty's commandment as to cause a commission to be drawn for a Provost Marshal, to be signed by Her Majesty, and certain letters to be written by us unto the said counties to give them knowledge of the commission and to require their services in the redressing of the said disorders, but because we do consider that this may in some sort appertain to your Lordship's office of the Earl Marshal of England, and would by no means take any course herein that may be prejudicial to the right and authority of your place, we have thought meet to acquaint your Lordship herewith before we go any further in the business, and do pray your Lordship to certify us both of your own opinion concerning your own particular right and interest (in the ordering the executing of this Service) by vertue of your office, as also in generality to give your good advice for our better proceeding herein."

The appointment of Sir Thomas Wylford as Provost Marshal was also mentioned to show that Provost Marshals were appointed under the Royal prerogative.

Essex replied, "For my own interest, I take it, under your Lordship's reformation, that all Provost Marshals are but Subaltern officers under the Marshal of England, and that they owe accounts to him, and he may be appealed to from them. Besides, the records of the Exchequer and the Tower do prove that the Marshal of England, 12 miles about the Prince's person, is to judge all criminal causes and persons, and to command those judgments to be executed.

"The Knight Marshal who is indeed but the King's Provost Marshal and is called in France ' Grand Provost de l'Hostel, ' hath been used in those kind of services, and so have other men specially chosen by the Prince's commission, as in the 37th year of her Majesty's reign, Sir Thomas Wylford. But this hath been in the vacancy or absence of a Marshal of England. For myself, I do assure your Lordships faithfully, I neither have cause or humour to draw trouble to me, and yet I had rather endure a great deal than that such an ancient office of the Crown should in me lose his authority and jurisdiction."

The first Provost Marshal of the Army, as distinct from the Provost Marshal who was an officer of State, was appointed in 1643 to the Royalist Army (the commission read "Provost Martial General of all the Forces in England"). The post became permanent in 1685. Although at this date Provost Marshals became Army officers, they were still appointed personally by the Sovereign.

The first Provost Marshal-General was Captain William Smith. Many attacks were made on this officer in pamphlets published by the Parliamentarians. One of these was entitled "The Inhumanity of the King's Prison-Keeper at Oxford, or a true relation of the most transcendant cruelties, cheatings, cozenings, and base dishonest dealings of William Smith, Provost Marshal-General of the King's Army . . . Written by Edm. Chillenden, who was a prisoner there 6 months."

Smith was charged with cruelty. His fees were alleged to have been excessive. He was also said to have shown ill-behaviour to his officer-prisoners in Oxford Castle, calling Sir William Essex, "old doting fool and ass," and some of the captains "barb," and other gentlemen "jackanapes."

From the Restoration to the end of the Stuart period the Deputy Provost Marshal (first appointed in 1663) undertook the duties now associated with that of Quartermaster, and from 1664 to 1680 this officer, known as the "Martial" or "Marshal," was appointed to every Regiment of Foot.

The earliest mention of a Provost Marshal serving in India is in 1678, when, in October of that year, Thomas Lott was nominated and appointed to that office at Fort St. George, Madras. He was succeeded by Tillman Holt, who was permitted to "have a licence gratis to keep a house of entertainment in his own dwelling-house, but not elsewhere." Tillman Holt was superannuated on the 29th July, 1703, being succeeded by Wheatley Garthorn, who died in 1707, and was followed by Ephraim Goss.

Assistant Provost Marshals are first mentioned in 1809, and during the earlier stages of the Peninsular War, police duties within the Army were carried out by Provost Marshals, helped by their Assistant Provost Marshals. These were non-commissioned and this custom seemed to have survived into the eighteen-eighties, as in the early Order Books of the Corps of Military Police there are to be found various notifications of Sergeant-Majors of the Corps being appointed to act as Assistant Provost Marshals.

The Army in the Peninsula was notoriously ill disciplined and the Provost Marshal's staff were hopelessly inadequate to cope with the situation. Wellington increased the provost force and on the 6th April, 1810, wrote ". . . The Provost's Establishment . . . was larger than was ever known in any British Army." He drew up the following orders for his Provost Marshals:

"The Commander of the Forces is concerned to observe that the power of the Assistants of the Provost Marshal of the Army has, in more than one instance, been abused; and that officers have thought themselves authorized to send orders to the Assistant Provosts, under which abuses have been committed, contrary to the established usages and rules of the service, and the intentions and orders of the Commander of the Forces.

"The Office of the Provost Marshal has existed in all British Armies in the Field. His particular duties are to take charge of the Prisoners confined for offences of a general description; to preserve good order and discipline; to prevent breaches of both by the soldiers and followers of the Army, by his presence at those places in which either are likely to be committed; and if necessary, he has, by constant usage in all Armies, the power to punish those whom he may find in the act of committing breaches of order and discipline.

MAJOR THOMAS TROUT, APPOINTED PROVOST MARSHAL IN 1861
The first Provost Marshal to be appointed from the ranks of the Military Police.

"The authority of the Provost Marshal to punish must be limited by the necessity of the case; and whatever may be the crime of which a soldier may be guilty, the Provost Marshal has not the power of inflicting summary punishment unless he should see him in the act of doing it. If he should not see the soldier in the act of committing the offence of which he may have been found guilty, a report must be made to the Commander-in-Chief of the Army, who would give such orders as might be deemed expedient, either for further enquiry, for the trial of the soldier, or for infliction of summary punishment according to the nature of the case, the degree of evidence of the soldier's guilt, and the existing necessity for an immediate example.

"The Commander of the Forces desires that it may be clearly understood that no officer whatever has a right to order the Provost Marshal or his assistants to exercise the authority entrusted to them; nor can the Provost Marshal or his assistants inflict corporal punishment on any man excepting they should see him in the act of committing a Breach of Orders and discipline. Their duty is, by vigilance and activity to prevent those breaches which the Commander of the Force is sorry to observe are too common, and to punish those they catch in the Act."

After the Napoleonic Wars the Provost Marshal played no outstanding part in military affairs. The appointment became that of a junior or semi-retired officer, but during the remainder of the nineteenth century three important changes took place which affected the office.

In 1829 the office of the Provost Marshal-General was abolished. The senior provost officer was the Provost Marshal, and those provost officers attached to garrisons and field formations were known as "Assistant Provosts," though non-commissioned.

Queen's Regulations for 1844 recognized the status of the Provost Marshal and laid down that "the officer appointed to act as Provost Marshal of the Army is to rank as Captain in the Army," and emphasized that "the appointment is one of great responsibility and requires the utmost vigilance and activity."

Section 74 of the Army Act of 1879 expressly forbids any Provost Marshal to inflict any punishment on his own authority, and from that date provost marshals lost their powers of summary punishment.

★   ★   ★   ★   ★

LET us examine now the origin and development of the Provost Marshal's assistants, now known as non-commissioned officers of the Corps of Royal Military Police, for they are the modern counterparts of men of the same calling 400 years ago. Barnaby Googe's unpaid yokels of "evil demeanour" and Markham's "under provosts" who were compelled to carry "halters, withs or strangling cords" were but the "Redcaps" of their time, and no doubt their methods of enforcing discipline seemed no more unusual to the soldiery then than the gentle hand of the modern military police.

Assistants of the early provost marshals were men of many sorts—tipstaves, jailers, hangmen, but rarely soldiers—but in 1810 a body of troops were ordered by the Duke of Wellington to perform the duties of military police under the Provost Marshal. These were the first professional soldiers to become military policemen.

It has been stated that the forerunners of the Corps of Military Police were the Corps of Mounted Guides and the Staff Corps of Cavalry, but this is not so. These Corps, however, do bear a certain relationship to the Provost, as they were raised to assist the existing Provost service. Police work did form a small part of their duties. In other respects they were the forerunners of the despatch rider service of the Royal Corps of Signals, of the Intelligence Corps and of the field security personnel of that service. Both Corps were disbanded before 1820.

Another fallacy connected with the origin of the Corps of Military Police is that it was born in 1877, and that there was no military police force in the Army between the Napoleonic Wars and this date. This presumably arose out of the fact that military police were not shown in the Army List, but this was because military policemen were shown on the muster rolls of the regiments to which they had originally belonged and the name of the Corps did not appear in their pay books.

During these years men from various units who volunteered for police duty were sent to the Provost Marshal at Aldershot for instruction and to be equipped. The force, however, was a small one and insufficient to police the whole Army. Aldershot itself was always policed by these qualified military policemen, but at the other stations discipline was maintained by garrison police, reinforced by regimental picquets. If occasion demanded, a posse of military police would be detached from Aldershot.

This small force also found the staff for detention barracks, but the men employed on this service became specialized and gradually broke away so that they eventually became a military prison staff. They are known as the Military Provost Staff Corps, and they still perform that part of the Provost Marshal's traditional duties as "chief gaoler in the Army."

In 1885 the Provost Marshal, in putting forward his recommendations for additional men, said he wanted good "policemen." This term was unknown in military circles and gave the impression that it was proposed to start a new service rather than augment and reorganize an existing one, and the War Office in a letter to officers commanding cavalry regiments referred to the formation of a Corps of Mounted Police for the Cantonment of Aldershot and asked for a return of N.C.Os. and men for this duty. They were to be men of not less than five years' service, if of ten the better, of sober habits, intelligent, active and capable of exercising a sound discretion. This development was the beginning of the existing organization of the Corps of Military Police.

Further correspondence about this time between the War Office and the general at Aldershot showed that reliable N.C.Os. and men were being transferred in increasing numbers to the Military Police. It was then, too, that corps pay—1s. 6d. for sergeants and 1s. for privates—was first granted.

It had been customary for some years for sergeants of the provost service to be appointed Assistant Provost Marshals, and in 1855 there transferred to the Military Police a cavalry N.C.O. This letter preceded his arrival:

Lieutenant-Colonel Commanding 7th Hussars to Major-General Knollys, Aldershot.

"I have the honour to acquaint you that, in compliance with an order from the Adjutant General the non-commissioned officer as per margin, proceeded by railway this day, mounted and fully equipped, *en route* to Aldershot to act there in the Mounted Police under your orders.

"I have further the honour to transmit herewith a Nominal and Descriptive return of T. Sergt. Major T. Trout and to state that he has been paid and settled with up to the 14th inst. inclusive."

Later Sergeant-Major Trout was commissioned (as an exceptional case) as Provost Marshal. Although the appointment was to be an "exceptional case," it seems to have acted as a precedent as the four next Provost Marshals, Captain Silk (1881), Major Broackes (1885), Major Emerson (1894), and Major Wood (1898) all appear to have risen from the ranks of the Military Police to be Provost Marshal and Commandant of the Corps. It was Major Broackes' wife who selected the red cap-cover subsequently worn by all military police.

Ten years later the first special instructions for Military Police were laid down by Provost Marshal Trout. They were:

"The Assistant Provost Marshals of Army Corps will keep a list of sutlers, etc., that are allowed to accompany their respective Army Corps, and will take immediate notice of any irregularity on their part, in order that the same may be notified for the information of the Assistant Quartermaster General.

"They will be careful to take every precaution to prevent soldiers or camp followers trespassing in game preserves, plantations, etc., or breaking in an unauthorized place.

"They will ascertain on the termination of each day's march the signs and locality of public-houses in the vicinity of the encampment, and take such precautions as will ensure order being preserved.

"They will make themselves acquainted with the position of private property in the vicinity of each encampment, and take such steps as may be deemed necessary to prevent cause for complaint.

"They will not allow the sale of intoxicating liquors in the markets of their respective encampments, and cause all persons selling articles to the troops to remain at the place indicated for that purpose, and the Markets to be closed at dusk.

"They will also comply with any orders or instructions that may be given them by General Officers Commanding their respective Army Corps.

"The Military Police are to prevent all soldiers and camp followers from cutting down trees, shrubs, furze on the commons, or damaging property of any description.

"They will see that the telegraph wires are not injured in any way.

"They will make the rounds of their respective camps at uncertain times, and eject all vagrants and women of loose character that may be found.

"They will at all times render every assistance to the civil police and work in conjunction with them.

"They must be particular not to give cause for complaint, be prompt and decided, but civil and temperate on all occasions in the performance of their duties; also use great care and discretion in dealing with members of the auxiliary forces."

On the 16th September, 1877, one sergeant, one corporal and six lance-corporals were dispatched to Portsmouth, and one corporal and five lance-corporals to Shorncliffe, Dover, to form permanent detachments for duty in those garrisons.

The military police were permanently stationed in Cairo by 1882. They accompanied the Field Force in the preliminary campaign before the occupation. In the keeping of the Sergeants' Mess at the Depot is a medal for the Egyptian Campaign, dated 1882, awarded to No. 1300 A. Gould, Military Mounted Police, with bars for Tel-el-Kebir 1882, Suakin 1884, and El-Teb; and in the casualty record it is noted that No. 75 Corporal J. Howze was wounded in action in the Battle of El-Teb. No. 113 Sergeant-Major J. L. Burke took a detachment to accompany the Nile Expeditionary Force in September, 1884.

It was during the Egyptian War of 1882, and for service in Egypt, that the Corps of Military Foot Police was raised. It was formed on 1st August of that year from N.C.Os. and men recalled to the Colours who had served with the London Metropolitan Police during the period of reserve service. They did not, however, become a permanent corps or serve at home for another three years. In 1885 the Corps of Military Police began to expand. It now became divided into the Military Mounted Police and the Military Foot Police, each with their own promotion rosters, but in other respects one Corps consisting of 263 N.C.Os. Detachments of Military Foot Police were stationed at Aldershot, Colchester, Dover, Shorncliffe, Chatham, Woolwich, Portsmouth, Gosport and Devonport.

Up to this time there has been no mention of officers within the Corps, other than the Provost Marshal. In 1889 the question was raised in correspondence started by Mr. J. E. Emerson, a future Provost Marshal, but at that time just appointed Quartermaster, and acting as Assistant Provost Marshal at the Curragh.

Lieutenant Quartermaster Emerson to the War Office.
March, 1889.

"On my being promoted to a commission my name appeared in the *London Gazette* as appointed 'Quartermaster in the Army,' and I am still shown as such in the Quarterly Army List. I observe however that the Army Estimates provide for the pay of two officers for M.M. Police and I presume I am one of the officers whose pay is thus provided for. I would be much obliged if you will inform me if I am to consider myself an officer of the M.M. Police or as a Quartermaster in the Army belonging to no specific Corps."

War Office to Quartermaster Emerson.

"Quarter Master and Hony. Lieutenant J. L. Emerson, is to consider himself as a Quarter Master in the Army, his pay being provided for as such, and not as an officer of the Military Mounted Police."

Emerson then put up a vigorous fight and eventually, after spirited correspondence, the War Office agreed that "Quarter Master Emerson was Gazetted a Quarter Master in the Army, but it has been decided that he shall be considered as belonging to the Military Mounted Police, and he will be so shown in future in the Official Army List."

So was set the precedent for the Quartermaster of the Corps of Military Police to be the only officer commissioned within the Corps.

In June, 1892, the War Office ordered that all promotions to and above the rank of sergeant in the Corps of Military Mounted Police and the Corps of Military Foot Police should be made in future within the Corps, and the Provost Marshal, as the Officer Commanding the Corps, was instructed to prepare and maintain seniority rolls of each Corps.

On the outbreak of the South African War, in 1899, the Military Police were posted as follows: 12 Military Mounted Police and 12 Military Foot Police to General Headquarters, 12 Military Mounted Police to cavalry divisions, 20 Military Foot Police to infantry divisions, and detachments of about 16 Military Foot Police on lines of communication.

In 1900 the Assistant Provost Marshal and all the Military Police in Egypt were drafted to South Africa. One of the most important duties was to be patrolling of watering-places, poisoned by the enemy. The Military Mounted Police also found most of the orderlies to the General Officers Commanding and Staff Officers, and General Buller's own personal orderly was a member of the Corps. Two Distinguished Conduct Medals were awarded to members of the Corps in this campaign.

The next major event in the development of the Corps was the Great War, which is dealt with in the following chapter.

After the Great War the strength of the Corps was gradually reduced. Detachments were posted at home and abroad in accordance with the number of troops at each station, until the number fell to 508 all ranks, conforming to the pre-war establishment.

Between 1919 and 1922, many military policemen found themselves posted for duty in Ireland, where their work was onerous, exacting and unpleasant. Much of the Army at home was sent to the Irish Command in connection with what Sein Fein called "war" and the British Government "disorder." They remained until the end of 1922, when the Irish Free State was inaugurated. That their work was appreciated and understood is apparent from a report to the War Office by the G.O.C.-in-C., General Sir Nevil Macready, Bt., who himself had been an A.P.M. in Egypt thirty-five years before, in which he wrote: "Provost work is seldom in the limelight, but it is largely due to Lieutenant-Colonel Ruttledge's organization and constant supervision that the Army in Ireland has maintained its good name throughout three years of distasteful duty in Ireland."

During "the troubles" a young artillery officer in Cork had attracted the attention of the provost authorities because of his energy and firmness. He was Lieutenant A. P. Green, later to become the well-loved and efficient A.P.M. of Belfast in the Second World War and to complete his provost service as Deputy Provost Marshal in Berlin.

On the 27th February, 1926, the Military Mounted Police and the Military Foot Police were merged into one Corps, under the title of the "Corps of Military Police."

In the following year the first self-contained and self-administered Provost Company for a specific purpose overseas was formed to accompany the Shanghai Defence Force. This company gained the admiration and respect of all in Shanghai, and the General Officer Commanding forwarded impressive reports of their usefulness.

In the light of recent history it is interesting that in 1932, when Colonel Bowles was Provost Marshal, the earliest mechanization of the Corps began. The first issue was ten motor-cycles, six horses, however, being withdrawn, presumably to pay for the innovation.

In March, 1933, the question of precedence and the Corps position in the Army List was raised, and the request that the prefix "Royal" might be affixed to the Corps was put forward, but it was arbitrarily decided that the Corps should remain non-combatant and the claim for combatant status was laughed out of court, it being mentioned that it was "ridiculous for certain units to imagine they were combatant merely because they were given arms with which to defend their own lives."

In February, 1933, a provost exercise was arranged by the War Office which was attended by eighteen officers designated to be A.P.Ms. on mobilization. This exercise was based on successful experiments carried out in 1931, during which provost work was co-ordinated into the organization of field formations. From this time forward provost practised their war role on manœuvres.

On 17th December, 1934, a Military Police section was dispatched from the Depot, under the command of Sergeant P. Stoddart, for attachment to the Headquarters, Saar Force. This section was fully equipped as though for active service and mechanized. All the N.C.Os. were selected for their ability to speak either German or French. Most were veterans of the Army of Occupation with a valuable topographical knowledge.

During the night of the 18th-19th December the section made a halt at Thiouville and was inspected by the French G.O.C. of that garrison. It arrived at Saarbrucken with the advance party of the force, where they detrained their motor-cycles and went by road to their billets. The sergeant in charge mentions in his report that the mechanized section, moving off and proceeding through the town in drill formation, seemed to cause a good impression on the local population and won the appreciation of the Stadt Police and Saar Special Police especially.

As soon as the heads of the various departments of Headquarters realized that the section not only spoke good German but knew the country, heavy demands were made upon them, and the following day they were kept busy acting as guides and despatch riders. Despite this, however, before the arrival of the main body, the town had been reconnoitred and divided into police beats and patrols, and guides were out operating in the city, able to act as interpreters to help the British personnel as soon as they appeared on the streets.

On 25th December the section was on duty, during which it covered fifty-five miles at top speed, escorting the Governing Commission President, the G.O.C. and the British G.O.C. on an inspection of the various British units.

On New Year's Eve the section was paraded and inspected by the G.O.C. British Contingent, who warmly complimented them on their work, turn-out and example.

Singapore was opened as a permanent station for Military Police in April, 1936. Before this the policing of Singapore from a military aspect had been carried out by garrison police under a provost sergeant, acting under the orders of a staff captain.

In November, 1934, two senior ranks of the Corps of Military Police were sent out as an experiment, which was extended over a period of one year. At this time there were many brothels and venereal disease was becoming a serious menace. At the request of the Roman Catholic Bishop of Singapore, the C.M.P. were ordered to make a maximum effort to put this down, backed by the authority of the G.O.C. After three weeks of concentrated effort, prostitution in the city area was reduced and kept down by maintaining a patrol wholly on this work.

Reinforcements arrived in 1936 in the form of twenty other ranks, with a C.S.M., after which Singapore became a permanent station. In 1935 Hong Kong became a permanent station.

In September, 1936, Nos. 1 and 5 Companies, a Corps section and Nos. 1 and 2 Line of Communication Sections were ordered to Palestine for service with the Emergency Force. No. 1 Company, the Corps section and No. 1 L. of C. Section went to Jerusalem, the rest remaining at Haifa. On the return of the force in 1936, No. 1 Company, reinforced by personnel from the remainder, remained in Palestine.

★   ★   ★   ★   ★

FROM 1511 to the present day the Provost Marshal and his assistants have been maintaining discipline in the King's forces.

When regiments which claim to be amongst the oldest units in the Army were not born, before indeed there was any standing Army at all, the coming of the Provost Marshal and his troop behind him was feared by the law-breaker, the deserter and the drunkard and respected by the good soldier.

In the Napoleonic Wars, in South Africa and in skirmishes elsewhere the military police had shown that they could maintain the proud traditions of the oldest service in the Army as well as in

THE ALDERSHOT DETACHMENT OF MILITARY POLICE IN 1896

peace, but war of a new kind was on the way, war which would develop the police service of the Army and thrust new duties upon it.

In 1914, 403 years after Henry Guylford had looked out over Cadiz from his ship, military police were again arriving in overseas ports to fight in the First World War.

Many further details about the earlier part of the 400 years summarized in this chapter are to be found in Major Lovell-Knight's "History of the office of the Provost Marshal and the Corps of Military Police," published in 1943.

C

CHAPTER II

THE GREAT WAR, 1914–1918

A T the outbreak of war the strength of the Corps of Military Police, mounted and foot, was three officers, a Provost Marshal Commandant at Aldershot and Assistant Provost Marshals at the Curragh and Tidworth, and 508 warrant officers, non-commissioned officers and men available for duty in the United Kingdom and overseas garrisons. The Headquarters and Depot of the Corps were at Aldershot, first at Stanhope Lines, and then at Mytchett Hutments.

On mobilization the strength of the Corps was increased by 253 reservists, many of whom had been civil policemen, making a total of 761. With the exception of a small staff to carry on the work at the Depot, all available military police were drafted to the B.E.F. To meet the urgent need for recruits, the Corps was thrown open to direct enlistment. The call met with good response, and many old soldiers enlisted. But the expansion of the Corps could not keep pace with the rate at which the Army was growing and it was necessary to transfer certain units *en bloc* to the Military Police. It has not been recorded that any of these units objected to this transfer.

An officer who later became a divisional A.P.M., whose unit was called up for guard duties, wrote, many years after the war, "We had not so much as a hint that we might be required to take on police duties, but the wheel of fortune turned that way and neither the men of the Wilts National Reserve nor their captain will ever regret that it did so."

In June, 1916, the Provost Marshal of the First Army in France was brought home and appointed Provost Marshal, Home Forces, with the rank of Brigadier-General. He received orders from the Adjutant-General to reorganize the Provost Service at home with a view to establishing a high standard of discipline among troops when away from their units, and to take special measures to reduce the wastage of manpower which resulted from the ever-increasing number of men who absented themselves at the end of their leave from the B.E.F. This reorganization meant a large increase in officers and other ranks, most of whom, other than those under training for overseas, had to be selected from those not fit for front-line service. The selection of officers for appointment was made at General Headquarters from officers for whom recommendations were received from Commands, and in many cases from direct applications.

To provide for the proper training of the military police, schools of instruction were opened in various commands, under the supervision of a selected officer, and a Manual for Military Police in Great Britain was compiled. For purposes of pay, rations, clothing and equipment, the Military Police were not, at first, organized as a self-accounting unit. The Aldershot Command and a few detachments made an exception to this rule, but elsewhere military police were attached to convenient units for pay, rations, etc. The objections to this method soon became apparent. Many detachments were far from the units to which they were attached, the units were constantly moving, and had little parental feeling towards the police. This led to difficulties in accounting, cash payments were delayed, and questions concerning individual accounts often entailed much correspondence and little satisfaction. These difficulties were overcome by the introduction of a centralized system of accounting within Commands.

At the end of the war a Deputy Provost Marshal paid this tribute to his men: "I should like to place on record how much I appreciate the services rendered by the personnel of the provost organization. The manner in which many of the military police, who were men of very low medical category, performed the long hours of work, showed a sense of duty which might well compare with the services performed in a more active sphere. They did their bit as well as they were able, often under circumstances which were far from easy.

"As for the officers who served in the branch, it is impossible for me to do justice to their efforts or to bring out fully the many hard and frequently thankless tasks which confronted them. Many of them had very little military experience, and those who took up A.P.Ms.' appointments when the branch was first reorganized had absolutely no text-books or instructions to guide them in the performance of their duties. They simply had to pick it up the best they could."

During the Great War military police served in France and Flanders, Gallipoli, Mesopotamia, Macedonia, Palestine, Egypt, Italy, North Russia, North-West Persia, and Afghanistan. Formations proceeding overseas had an A.P.M., and small establishments of Military Police at the Headquarters of Corps and Divisions. These were looked upon as useful for security duties at Headquarters of the formation and in some cases were made available for duties as orderlies or grooms. A serious difficulty was that no consideration had been given before the war to the work which they might be called upon to perform during operations, nor was there any manual of regulations that could furnish a guide to provost duties in the field. This was partly caused by the fact that the tasks the Corps of Military Police were to be called upon to fulfil were entirely unforeseen, nor was there any officer sufficiently experienced in this work to be accepted as an authority; consequently those officers, like General Rogers, who suddenly found themselves saddled with the strange and almost unknown appointment of Assistant Provost Marshal had to rely on their wits and do what they felt to be right—often in the face of strenuous opposition and orders countermanded by Staff Officers who wished to use the police as orderlies.

On landing in France the duty on which there was general agreement was the necessity for providing security patrols at formation headquarters, and this was given to provost. Unfortunately, a precedent was established which was to die hard; and, as every military policeman knows today, this improper use of police is a trouble to every provost staff officer and police unit.

Indeed, during the voyage from Southampton to Havre the Brigadier-General, General Staff, of I Corps, asked the A.P.M. of the Corps what he thought his operational duties would be. The A.P.M. replied that he had only taken up his appointment a few days, and that he had no idea. "No doubt," said the B.G.G.S., "we shall find something useful for you to do."

Subsequent events were to prove the accuracy of this, for at a very early date the collection and control of stragglers and traffic control, which were essential for the success of any operation, fell to the lot of provost to perform. Right from the start, provost officers found themselves up against a certain prejudice which surrounded the word "police" and also against many staff officers who were jealous of the dual control which resulted from an A.P.M.'s responsibility to his G.O.C. through the "A" staff and to the Provost Marshal at G.H.Q. in connection with the technical supervision of certain military police duties.

All these difficulties were overcome with varying degrees of success by tact and firmness, and events proved that the greater the prestige afforded to the appointment of A.P.M. by the staff, the better the results of the work of the military police and the greater the operational value of the formation concerned.

It was during the retreat from Mons that the problem of how best to deal with stragglers first presented itself. The military police, reinforced by cavalry as required, collected and brought on many hundreds of men who had fallen out from sheer exhaustion and who would have fallen into the hands of the advancing Germans. It was remarkable how these men responded to the efforts of the police, who adopted various methods to help them make a special effort; in some cases an emergency ration, in others a few minutes' drill or singing; in a few extreme cases, threats.

It soon became recognized that wastage of manpower, of arms and ammunition, could be prevented by the military police. This work, which continued until static warfare set in, then developed into manning stragglers' posts, collecting stations and what in those days were called "battle-stops." The military police were required to establish posts immediately behind the front line in which to collect and sort men found returning from the front without legitimate reason. Wounded were directed to first-aid posts, the weapons and ammunition being retained, and, at intervals, returned to forward units. Stragglers might be either genuinely lost men or men in a state of temporary fright but not intentional deserters. These were collected into groups, fed, rearmed if necessary, and sent back. In this way units received a constant supply of manpower and ammunition, which on more than one occasion just tipped the balance in necessary strength at a vital moment.

On one occasion during an enemy attack military police manning stragglers' posts held, defeated, captured and disarmed over 800 Germans who had overrun our front line.

Stragglers' posts also served as guide posts for relieving units, ration parties and rendezvous. The military police of one battle-stop gained the Military Medal for maintaining a particularly difficult post and at the same time keeping clear neighbouring roads for the artillery traffic.

Several N.C.Os. at the battle-stops were mentioned in despatches for their valuable work. In one instance the front line gave way, but the N.C.Os. in charge of the battle-stop to the immediate rear interpreted the name of the posts literally and proceeded to make a most effective battle-stop. Hastily organizing their stragglers, they successfully blocked all roads leading from the front to impede the expected hostile advance from that direction. They then directed the stragglers into defensive positions astride these roads and held on. This enabled the front line to use the posts as rallying points and to reorganize, with the result that the line was held.

The need for control of traffic and clearance of roads had become apparent during the early days of the retreat when thousands of refugees had to be turned off the roads daily to enable the troops to march. Many a heart-rending situation had to be dealt with by the police, who could show no sympathy for the frightened civil population. But traffic control on any planned or general basis was hardly appreciated in these early days. On the roads every brigade fought for itself, and its police were expected to clear a way exclusively for the formation to which they were attached.

The control of one-way traffic during the retreat proved a simple matter compared with the position which arose when the advance began and the battles of the Marne and Aisne were fought, when arrangements had to be made for forward and rearward movement, for supply and ammunition lorries, and for the evacuation of the wounded as well as the tactical movements of troops. No matter how good the staff work so far as time and space were concerned, strict police control proved essential, for nearly every commander, however small his unit, was convinced that he should be given the priority which he demanded.

Brigadier-General Rogers, who started his war service as a divisional A.P.M., and eventually became Provost-Marshal, B.E.F., reported:

"We landed at St. Nazaire on 9th September, 1914, when the battle of the Marne was being fought; we hurried up by trains to near Paris and marched from there.

"This brings us to the question of how to distribute military mounted police on the line of march with a division advancing. Since the early days there has not been much in this way; I mean a complete division with its artillery going forward into an unknown area, with an unknown destination. I say unknown destination because one didn't know where one was going, as the General Staff might expect to get orders to divert at any moment.

"The length of an infantry division was fourteen miles. It was my practice on these marches to remain behind until all the headquarters had cleared the village. Together with several M.Ps., I searched the place for absentees. We left when we had cleared up the situation.

"The distribution of our personnel was as follows: Two in front of a brigade and three in the rear. With Headquarters of division there were usually three in front some way ahead in order to ensure a clear road. There were three in rear and the remaining six were split amongst the artillery. The duties varied according to circumstances; mounted military police were warned that they had to be ready to cope with any situation, but ordinarily those in front of divisions and brigades were responsible for a non-check march—to clear the roads. When near the destination they were required to ride forward with the staff officer responsible for billeting and to put up sign boards.

"The mounted military police in the rear had a much more difficult task. They were continually riding forward to check some fault or give some help. They were responsible for the collection of all stragglers.

"After one of our marches a brigade major came up to me and said that he thought I ought to be continually riding up and down the column. I pointed out to him that I always did ride up the column, but as it was fourteen miles in length, by the time I got to the head it was time I went on to the billeting area and saw to things there."

As static warfare developed after the battle of the Aisne, so traffic control difficulties increased, and the early days of the first battle of Ypres presented an entirely new problem.

This was solved partly through the introduction of traffic circuits by Colonel Marker, a senior staff officer who was killed a few weeks later, and partly by trained military police supervision.

Night after night military police, reinforced by troops where necessary, were on duty in rear of the trenches at road junctions, frequently under shell fire, sorting and directing traffic not only of different formations but of different nationalities. Without the efficient performance of this duty, relief of troops, provision of supplies and ammunition and the evacuation of sick and wounded could not have been completed during the hours of darkness.

Traffic control was now gradually becoming one of the most important duties of the military police and during 1915 was brought to a high pitch of efficiency. It proved invaluable when any special attack was launched. The first time that traffic control by military police was employed to any extent in the battlefield was at Neuve Chapelle in 1915. Ammunition and supply circuits were worked which resulted in lorries doing the distance in forty minutes less time than before. Posts were put out and all civilian traffic stopped at 3 a.m., which ensured a clear run for transport and avoided the inevitable ditching of lorries in attempting to pass farm wagons. This was also the first occasion on which organized stragglers' posts were maintained with supplies of food facilities for returning stragglers.

It was soon recognized by Commanders and their staffs how largely the success of any operation depended upon freedom of movement in rear of the actual fighting, and from that time the importance of the work of the military police was more generally appreciated and traffic control companies were organized. The battle of Loos, however, in September, 1915, was a tragic example of failure to appreciate this. Two highly trained divisions, just out from home, who had been marched into the battle zone were thrown into the battle without proper rest and food because lack of arrangements for keeping the roads clear resulted in complete confusion during the evening and night before the battle. The fighting efficiency of the troops was so seriously impaired that through no fault of their own their attack failed.

During the struggle for the Somme in 1918 traffic control personnel manned the bridges over the Somme for thirty-six hours under continuous heavy shell fire and not one man left his post until all the fighting troops were across. They then fell back and were the last over. In one case a man was blown over the bridge into the river twice in a few hours by shell fire but climbed back to carry on with his duty of getting the traffic through. These men were later called upon to fill a breach in the line.

The duties of the Provost Service in the B.E.F. were many and varied. Besides stragglers' posts and the ever-increasing traffic control duties they embraced:

Detection of crime, and the arrest of offenders;

Maintenance of order under all circumstances;

Surveillance and control of all civilians within the area occupied by their formations;

Custody of prisoners of war until their transfer to railhead or to a P.W. working company;

The protection of the indigenous population against acts of violence by soldiers or camp followers.

The shooting of dogs found unattended near the forward lines, and search of the bodies for messages.

Seizure of carrier pigeons.

The work of the military police during 1914-1918 shows that the Provost Branch at that time laid the foundation for its much more extended work in 1939-1945.

Brigadier-General H. S. Rogers left on record an account of the activities of the Provost Marshal in the Great War, which he introduces with a quotation by Napoleon. "You cannot have a good army without a good police force within."

He recommends that "every high Commander should insist on seeing his senior provost officer frequently, because on him depends to a very large extent the prevention of crime and the prevention of disease which go a long way to keeping an army fit for action."

But the military police also had their front-line duties, and the following account of a day in the life of an A.P.M. and his divisional provost company can be regarded as typical:

In an attack it was necessary for the provost to be well up in order that they should be the first to get hold of civilians in captured villages and round up hidden enemy agents. During the battle of Hermies, at dawn of the day of attack, the A.P.M. with twelve military police took up his position behind a hill. As the attack was put in they moved in with the fighting troops and were actually in the village before the assaulting troops had finally captured it.

KING GEORGE V WITH THE PRINCE OF WALES TALKING TO A
MILITARY POLICEMAN AT BETHUNE, 11TH AUGUST, 1916

THE COMMANDER-IN-CHIEF, ARMY OF THE RHINE, INSPECTING
THE COLOGNE MILITARY POLICE IN JUNE, 1919

The police immediately set to work on a house-to-house comb-out for civilians and hidden agents, then took over all prisoners of war, thus saving the necessity of escorts. They made the prisoners carry back our wounded, and consequently by 8 a.m. the battlefield was entirely cleared of prisoners and wounded. The returning escort was able to guide reinforcements and thus avoid a German machine-gun which they had located, and was then able to send back and direct the wagons of the Royal Engineers which had come up for bridging and other services.

They picqueted wells which, according to Intelligence officers, had been poisoned.

The A.P.M. was back almost immediately after the battle, reporting in person to the G.O.C. what had happened, the number of prisoners taken, etc. For this he was awarded the D.S.O.

The Corps of Military Police suffered many casualties and was awarded many honours. The Adjutant-General, B.E.F., wrote this letter to the Provost Marshal in 1918:

"The Field-Marshal Commander-in-Chief has expressed his satisfaction with the work of the Corps of Military Police. . . . He congratulates you on the efficiency of your organization, and wishes you to convey to your P.Ms. and A.P.Ms., and those serving under them, his appreciation of the manner in which they have discharged their duties and stood to their posts. The orderliness which has prevailed behind the front is directly attributed to their efficiency and devotion."

The Commander-in-Chief in his final despatch, said this of the Corps:

"In the battle zone, where frequently they had to do duty in exposed positions under heavy fire and suffered severe casualties, the military police solved an important part of the problem of traffic control by preventing the unavoidable congestion of troops and transport on roads in the vicinity of active operations from degenerating into confusion. In back areas their vigilance and zeal have largely contributed to the good relations maintained between our troops and the civilian population."

On 1st December, 1918, British troops marched into Germany. The 1st Cavalry Division entered the Rhine Province near Malmedy, accompanied by their normal complement of military mounted police. A military policemen was actually the first British soldier to cross the Rhine, motor-cycling across the Hohenzollernbrucke and talking to the German sentry on the farther side.

The difficulties of the military police at once began. Precautions against treachery on the part of the enemy inhabitants had to be taken. The persons and property of the inhabitants had to be respected in accordance with the proclamation issued by the

Commander-in-Chief and General Sir H. Plumer, G.O.C. Second Army, to the population, and the inhabitants themselves protected against the natural desire for reprisal which was felt by every British soldier who had marched through devastated Belgium. The subsequent attitude of the inhabitants of the occupied zone seems to justify the conclusion that the military police skilfully carried out their role.

The immediate difficulty encountered on crossing the frontier was the lack of interpreters, but the posting up of proclamations to the inhabitants, carried out expeditiously by the first provost officer to enter each village, greatly eased the subsequent work of the police.

The police of the Army of Occupation were controlled by Brigadier-General Rogers, Provost Marshal, B.E.F., and Lieut.-Colonel Percy Laurie, D.P.M. Second Army.

*   *   *   *   *

ON the capitulation of Turkey in October, 1918, Constantinople and the shores of the Bosphorus and Dardanelles were occupied by a mixed force of British, French and Italian troops from the Salonica front. A detachment of military mounted and foot police which accompanied the British Force was later reinforced by drafts from the United Kingdom up to a strength of about one hundred and eighty all ranks.

The D.P.M. of the Force, Lieut.-Colonel W. F. O. Faviell, was established at G.H.Q. in Constantinople with a D.A.P.M. for Constantinople, Base H.Q. and Haidar Pasha, situated on the Asiatic shore. In the later stages of the occupation D.A.P.Ms. were also located at Chanak and at Kilia in the Dardanelles zone.

Constantinople has been described as the most immoral city in Europe at that time. The cosmopolitan population, in which was to be found some of the worst elements from the Balkan States and the countries bordering on the Black Sea, was swollen by the large influx of refugees—Armenians and Greeks from the Turkish massacres in Asia Minor and the many thousands of "White" Russians seeking refuge from the Bolsheviks.

Under these circumstances the duties of the military police were arduous and often hazardous. Patrols, strict supervision of "Out of Bounds" areas, anti-V.D. measures, security duties at Army and Allied Corps Headquarters and dock duties were among the chief commitments. The investigation of crime, principally thefts of Army stores, was undertaken by selected N.C.Os. working in co-operation with the civil police.

The Force was withdrawn in October, 1923, under the Treaty of Lausanne, and the military police were paid a particularly handsome tribute by the Allied Commander, the late General Sir Charles Harington.

★ ★ ★ ★ ★

IN the four years of the Great War the Military Police had developed from a small body of professional soldiers, concerned solely with the enforcement of discipline at military stations and in the base towns of overseas theatres of war, to a Corps containing thousands of men, which had acquired an essential operational role both in the rear and in the forward areas.

CHAPTER III

SECOND WORLD WAR:
MOBILIZATION AND THE B.E.F.

IN the years of peace after the Great War a mobilization scheme was maintained at the Depot. This scheme was designed to absorb reservists rejoining the Colours on mobilization and to organize and equip the various provost units that were to come into being on the outbreak of war.

In 1936 when the Nazi power in Germany made war more likely, a supplementary reserve was formed, and in 1938 with the support of the late Sir Stenson Cooke, Secretary of the Automobile Association, a reserve of 500 A.A. scouts, later increased to 850, was created.

Earlier, in May, 1937, the Field Security Wing of the Corps of Military Police was formed. Under Captain F. C. Davies, M.C., a small cadre of C.M.P. N.C.Os. trained selected Regular and Territorial Army soldiers in Field Security Duties. Subsequently, the Wing was transferred to the Intelligence Corps.

The introduction in 1938 of direct enlistments from civil life into the Corps marked a further step in the effort to increase provost resources. Probationer E. Vaughan was accepted as the first recruit under the scheme in August of that year. A high physical standard was required, and applicants had to pass an educational test and produce references of irreproachable character in lieu of the qualifications required of the soldier transfer.

In February, 1939, a provost company was allotted to each of the Territorial Army Divisions, and local recruitment for these units proved popular. Companies quickly came up to full strength and, indeed, some units had a waiting list. These Territorial Army provost companies were ready to carry out their allotted role on the outbreak of hostilities.

To overcome any immediate shortage of officers in the event of mobilization, a "post-mobilization course" in provost duties for officers of the Regular Army Reserve, the Territorial Army, and the Emergency Reserve was held at the Depot in May, 1939, and a number of those attending were earmarked for provost appointments on mobilization being ordered.

Arrangements were also made about this time for reservists from the Brigade of Guards, then serving in police forces throughout the country to be transferred for duty with the Corps of Military

Police on mobilization. In this way the provost potential was built up.

In July and August, 1939, Section "A" Reservists were called to the Colours, so that in the days immediately before the declaration of war the Corps contained 769 warrant officers and non-commissioned officers, 500 "Corps" reservists, 850 supplementary reservists (A.A. Scouts), 1,002 territorials, 500 Guards reservists and 500 reservists of other arms, thus making a grand total of serving men and reservists of 4,121. During the years immediately preceding the Second World War traffic control training was greatly intensified as a result of the mechanization of the Army.

The mobilization scheme included some rearrangement of the Provost Staff, Colonel S. V. Kennedy, the Provost Marshal of the United Kingdom, who was also Commandant of the Depot, and officer i/c Records, becoming Provost Marshal at G.H.Q. of the B.E.F., his place being taken by Colonel W. B. Hayley. The A.P.M. Depot, Major R. T. S. Kitwood, became Second-in-Command and Chief Instructor, and the Quartermaster, Lieutenant L. Stewart, Assistant Officer-in-Charge of Records. Provision was made for the formation of an administrative wing and a training wing.

The provost component of the first contingent of the field force, which formed on the outbreak of war and later went to France as part of the British Expeditionary Force, consisted of Nos. 1, 2, 5, 6 and 7 Provost Companies and No. 8 H.Q. Provost Company, mobilized at the Depot, and Nos. 3 and 4 Provost Companies, mobilized at Bulford and London respectively. In addition to the formation of these field force units, certain ports detachments had to be formed and some garrisons reinforced with reservists to replace the regulars withdrawn.

On the outbreak of war, therefore, provost units, with the exception of those in overseas garrisons, were in general of two kinds —the home command or static company, and the field formation company.

The static companies were home units whose duties were mainly of a garrison nature. A company was located in each Command and the men selected for these companies were those whose age or medical categories rendered them less fit for the more rigorous duties on active service. Their primary duty was the maintenance of discipline among the troops stationed at Home.

Field formation companies were allotted to army, corps, division and lines of communication, and were at that time, and with the exception of the latter, on a standard establishment consisting of a company headquarters and six sections, all fully mechanized.

On arrival in France the military police were immediately

confronted with much vaster problems of traffic control than had ever before been experienced. On disembarkation provost companies were at once heavily committed in the task of traffic control during the move forward from the ports. The road movement, the largest ever undertaken with motor transport by the British Army, was completed in a satisfactory manner. The late E. A. Montague, correspondent of the *Manchester Guardian* with the British Forces in France and son of C. E. Montague, the novelist, who was himself an A.P.M. in the Great War, described in a despatch to his newspaper in October, 1939, the part which the Military Police played in it:

"Visitors to the Aldershot Tattoo may hardly have noticed the military policemen who have shepherded them so efficiently round the right corner and into the right car park. These same men have carried out equally unobtrusively in the last few weeks a far bigger traffic job with brilliant success. They have steered and signalled the British Army across France.

"In cold figures, some 720 men of the Corps of Military Police have brought 25,000 vehicles many miles across country which they themselves had never seen until the day before the operation began, and they did so without any block or hold up or serious inconvenience to the normal French traffic. Never at any time did the driver of a vehicle have to open a map; his way had been marked for him by signs and Military Police at cross-roads.

"To each section of police was allotted a stretch of about fifty miles of road, to which it went on the day before the march began, explored its ground, stuck up its signs, and posted its human traffic controls. With the aid of its gendarme, it had to make itself known to the local French authorities and arrange common problems with them. In other words, it had to act for itself, and if it had acted wrongly no amount of good organization higher up would have saved the general movement of the Army from being blocked, perhaps seriously. The success of the operation was a tribute not only to fine organization which had been going on for a whole year, but also to the qualities of the men who carried it out.

"The Army is the first to admit that it owes much to the help of the Automobile Association, which organized 800 of its patrols a year ago as a special reserve of military police. More than half of the men who controlled the drive across France and are now controlling traffic in the British area are former A.A. Patrols. No vehicle took more than ten days over the journey, though there were several rest days when maintenance was done, and the speed of the vehicles in convoy never exceeded twenty miles an hour.

"In this, as in everything else, the co-operation of the French has been ungrudging and invaluable. It was originally arranged that the French should continue to control their own vehicles, and at first British and French controls worked together, but after the first twenty-four hours the French withdrew many of their men, seeing that the British military police were able to do the work alone, and now all but one in ten of French controls have been withdrawn. It is remarkable and delightful to see how efficiently the British military police controls the traffic even in big cities, and with what amiable docility the French obey them. The military police also have what they call their 'courtesy cops' who fulfil the same functions as at home (but, of course, confine themselves to British drivers), and if necessary report offenders to their commanding officers.

"Anglo-French co-operation is most marked when the British Forces take up positions in an area which includes a town. The Captain of the French gendarmerie who accompanies every company of British military police confers with the mayor of the town and the local chief of police, who give him all the information that a policeman needs about a new district, and helps him to allocate hotels, cafes and estaminets to the different ranks."

By November, 1939, the B.E.F. was settled in its defined formation areas. G.H.Q. had been established at Arras, where the Provost Marshal B.E.F., Colonel S. V. Kennedy, assisted by an A.P.M., Major C. F. O. G. Forbes, and a D.A.P.M., Captain V. A. D. Dunkerly, set up his Headquarters. Other holders of Provost appointments at the time were: A.P.M., 1st Corps, Major G. Ingham. D.A.P.Ms., 1st Division, Captain M. Baird; 2nd Division, Captain T. Cooper. A.P.M., 2nd Corps, Major M. Sykes, later to become Provost Marshal of India. D.A.P.Ms., 3rd Division, Major Dean; 4th Division, Captain H. V. McNally (later Provost Marshal, A.F.H.Q., and B.A.O.R., and D.P.M. War Office).

Lieut.-Colonel J. A. Jervois, was D.P.M., H.Q. Lines of Communication, which had been divided into sub-areas with D.A.P.Ms. installed at Brest, Rennes, Nantes, St. Nazaire and other important key towns in the rear areas. An A.P.M., Major Bassett F. G. Wilson, later to become Provost Marshal, 21 Army Group, was established in Paris.

About this time, in order to assist in the identification of provost units, provost companies allotted to divisions were ordered to include the number of their divisions in their own designation and companies allotted to Army and Corps were given serial numbers beginning with 101. No. 8 H.Q. Provost Company became No. 1 H.Q. Provost Company (L. of C.).

During the first few months of the war, the intake of recruits to the Depot of the Corps at Mytchett far exceeded the available quantity of uniform and equipment and it was sometimes saddening for the skilled motor-cyclists of the Corps to see their intellectual cousins of the Field Security Wing riding away to the B.E.F. on magnificent new motor-cycles which they had, in many cases, neither the skill nor the desire to use, while they themselves had to leave for their units without transport. The shortage which was, perhaps, most acutely felt, was of red cap-covers. One recruit who began duty in February, 1940, records that he did not receive an issue of a red cap-cover until July of that year.

Training at the Depot had been intensified from the outbreak of war and recruits and transfers, on passing out as trained military policemen, were posted to the new provost units then being formed for the later contingents of the Field Force and to the B.E.F. to fill vacancies caused by accident and illness.

During the period of inactivity of the B.E.F. in France and Flanders, police duties were similar to those at home with the additional responsibility of maintaining cordial relations with the French civilians—relations liable to be frayed by bad behaviour on the part of the British troops. Brothels had also to be kept under surveillance. Liaison with the French police was quickly established and the Corps of Military Police became the symbol of fair play to the British soldier and French citizen alike.

Pilfering of stores at the ports in France and in transit reached such alarming proportions that early in December, 1939, after a visit by Colonel Kennedy, Provost Marshal, B.E.F., to the War Office and to the Commissioner of Police, Scotland Yard, the Home Office sent Chief Inspector Hatherill to France to make a report.

Accompanied by Detective Constable Nicholls, Chief Inspector Hatherill made an extensive tour with Provost Marshal, B.E.F., and recommended that the military police should be augmented, and that the Provost Service must have a C.I.D. of its own.

The first detachment of the S.I.B. (Special Investigation Branch), under Major Campion, was posted to the Provost Service, B.E.F., and arrived in France on 29th February, 1940.

Towards the end of March, at the Provost Marshal's further request, Colonel Seymour Mellor, Chief Constable of the War Department Constabulary, accompanied by Captain Cheney, his Assistant Chief Constable (later to become Provost Marshal of the U.K. and Provost Marshal B.A.O.R. respectively) visited France to make recommendations, based upon W.D.C. methods, for the policing of docks, entrance-guarding, passes, etc. Amongst other things in his report, Colonel Mellor recommended an increase in the numbers of S.I.B. sections who were at the time of his visit already doing a great deal of work.

By February, 1940, the lines of communication had been

A MILITARY POLICEMAN WITH FRENCH SOLDIERS AND A
HOTCHKISS TANK, FRANCE, 1940

MILITARY POLICEMAN ON TRAFFIC DUTY IN CHERBOURG

reinforced by No. 2 H.Q. Provost Company (L. of C.), late Armoured Divisional Provost Company (T.A.), and No. 3 H.Q. Provost Company (L. of C.), renamed from 1st Armoured Divisional Provost Company. In April, 1940, the strength of the B.E.F. was increased by the addition of III Corps A.P.M., Major G. T. Senior, with 104 Provost Company, the 46th Division D.A.P.M., Captain H. L. Lofthouse, and the 48th Division D.A.P.M., Captain R. E. L. Warburton, with their respective divisional provost companies. 23rd Division D.A.P.M., Captain Watson, the 50th Division D.A.P.M., Captain N. A. H. Jordan, and the 51st Division D.A.P.M., Major C. L. Carlos-Clarke, with their Provost Companies, also came into the theatre at this time. The 53rd Division Provost (T.A.) was redesignated 105 Provost Company and allocated to the newly created First Army.

So far the military police in France had been guiding the ever-growing British force from the Channel ports to their dispositions in the British line and there attending to their many duties among the troops in a foreign country; but when the enemy advanced the Provost Service began to perform those duties for which they had so long been waiting.

With the opening of the enemy offensive in May, the B.E.F. moved forward to the River Dyle from Wavre to Louvain, a move of sixty miles across the Belgian frontier over unreconnoitred routes. Despite traffic difficulties, the manning of the Dyle defences was completed.

On 10th May the 12th Royal Lancers crossed the frontier on their dash to the Dyle; following them, and some six hours ahead of the main body, came the military police. With them was Captain S. A. Ralli, D.A.P.M. to the Provost Marshal, representing the Provost Service at Advanced G.H.Q. They had to find and sign the routes and lay down a system of traffic control. This was quickly done and the main body were able to move forward over a controlled routing system—signed right through to their positions.

Then down these routes broke a tide of refugees constantly increased and urged forward by ever-growing human floods at every side and cross-road. The numbers of the refugees and the assortment of vehicles from farm wagons to high-speed cars, intermingled with cyclists and pedestrians, all converging on to the main routes from every junction and track, blocked them and rendered them useless for military movements.

After eight months' study of traffic problems in France, it had been decided in April that the British Army needed something equivalent to the French "Regulatrice Routiere" system. Early in May, therefore, by transferring older men (many of them ex-A.A. scouts) from the provost companies in the B.E.F., the Provost

D

Marshal B.E.F., formed 151 Provost Company for traffic control duties under No. 1 Traffic Control Group, which took its orders from "Q" (Movements).

This was the first traffic control company to be formed in this war; and on 11th May, immediately after operations commenced, 151 Provost Company was deployed in the Amiens-Abbeville area. During its short but lively existence many of its N.C.Os. became casualties or prisoners of war in the German enveloping movement which ensued.

Almost before the military police had completed their task of freeing the roads of refugees they were called upon to undertake an even more exacting task—the evacuation of the British Army.

Everywhere in France and Belgium policemen were standing unrelieved at cross-roads while the armies rushed back to escape the closing German pincers. When the last vehicle had passed him the "Redcap" would discard his white traffic sleeves and, taking a rifle, would join the infantry covering the retirement. Nowhere did the military police take a more prominent part in active defence than at Arras. Here a section under command of Corporal Lucas, later of the Depot Staff, helped to man the defences in front of the town, armed with Bren guns and anti-tank rifles. Here is Corporal Lucas's own account of the action:

"By this time, I had managed to get all my men armed, mostly with rifles, for which there seemed to be a scarcity of ammunition. However, by stripping the dead and picking up odd stuff lying about, each man soon had a hundred rounds or so.

"We were actively engaged from about 13.30 to 20.00 hours, mostly with enemy motor cyclists, light tanks and infantry. Enemy planes, of course, were over all the time. About 14.00 hours a group of tanks came forward, but a C.S.M. of an infantry unit who was with us scored two direct hits with an anti-tank rifle on the leading one. Our gunners then got direct on the target, knocked out two, and the others withdrew.

"This sort of thing, interspersed with infantry attacks, kept on spasmodically up to about 7 p.m., by which time I had lost five of my men. Then a lone motor-cycle combination approached (I think the poor devils were dazed and lost). I waited until it got within 200 yards, and then let go a magazine out of the Bren. It must have killed all three Jerries outright, but the machine kept turning round and round in the road before it went into the ditch."

At Hazebrouck, too, military police N.C.Os. were detailed to various points to guard the roads against enemy tanks. The lack of defensive weapons was acute.

One party under a corporal was detailed to occupy the upper rooms of a house at a road junction, and by throwing bottles of lighted petrol on the tanks managed to stop them. Another three members of the section were engaged on reconnaissance work, riding out in the direction of the enemy and reporting their position.

At Dunkirk the British Army was assembling to embark for England. Weary, hungry, constantly harried by German fighters, the exhausted troops gained confidence from the unmoved "Redcaps" directing traffic and men in Dunkirk and on the beach. One corporal, after five N.C.Os. of his section had been killed, removed the white sleeves from his dead predecessor and, still wearing his service dress cap and red cap-cover, maintained a vital post at a cross-roads for twelve hours until all the British troops had passed through. The city around him was burning. He was the last soldier to leave it. As he did so he collected his traffic signs so that they should not act as pointers to the enemy.

On the beaches the military police achieved their highest peak of service and self-sacrifice. One after another, as divisions arrived at the beach, their own provost companies saw them embark and then fell out, staying back to assist others. They acted as marshals to the waiting queues, collected and caused to be brought back many thousands pounds' worth of arms and equipment, organized the evacuation of wounded and acted as messengers up and down the beaches. As a last duty they carried the wounded on board before sailing for England.

The final boat to leave the beaches before General Alexander's final inspection about midnight on Sunday, 2nd June, contained many military police, but many there were whose bodies marked the site of their duty.

Military policemen accompanied the Calais force and in the opening stages carried out their normal role, route reconnaissance and dock duties being perhaps the most important. Towards the end, however, their main and self-imposed function was that of anti-fifth-column patrols. In twos and threes, armed only with revolvers, they undertook a complete search of the city, rounding up and disposing of the legion of snipers who were shooting at our troops from the rear. Many an unseen fight to the death took place in garret and cellar in Calais between individual M.Ps. and snipers.

Finally, after all communications were cut, two volunteers were called for to carry a message from the encircled city to Dunkirk. Two C.M.P. corporals undertook the duty. One was killed, but the other, Corporal Illingsworth, completed his task. When he last saw the remainder of his comrades they were forming themselves into an infantry platoon with the intention of reinforcing the Rifle Brigade in the line.

★ ★ ★ ★ ★

THE Provost Service gained much in experience during the short campaign in France. Two things were clear. One was that military police could no longer be regarded as base troops who would never be in contact with the enemy, and the other that control of the traffic of a modern war demanded more men than the existing Provost Service could supply.

The gallantry of the military police and the tireless efficiency of the traffic control companies at El Alamein and on the Normandy beaches, and indeed in every theatre of war during the next five years, had their beginnings in those dark days immediately before Dunkirk.

CHAPTER IV

SECOND WORLD WAR: AT HOME

BY the end of June, 1940, the evacuation from Dunkirk was over; most of the soldiers of the British Expeditionary Force were back in the United Kingdom, but practically all transport, equipment, ammunition and stores were lost. Holland, Belgium and France had capitulated; Russia and the United States were neutral; we stood alone.

In the United Kingdom were a certain number of mobilized divisions and corps and many new ones forming; thousands of men were passing through infantry and other training centres; military camps and new H.Qs. were springing up everywhere and there was activity in planning and preparing coastal and inland defences against the expected invasion. But in June, 1940, we were practically defenceless; the menace of invasion loomed over us and the defence of Britain was the order of the day.

There were striking differences between the military commands at home, which considerably affected the training and development of military police during the next four years.

The Eastern Command in June, 1940, covered the Eastern counties north of the Thames, and also south-eastern England, Kent, Surrey, and Sussex; those points of the United Kingdom, in fact, nearest the enemy; and because of this, most favourable for landing, most tempting to Germany and vulnerable to us. Inevitably Eastern Command and the more easterly portion of Southern Command became the potential front lines and forward areas. The other Commands, removed from the threat of initial shock, were organized as the main base.

In Eastern Command there were few main depots or big manufacturing districts, most of which were concentrated in the other Commands, which, incidentally, were far larger in area and contained most of the big cities and long road distances in this country.

The lightning German campaign through Holland, Belgium and France had illustrated the appalling dangers of the refugee problem. In France we had seen thousands of refugees driven ahead of the German forces to mask the fire of the defending armies. We had also seen vast French armies virtually immobilized by roads blocked by the civilian refugees and their vehicles forming an impenetrable barrier to military movement.

This refugee menace obviously produced a military traffic-control problem of the first importance, and in addition to this problem all road signs and place names in the United Kingdom had been removed for security reasons. This added to the difficulty of controlling and organizing our own military traffic routes. The need to solve these problems was to lead to the formation of the C.M.P. (Traffic Control Wing) in July, 1940.

It was evident that the closest liaison would be necessary between military and civil police and the regional police staff officers, who had been appointed in all the civil administrative regions into which the country had been divided for the war. A great number of recruits from civil life were now stationed all over the country under military discipline. This raised a problem for the police particularly in big towns and crowded areas.

With regard to "civil" as opposed to "military" crime it was obviously desirable that the Army should, in the interests of discipline, deal with soldiers so far as it was possible. In the case of serious crime, military offenders would, of course, have to be dealt with in the ordinary civil courts; but a good understanding with the civil police should permit petty offences to be handled by C.Os.

There is necessarily a big difference between the employment of the provost service under peace conditions and in war time. What might be called the "policeman" complex was, of course, a form of hangover from peace conditions, where the military police were chiefly conspicuous in carrying out disciplinary street patrols in Aldershot and other big military centres and when their activities were apt to be associated, by other troops, primarily with guard-rooms and charge-sheets.

The Army as a whole did not, at this stage of the war, appreciate either the difficulties or scope of the operational role which traffic control in modern mechanized warfare was to cast upon the provost service. This lack of understanding was to prove an obstruction to the operational development of the use of military police in the early days. Further, it was to lead to mis-use of the military police on duties for which they were not designed, a habit which took a long time to eradicate.

For a long period during the war the status of most provost officers was below that of officers of other important services. Some appointments remained undergraded at the end. This was mainly because of the failure to appreciate the provost war-time role; but from the outset it put provost officers at a disadvantage in conference as it caused a loss of weight in argument.

From the start it was clear that manpower was to be a difficult problem. It was soon found that too many "A" category men were employed guarding depots, dumps, installations, H.Q.s., etc. The double need to release all fit men from these duties, and to enable them to be carried out with fewer men was to lead to the formation of the C.M.P. (Vulnerable Points Wing) in February, 1941.

In July, 1940, Colonel W. B. Hayley retired from the office of Provost Marshal of England and Sir Percy Laurie was appointed as his successor and promoted Brigadier.

In January, 1941, A.P.Ms. Commands were upgraded to D.P.Ms. Lieutenant-Colonel's appointment. At this time the D.P.Ms. in the different Commands were as follows:

Northern Command, Lieut.-Colonel P. J. J. Pickthall, succeeding Lieut.-Colonel Bryant appointed P.M., Middle East, in April, 1940.

Southern Command, Lieut.-Colonel G. C. Firbank.

Eastern Command, Lieut.-Colonel C. T. O'Callaghan.

South-Eastern Command, Lieut.-Colonel W. D. A. Hall.

Western Command, Lieut.-Colonel W. H. Diggle.

Scottish Command, Lieut.-Colonel W. T. F. Holland.

London District, Lieut.-Colonel C. R. Gerrard.

Northern Ireland District, Lieut.-Colonel J. N. Cheney.

In 1940, for tactical reasons of command in the event of a German invasion of south-east England or the eastern counties, Eastern Command was split into two; Eastern Command retaining the eastern counties north of the Thames and a new South-Eastern Command being formed, and including approximately Kent, Surrey and Sussex and the old Aldershot Command, which now became a district under South-Eastern Command. Lieut.-Colonel Senior was appointed D.P.M. of South-Eastern Command.

Commands were, in general, sub-divided into areas of administration and operational responsibility under newly formed corps, districts, sub-districts, independent brigades, garrisons, etc.; districts and sub-districts were sometimes administrative only, sometimes with limited operational roles.

The provost service settled down quickly into this new pattern, but except in Eastern Command, South-Eastern Command and Northern Ireland disciplinary duties were predominant.

The potential "front-line" character of Eastern Command and South-Eastern Command gave a far greater impetus to the operational training of military police than it was to enjoy elsewhere. This distinction, coupled with the comparative absence of big towns and manufacturing districts and their disciplinary problems, naturally led in time to traffic control companies trained in these two commands becoming more operationally efficient than those in other commands, where road distances were much greater, and where traffic control companies accordingly were spread over larger areas and deployed on a more rigid and static plan.

The arrival in Southern Command of Dominion troops and,

later in 1942, of American Forces, at first increased the burden for provost until the respective Allied Provost Wings became operative, and even then the "Redcap" was frequently called in to mediate and advise. As was to be expected, friction occasionally resulted and the duty of the military police was to prevent incidents and endeavour to keep the relationship as amicable as possible. Their tact proved equal to the task. In the latter part of 1940 the newly formed traffic control companies helped civil police in the control of traffic in bombed areas. Practices with the Home Guard and civil police reserves, of action to be taken in the event of invasion by the enemy, took place.

Compared to those in operational formations, the London "Redcap" undeniably had a more interesting job than many of his less fortunate comrades hidden away in comparative backwaters. Just as the London "Bobby" has rightfully earned for himself a reputation for reliability, so did the London military policeman come to be regarded as a fair if firm disciplinarian on the London streets.

From a 1939 establishment of three officers and 116 other ranks the London District Provost Company increased steadily until in June, 1945, its complement was 598 other ranks controlled by a D.P.M., 5 A.P.Ms., 2 D.A.P.Ms., 1 A.P.M. (V.P.) and 1 D.A.P.M. (V.P.). The following extract from a letter written by a retired Colonel to the Editor of *The Times* is a tribute to the London "Redcap":

"There must be many ex-officers like myself who served in the regular Army as far back as 40 years ago and who have observed with great pleasure the remarkable improvement in the conduct of the troops, especially in such places as railway stations, trains, restaurants, cafes and public-houses, etc., where large numbers congregate from time to time.

"I should like to pay tribute to a particular branch of the Services which I feel has played a most important part in helping to maintain this remarkable display of general good conduct. It is one of which little is heard, and is known as the Corps of Military Police. The Provost Marshal and his assistants have without doubt inculcated a remarkable spirit of 'first-aid' in the Military Police. There is a striking resemblance in this Corps to the London 'Bobby,' who has a reputation of being, first and foremost, always helpful. I have watched the Military Police carrying out their duties in railway stations and other places. They appear to be imbued with the spirit of helpfulness and advice rather than seeking for offenders. I recently watched two of them examining leave passes at one of the London railway stations, and could not help but notice the friendly spirit in which they stopped troops for the inspection of their passes, and in returning the passes to them often gave advice regarding such matters as to the buttoning up of coats or the wearing of hats at the correct angle, etc. A smile on both sides, and the soldier buttoned up his coat and walked off. I am sure there must be many others who have observed the work of the Military Police and who can testify to the same effect. The absence of military offences in the Army today is due to many reasons, but the Corps of Military Police can certainly be credited with their share of minimizing offences outside barracks and camps."

During the bombing of London the C.M.P. proved that the discipline they expected in others was inherent in themselves. Throughout the bombing, beats were maintained. All available men were standing by with first-aid kit and traffic direction equipment to assist the civil police.

Within a comparatively short time after the formation of the Traffic Control Wing in July, 1940, thirty-two companies were formed in the United Kingdom. They were organized in groups, usually of four companies, under a group commander, with a group H.Q. and a small administrative staff.

Although initially raised for traffic control duties at home, most of these companies ultimately saw active service in the North African and European theatres of war. The skill and devotion with which they carried out their duties at home and overseas was to bring distinction to the Corps.

These traffic control companies were formed on somewhat similar lines to a divisional provost company, but the rank and file were privates instead of lance-corporals. The sections were seventeen strong instead of sixteen as in a divisional provost company. One extra subaltern and one extra sergeant were also on the strength, making the total traffic control company strength 123 as compared with a divisional provost company strength of 115. The transport was mainly buses and charabancs to take sections to their posts along the road.

The personnel were usually recruited from Infantry Training Centres and therefore consisted of men with little or no military background, and of course, no police training whatever. They were selected by D.P.Ms. in each Command. Group and company commanders, C.S.Ms. and section sergeants were, whenever possible, individuals with previous military police experience; in most cases the section sergeants were good military police lance-corporals promoted for the purpose, who filled the bill admirably.

For the rank and file the only qualifications were that the men should be of good average intelligence, and be capable of being trained in map reading and writing reports; they were not at that time required to ride either a motor-cycle or pedal bicycle and there were no special requirements as to character. Both these last points were wisely amended at a later date.

Each C.M.P. (T.C.) Company was allotted by Commands (or by Corps) to a specific area, in which they were made responsible for signing, patrolling, facilitating and logging the passage of convoys, and furnishing road information on specified military routes. This was a purely static role; and indeed their function was, at that time, to be little more than human sign-posts. They were formed as a matter of high priority in July, 1940; but it was not until 10th October that it was decided they should become a new wing of the C.M.P.

Provost officers were, however, given only a limited control of this new wing; for whilst D.P.Ms. were responsible for discipline, individual training, administration and supervision of duties, the operational training of C.M.P. (T.C.) companies, their disposition and tactical use were the direct responsibility of the staff; *i.e.*, of "Q" (M.) in commands, or of a staff officer, usually a D.A.A.G. in corps.

In the B.E.F. corps and divisional A.P.Ms. and D.A.P.Ms. had already won their spurs and gained their Commander's confidence in their ability to carry out difficult operational duties under war conditions; but, at home, it was not until March, 1943, nearly three years later, that Exercise "Spartan" showed that dual control spelt disaster, and the provost service was at last made master in its own house, and given effective command over its own troops.

During the defence period there was the greatest activity in Northern Ireland, for not only had precautions to be taken against I.R.A. activity but a field force had to be mounted to advance into Eire in case of a landing by the Germans.

In this plan the military police played an important part. On receipt of information that the Germans were about to invade Eire the border between Southern and Northern Ireland was to be closed and the Army concentrated upon it before advancing upon the Germans, with the possible approval and assistance of the Eire Army.

The military police forces in Northern Ireland at this time were comparatively larger than those in the United Kingdom. Corps and each of the three divisions had their own provost company. In addition there was a Command provost company in Belfast and an Army Company at H.Q. British Troops in Northern Ireland.

The provost resources at the D.P.M's. disposal were increased by one of the newly formed T.C. Groups (three companies) which was sent over to Ireland, to assist the great movement of the

British Forces south if invasion took place. Fortunately the I.R.A. gave no serious trouble, but from time to time their activities were troublesome to the traffic control companies. When controlling an exercise or other road movement the traffic control patrols would in the usual way put out signs and arrows. Within an hour they would either have had their direction altered or be missing altogether.

The culprits were never caught, but the traffic companies had to change their method of signing. A red dye was produced by a local chemist. This was placed in powder form in a large number of small paper bags. A truck would be loaded with these bags and whenever it was desired to indicate a direction round a corner an N.C.O. would throw out one or two bags which left a red streak in the direction required. This successfully foiled the I.R.A.'s activities.

On the whole the I.R.A. had a healthy respect for the military policeman and, while shots were quite often exchanged with members of the Royal Ulster Constabulary, the "Redcap" patrols remained always unmolested.

It was fortunate that there were few disciplinary troubles among troops at home so that the police were, on the whole, able to concentrate on traffic control training. Commanders were naturally apprehensive that the colossal intake of raw civilian recruits into the new armies forming at high speed might be little amenable to Army discipline and cause a major problem. On the whole their fears were not realized, as both young and middle-aged men who were called up to the colours came in with a sense of urgency and defiance of the enemy, which caused them for the most part readily to accept Army ways, dress, routine, and discipline.

On the other hand, in a few cases, this apprehensiveness of some Commanders led to their provost companies being employed upon disciplinary duties to an extent which left little time for that vital operational training which these companies, many of them newly formed, so urgently needed.

Corps and divisional provost companies were, in the main, fully occupied with troops of their own formations; but in garrison towns, big cities and areas of troop concentrations there was a growing general disciplinary problem which brought about a considerable increase in Command provost companies.

Command provost companies were organized in varying numbers of small sections and had less mechanical transport and therefore less mobility than formation provost companies. The Command military police were for the most part allotted for static police duties to garrisons and big towns where they worked under the orders of the local Commander. Their duties were purely concerned with local discipline; and a slightly lower medical category was accepted for Command military police than for formation military police.

The Ports provost companies formed for police work in ports and harbours and the S.I.B. (Special Investigation Branch), which was mainly formed from detectives, are dealt with elsewhere in this history.

During the Defence period, military exercises, if not actually testing and practising local defence schemes, were usually defensive in character. The development of the operational role of military police gained little assistance from these exercises; which were, too often, rehearsing the withdrawal in as good order as possible from a prepared defensive position to a switchline or vice versa.

Indeed, the police of at least one divisional provost company were the only troops upon which the Commander could call for the defence of his H.Q. in the event of an attack by parachutists. An N.C.O. of one of these companies has described the activities of his company in those early days:

"We were a mixed lot of N.C.Os., racing motor-cyclists and ex-civil policemen, mostly, with a few regulars. Some of us knew all there was to know about how to get the best out of our motor-cycles and others all about the laws of evidence and the Larceny Act, but I can't say that many of us had much idea of military discipline. Between the Company we had four red cap-covers. These were allotted to the men on the Divisional H.Q. gate. Town patrols just did without. Soon after Dunkirk when the invasion scare was at its height we were issued with revolvers and six rounds of ammunition. There weren't any holsters and we went around with our pistols, old fashioned 45's, stuck in our belts like pirates.

"Most days, sometimes several times a day, we were called out to defend Div. H.Q. from imaginary parachutists."

At this time also the unsound habit of attaching sections from the divisional provost company to brigades became prevalent, and was to prove one of the hardest evils to eradicate. Many divisional and brigade Commanders at that time gaily but unwisely insisted upon decorating their gateposts with smart "Redcaps," and employed them to check passes in H.Qs. of minor importance.

They learned by later war experience that there were never enough military police to do their legitimate jobs; and that the breaking up and dispersal of a divisional provost company out of the control of its own officers was not only bad for its internal discipline but made it impossible for the A.P.M. or the O.C. company to handle it economically or efficiently in operations, or even to train it properly for battle.

Corps and divisional provost companies as organized and formed before the war proved a complete success. Only a few improvements and additions were made from time to time in personnel, transport and equipment; and it can be fairly claimed that they fully justified the foresight of their original creators. One of the principal improvements was the substitution of jeeps for the unsatisfactory motor-cycle side-cars.

Towards the end of 1940, owing to shortage of officers, D.A.P.Ms. were struck off the War Establishment of corps H.Q. and A.P.Ms. corps were left to compete alone. This was, operationally, a retrograde step: especially as the new C.M.P. (T.C. Wing), having just been formed, the chances of Provost Service to assert their influence and attain full executive responsibility for the employment of this Wing became even more remote.

In February, 1941, the second big addition to the C.M.P. strength was made by the formation of the Vulnerable Points Wing. The V.P. Wing was designed to carry out purely static guard, patrol, gate and security duties (on the lines of the W.D. Constabulary) at vulnerable points such as depots, dumps, wireless stations, secret installations, tunnels and bridges.

There were many places of this character throughout the United Kingdom which had to be permanently under guard against sabotage, espionage and kindred risks; many of them, indeed, contained papers, apparatus and installations of a highly secret nature; which, in the event of the defence of the vulnerable points themselves becoming overborne by an attacking enemy, must without fail be either removed or destroyed.

The vulnerable points were classified under different headings, some to be held at all costs to the last; others, in the event of invasion, to be dismantled and evacuated; but, in all of them, patrol duties, security duties and in some cases a certain amount of traffic control, were necessary. Before the formation of V.P. Wing these tasks were performed by local infantry detachments. This caused an unacceptable interference in the battle training of the infantry; and, moreover, was wasteful in manpower as it was found that one trained C.M.P. (V.P.) working on War Department Constabulary methods could replace satisfactorily three or four infantrymen who carried out guard duties in the manner normal to their own type of training.

D.P.Ms. Command were responsible for their technical training, their discipline and technical supervision and partly for their administration. To help them in this task A.P.Ms. (V.P.) were added to the staff of D.P.Ms. Command; actual working orders and, in the main, local administration of the V.P. police was the duty of the local Installation Commanders to whom they were attached.

The allotment of V.P. sections to the various installations was the task of the "G" Branch of Commands with the technical advice of the D.P.M.

Men of higher age-groups and also of low medical category were acceptable and a minimum height of 5 ft. 3 ins. was laid down.

When the Wing was first formed the character requirement was "no bad characters"; but this requirement was, owing to the responsible nature of their duties, very properly changed to "not less than very good."

The V.P. Wing was at first organized into sections of eight men each with a sliding scale of N.C.Os. which varied according to the number of sections employed together in one locality.

Several hundred police dogs were trained (together with their handlers); they were organized in sections and attached as a rule to vulnerable point companies. They were first used in the U.K. to give increased protection at vulnerable points, and to economize manpower. Later they were used effectively in Egypt, the Middle East, Central Mediterranean, and in North-Western Europe.

Brigadier Sir Percy Laurie, upon his appointment as Provost Marshal, was at once confronted with a gigantic task of organization and expansion. Within his first twelve months he organized and expanded the S.I.B., the T.C. and V.P. Wings; and throughout his three years of office, the whole Provost Service was in a rapid and constant state of growth.

The figures speak for themselves. When Sir Percy Laurie assumed office on 17th July, 1940, the total Provost strength was 194 officers and 8,350 other ranks; on his retirement on 2nd July, 1943, it had risen (including the new wings) to 553 officers and 32,000 other ranks.

No one without an exceptional degree of administrative ability, driving power and tact could have succeeded in this formidable task. There is no doubt that Sir Percy Laurie's wide experience and tireless energy in building up this great force, and in securing for the Corps the right types of officers and other ranks, laid the sure foundation for that highly trained and well-disciplined body of provost officers and men of all three Wings, who gave such a good account of themselves in the later and more critical phases of the war.

*   *   *   *   *

IN June, 1941, the main German armies became involved in the invasion of Russia; in December, through the aggressive action of Japan, the United States entered the war as our active ally. Within a short time American troops began to pour into this country via Northern Ireland. The menace of German invasion had now receded; nor was it likely to recur on a major scale, unless Russia collapsed and thereby set free the main German armies.

During the next two years provost commitments were to be a continued preparedness against the reduced risk of German invasion of the United Kingdom; campaigns in Greece, Crete, Syria, Abyssinia and Madagascar, etc.; defence of Egypt and the Eighth Army campaigns in Libya, and other commitments in the Near East; the war against Japan; allied landing and campaign in North Africa; preparations for the Second Front in Europe.

Of these commitments, defence measures involved the continued deployment in the United Kingdom of a considerable number of traffic control companies and the manning of many vulnerable points with C.M.P. (V.P.), nuisance raids by the enemy on a big scale being still considered a possibility. The preparation and mounting of First Army and the armies for the Second Front were full-scale major commitments which could not be allowed to fail.

The preparation of provost forces for the First Army and the allied landing in North Africa produced no major problems for the provost staff as there were still ample resources in this country to draw upon; it was, however, to produce two interesting and significant innovations.

They were the addition to the military police resources of a C.M.P. (T.C.) Group consisting of a Group H.Q. and six companies, and also a few beach "bricks" which consisted of provost sections specially trained for police work on the beaches and in the bridgeheads. Both these innovations were subsequently greatly developed during the mounting of 21st Army Group for the Second Front.

After the allied landing in North Africa the preparation of the Second Front forces became the principal task to which everything else was subordinated. In the early stages, the only guides to intelligent anticipation were that the forthcoming invasion involved an assault landing upon a number of beaches, the capture of a port or ports, two lines of L. of C. each 250 miles long, and an Order of Battle consisting of G.H.Q., two armies, and a large L. of C. organization.

G.H.Q. Home Forces were charged with the formation of the Order of Battle and raising, equipping and training the forces and units which it comprised. In February, 1943, a D.P.M. Home Forces was appointed to cover the provost side, which had hitherto had no direct representative.

The development of the military police machine had to be moulded upon a just mixture of lessons drawn partly from provost reports from overseas (particularly from Eighth Army and First Army) and partly from large-scale assault and invasion exercises in the United Kingdom.

A continental assault was a fairly safe assumption; hence planning proceeded upon the assumption of a landing and subsequent campaign in an enclosed country with all the complex traffic problems which a network of main roads, lanes, rivers, bridges, towns and villages would provide.

The preparation of the Second Front provost force was attended by many difficulties. Bids for officers and men had to be sustained against an ever-growing manpower problem, and the natural reluctance of C.Os. to part with good officers or N.C.Os.; whilst bids for essential transport and equipment were made against the conflicting claims of other arms out of a pool insufficient to satisfy the needs of all.

Provost staff officers were still out-ranked by their opposite numbers in other services; their voices in conference and bidding continued to suffer, therefore, from this disadvantage.

Only after stringent measures following Exercise "Spartan" in March, 1943, and the publication by G.H.Q. Home Forces of the *Common Doctrine*, was the correct relationship between the staff and provost in traffic control matters to be finally and satisfactorily established.

A thorough examination by the provost staff in the spring of 1943 of the earlier edition of the Order of Battle for the Second Front was to reveal that the proposed allotment of traffic control companies, L. of C. provost companies, ports companies and Special Investigation Branch fell far short of bare necessities. The organization of L. of C. companies needed drastic revision if these units were to be able to sustain their destined roles.

Traffic control companies, allotted for service overseas, had to be weaned from their static and defensive state of mind, retrained in operational and disciplinary duties and largely re-equipped; so that in a theatre of war they should become as far as possible interchangeable with provost companies.

Provost resources being insufficient in the Second Front Order of Battle, and fresh sources of supply of military police personnel in the United Kingdom being unobtainable, the question arose whether use could be made of the only remaining source of supply, namely the C.M.P. (Vulnerable Points Wing).

The military police role in the assault, in the beach maintenance areas and in the bridgeheads would clearly be a vital factor in consolidating and exploiting a successful landing. Military police detachments had therefore to be organized for this role. These military police beach units had, owing to manpower shortage, to be found from the L. of C. companies allotted in the Order of Battle, which were planned to revert to their normal L. of C. role after the bridgehead phase was over.

The assault plan called for more beach provost units than the allotted L. of C. companies could arithmetically provide. Each company had only one officer, the company commander, practically no transport and no signing equipment; but all these were vital, first for the beach units, and later for normal military police work in the L. of C.

The question of communications for military police and particularly for traffic control companies was recognized by the staff to be of great importance. For technical reasons of overloading the radio telephone net was denied to the traffic control companies as a matter of general routine, though for some specific operation the staff might order its use. In the end a solution was found.

*   *   *   *   *

IN November, 1941, Lieut.-Colonel Pickthall, then D.P.M., Northern Command, was appointed D.P.M., War Office, within the Provost Marshal's staff with the local rank of full Colonel. He was succeeded in Northern Command by Major Bassett Wilson, then A.P.M., 12 Corps.

All Commands had by now their own C.M.P. training depots, which had been primarily formed to train the C.M.P. (V.P.) intake during the building up of the V.P. Wing. They soon began to be used for training recruits to T.C. Wing and suitable personnel from the T.C. Wing for transfer into the Provost Wing and for refresher courses of all three. They proved a particularly valuable training asset during the building up of the Second Front forces.

In December the A.T.S. Provost Wing was formed. Eight D.A.P.Ms. were appointed, one to each Command and to London District. Probationer auxiliaries went through one month's course in police duties under provost instructors at the C.M.P. Depot at Mytchett.

The influx of the American troops, vehicles and stores into the United Kingdom began early in the year and proceeded apace. They were landed in ever-increasing numbers in Northern Ireland, and from there went to their various areas in Great Britain, where they carried out their training and formation. They brought their own military police with them.

The sudden arrival of American troops in Northern Ireland set the police there the biggest problem they had yet had to tackle—a vast disembarkation of troops in the comparatively small port of Belfast. However, all went well largely owing to the energy and ability of Major A. P. Green, A.P.M., Belfast.

A military police officer who was in charge of arrangements in one of the docks has described the landing:

"It was a typical grey Northern Irish day—drizzling rain and a

E

chilly wind. Everyone was in position—the movement Control Officer, the military police, the Royal Ulster Constabulary, transport—all waiting impatiently for the first ship to arrive. Outside the dock gates a great crowd (who, of course, knew exactly what was going to happen, although the arrival of American troops had been kept a secret) collected and began to sing 'Yankee-doodle.'

"At last the first ship arrived, the British and American Generals greeted each other—the band struck up and the U.S. soldiers got their first glimpse of the United Kingdom."

The first contingents of U.S. troops were accompanied by M.P. companies, some of which, at that time, had received but little police training. Many were the problems which confronted the D.P.M., British Troops, Northern Ireland, Lieut.-Colonel J. N. Cheney. In Londonderry disorders between U.S. marines and British sailors were frequent—too often British soldiers joined in to support their naval comrades. Eventually a picked detachment of military police under the command of a staff lieutenant, all of them big men and ex-civil policemen, were sent to Londonderry. In a few weeks' time, with the ready help of the Royal Ulster Constabulary and other Service police, they had suppressed the worst disorders and arrested the trouble-makers, but it was not until the arrival of the United States Marine Shore Patrol that really effective measures were taken against obstreperous U.S. troops.

There were, of course, the usual troubles between U.S. and British troops over girls—one incident unfortunately resulting in the killing of a British pioneer. However, owing to expert S.I.B. work, the culprit was eventually arrested.

The Americans poured into Ireland in vast numbers—stopping in Northern Ireland for a time and then moving on to the United Kingdom to take their place in the ever-growing army waiting to invade Europe.

Within a very short while a system of combined patrols (one British and one American military policeman) was introduced throughout the United Kingdom; a system which served to initiate American police into our methods of patrolling, which helped them and was effective in establishing good comradeship between the two military police forces.

Meanwhile, preparations had started in the United Kingdom to build up First Army and to train them for operations for which they were about to undertake.

In April Lieut.-Colonel Senior, D.P.M., South-Eastern Command, vacated this post to take up the appointment of Chief Constable of East Suffolk, and Lieut.-Colonel Bassett Wilson, D.P.M.,

Northern Command, was moved down to South-Eastern Command to replace him. Major J. P. Moreton, previously A.P.M., Northern Command, was promoted D.P.M., Northern Command.

Provost Marshal, War Office, Brigadier Sir Percy Laurie, was granted the local rank of Major-General. This was a step in the right direction, followed in May by the upgrading to A.P.Ms. of D.A.P.Ms. in divisions.

Exercise "Tiger" was staged in South-Eastern Command by General B. L. Montgomery. It was of great interest to the provost service. 12 Corps and Canadian Corps were fighting. 12 Corps, which was the first to attack, carried out a large dumping programme, followed by a precipitous fighting advance, in the middle of which they were suddenly and unexpectedly ordered by the Director to withdraw. The roles were immediately reversed, and 12 Corps had to conduct a fighting retirement at high speed, relentlessly pursued by Canadian Corps.

The exercise was, therefore, a high test for both staff and troops in rapid advance and rapid retirement, over a poor road system; first at short but reasonable notice, and afterwards (when the roles were reversed), at practically no notice at all. The exercise strained and tested to the full the traffic control arrangements of the corps and divisions which were taking part. For the first time traffic control companies were employed in an exercise of this kind, one company being allotted to the A.P.M. of each of the competing corps.

The provost report on "Tiger" which was included in the official administration report of South-Eastern Command recommended:

1. That in modern warfare a corps cannot function without the addition of a traffic control company to its normal military police resources.

2. That the proper and economical use of T.C. involves the setting up of a central corps traffic control plan, which must be co-ordinated by A.P.M. Corps, and have firm links between corps and divisional areas of responsibility.

3. That the directional discs issued to provost and traffic control companies for road signing should be exclusively confined to operational and administrative routes laid down by the staff; and that a new square sign with a red arrow be used in future for all subsidiary routes.

4. That a D.A.P.M. or a Staff Lieutenant should be added to the staff of A.P.M. Corps.

In July Lieut.-Colonel Mark Sykes, D.P.M. and Commandant of the C.M.P. Depot, Mytchett, was appointed D.P.M., First Army. He was succeeded by Lieut.-Colonel Frank Wright.

A Traffic Control Group consisting of six picked traffic control companies under command of Major Hart were detailed for special training and preparation for the forthcoming operations with First Army. These companies were concentrated, mobilized and their operational training completed in Eastern Command and South-Eastern Command. Each company was equipped with the full number of jeeps, now authorized for traffic control companies. They were to become part of the normal transport of all provost and traffic control companies.

Three provost beach bricks (consisting at that time of two provost sections and no officers) were formed and trained under Combined Operations Headquarters on the coast of Ayrshire, for the work which they would have to do during the assault and the subsequent development of the bridgeheads.

Their task was one of great responsibility and difficulty. Immediately after the first landings upon the beaches, successive waves of craft, would continue to arrive carrying troops, vehicles and stores. The task of the military police beach detachments was to get ashore in the early stages, bringing with them sufficient signs and signing equipment to lay out, organize and control the traffic routes for wheeled and tracked vehicles and walking personnel from the beaches into their respective transit areas, and thence on to the various assembly areas.

These routes followed a key plan which was prepared beforehand by the staff from aerial photographs and other forms of reconnaissance, and developed inland as the attack progressed.

In addition to these routes there was the important task of signing and controlling traffic circuits covering the ammunition and supply dumps, vehicle parks, field dressing stations, prisoner-of-war cages and many other installations comprised in the beach maintenance area which had to be developed at top speed. Experience was to show that two military police sections without an officer was inadequate for this difficult task.

The build-up and the preparation for the provost resources of First Army were completed by the end of the autumn, when the force embarked and left the United Kingdom. On 23rd October the battle of El Alamein took place and Eighth Army advance began. On 8th November the allied forces, including First Army, landed in North Africa.

It had been decided at Casablanca to resume the concentration of forces in the United Kingdom and to begin detailed planning. A joint Anglo-American staff therefore was set up for this purpose under a Chief of Staff to the Supreme Allied Commander. This staff, taking the initials of its leader's appointment, became known as Cossac.

Meanwhile, the preparations for which the G.H.Q., Home Forces, were responsible continued and included the building-up of the order of battle, and the training of formations and units.

On 16th February, 1943, Lieut.-Colonel Bassett Wilson, then D.P.M., South-Eastern Command, was appointed D.P.M., Home Forces. Major B. D. Armstrong, A.P.M., Western Command, was appointed D.P.M., South-Eastern Command. Later, in May, Second Army was formed with its H.Q. at Oxford. Lieut.-Colonel F. C. Drake, who had been Commandant of the South-Eastern Command C.M.P. Training Depot, was appointed D.P.M.

The first fortnight of March was taken up with a great exercise called "Spartan." Two armies were in conflict; one represented a British invading force, under the command of Lieut.-General McNaughton, with a Canadian Army staff reinforced by some British staff officers, including a British "Q" (M.) staff. The British Army was composed of British and Canadian corps, with port and base depot installations and administrative troops which functioned along an L. of C. from Southampton to a line north of the Thames. This tested the operational and administrative traffic problems which arise from the capture of a port and swift penetration into an enclosed country. The other army was based in the Eastern counties and represented the forces of an invaded enemy country.

The importance to the provost service of "Spartan" cannot be over-emphasized. The confusion on the roads in the rear of the fighting formations showed the fundamental weaknesses of the existing traffic control system; but this time the lessons were learned, and the sequel defined the practical and proper relationship between staff and military police, and put the provost service in a position to carry out, on their own responsibility, the taxing operational role for which the development of modern mechanical warfare had cast them.

It was not difficult to put a finger upon the contributory causes of the traffic control inefficiency in "Spartan." The chief and overriding cause was dual control; it was inevitable that, at some point, a complete breakdown must arise in a rapidly expanding traffic control system where two masters were in the saddle with divided and conflicting responsibilities; and where the master who sought to exercise control of allotment, dispositions, and even the giving of executive orders, was a staff officer sitting in his office and not the senior provost officer of the formation, who was, in fact, in control of the troops involved.

The next cause was the absence of any guiding principles governing traffic control in the back area. The staff had not decided what they wanted; there was no *Common Doctrine* setting out either the staff requirements, the information and orders which the staff must give to provost, or the service which provost must provide to implement those orders.

Finally was the fact that, while the traffic control companies were able to handle with speed and efficiency the clearing of traffic jams and other local problems, they showed for the most part a lack of ability to provide or maintain any linked system of service and control over the ever-lengthening operational and administrative routes; nor, in some instances, were they able to move at speed to a new sector, and without delay or confusion, take over and control an existing traffic control layout or set up a new one.

This last criticism principally affected groups from Northern Command and (to a lesser extent) Southern Command, whose traffic control companies were normally deployed, for convoy duties, over widely spread posts covering huge road distances. Groups from Eastern Command and South-Eastern Command, where distances covered by companies were far less, and where normal company duties were always more identified with operational conditions, not unnaturally were able to put up a better show.

In the British Army in Exercise "Spartan," operational orders to traffic control companies were issued direct by "Q" (M.) to the traffic control Group Commander concerned without reference to the D.P.M., who often was unable even to ascertain where they were. The resulting chaos had to be seen to be believed; but it proved in the end to be a blessing, even though in somewhat unpleasing disguise.

The use in "Spartan" of the traffic control companies by the British Army was purely on a hand-to-mouth basis; there was no ordered plan or development of T.C. over the lengthening road communications, no organized system of linked traffic posts, information posts, communications, road intelligence or road services.

Even the road signing was unco-ordinated; the base sub-area staff adopted numerals 1-7 for the road nomenclature in their area; when these roads broke into army areas they were marked by letters of the alphabet. In corps areas farther ahead, the same through roads received yet a new set of alphabetical letters; a system which appeared to be devised for the sole purpose of ensuring that drivers of lorries would inevitably lose their way. Not only were the drivers and convoys lost but the traffic control companies were utterly at sea and hopelessly befogged.

Full provost reports upon "Spartan" were submitted by D.P.M., Home Forces, to the chief administrative umpire and to M.G.A.,

Home Forces, Major-General Lorie, who called a conference to deal with the important points which "Spartan" had produced. Decisions were taken on all the vital issues. As these decisions represent a landmark in the development of the traffic responsibilities of the military police, the most important are set out below:

Organization.

(*a*) Traffic Control Group H.Q. to be abolished.

(*b*) An A.P.M., Traffic Control, to be added to staff of D.P.Ms. having traffic control companies in their formation.

(*c*) A.P.M., Traffic Control, to be located during operations near "Q" (M.) at Formation H.Q.

Executive Responsibility.

(*a*) D.P.M. or A.P.M. to be executively responsible for traffic control and for the fulfilment of the traffic plan in accordance with orders issued by the staff.

(*b*) The D.P.M. to be responsible for technical training, "Q" (M.) to see that operational training is carried out.

Operational Employment.

(*a*) System of traffic control to be linked vertically and horizontally.

(*b*) Logging requirements and the minimum information to be given by the staff to the T.C. organization were laid down.

(*c*) Principles for the control of bridges, bottle-necks, field maintenance centres, etc., were approved.

Traffic Office.

It was decided that War Office should be recommended to appoint a D.A.A. and Q.M.G. (M.) to run a traffic office in each corps.

Communications.

The principle was established that it must remain the responsibility of the General Staff and Signals to see that T.C. were provided with adequate signals communications.

Road Signing.

A definite code of road signing was agreed, the main features of which were the strict limitation of the use of C.M.P. directional discs to the main operational and administrative routes and the provision of rectangular signs with red arrows for local and subsidiary routes. (This had already been recommended in June, 1942, after Exercise "Tiger.")

TRAINING.

Central School under G.H.Q., Home Forces.

It was agreed that a central school in traffic control work should be set up by D.P.M., Home Forces, under G.H.Q., Home Forces.

Command Training.

It was decided that two traffic control companies in rotation should, whenever possible, be taken off normal duties and given operational training.

Equipment.

(*a*) It was decided to increase the holding of directional discs, Franco signs, stencils and guards' lamps for both provost and traffic control companies, and to standardize this holding so that the companies of each wing had the same allotment.

(*b*) It was decided to issue loud-speakers to every provost and traffic control company.

Medical Categories.

It was recommended that the policy of substituting lower medical category for "A" category for traffic control should cease.

Armlets.

It was agreed that traffic control personnel should be supplied with M.P. armlets so as to increase their authority.

The *Common Doctrine* which resulted from the conference was published in May, 1943, under the title "Notes on the Control of Military Road Movement in a Theatre of War." The general object was stated as being "to attain uniformity in the control of military road movement in the theatre of operations." The pamphlet was ordered to be studied by the staff "who prepared each movement plan, by provost and traffic control units who are principally concerned with its execution and by units who have responsibilities towards the traffic control organization."

The traffic control courses ordered by the M.G.A.'s conference were held during four successive weeks.

Exercise "Spartan" and its immediate sequel were mainly concerned with the reorganization of the traffic control wing, the new appointment of A.P.Ms. and D.A.P.Ms., Traffic Control, the relationship between staff and provost, the preparation of the *Common Doctrine* and the training necessary.

It did not, however, touch the question of the general sufficiency of provost resources, as allotted in the order of battle for the Second Front. A close examination of the order of battle revealed a shortage in the allotment of traffic control companies, ports companies, S.I.B. and the L. of C. companies from which beach units had to be provided. It also revealed the defects in the war establishment of the allotted L. of C. companies as already described.

The first step taken was to press for an increase in traffic control companies, of which only eight were allotted in the order of battle, and in the end the allotment of traffic control companies was doubled and thus raised to sixteen.

This would leave eight traffic control companies in the United Kingdom which were earmarked primarily for reinforcements and for Operation "Harlequin," the code name for the complicated business of assembling, sorting out, marshalling and embarking the Second Front expeditionary forces.

It was agreed by the War Office that, after the invasion was launched, up to four further traffic control companies would, if need arose, be made available for the Second Front, leaving the four remaining companies as emergency and drafting companies in the United Kingdom.

The War Office were then asked for C.M.P. (V.P.) companies for overseas duties. A case was put up asking for ten special C.M.P. (V.P.) companies to be raised and trained as auxiliary police to assist provost and traffic control companies in P.W. escort duties, static traffic control duties in towns, auxiliary military police work in big towns and congested areas and normal vulnerable point duties.

The need for increasing the three allotted sections of the Special Investigation Branch was, of course, obvious; but the difficulty in this case was not in convincing the War Office of a patent truth, but the provision of men holding the necessary qualifications.

This question was, however, being tackled by the Provost Marshal, War Office, who obtained all the suitable men possible with the requisite civil police experience, trained them at Mytchett to give them a military background, and produced, as the war continued, considerable additions of first-class material to this most important branch.

A certain number of men who had little or no previous civil police experience but a definite flair for this work were also trained and proved a success. Notable amongst them was Lance-Corporal F. W. Buckland, a business man in civil life, who became one of the most efficient of S.I.B. Sergeants, with a standard of personal integrity and devotion to duty which brought great credit to the Corps.

There was a similar need for increase in the case of ports companies. The single ports company allotted would be clearly far short of the minimum needs as the invasion progressed. Ultimately, two additional ports companies were provided.

The formation of L. of C. companies and beach provost units proved a troublesome question. Owing to the acute shortage of personnel the provost beach units had to be provided from the allotted L. of C. provost companies, the intention being to re-form the L. of C. companies as such as soon as operational conditions permitted.

The War Office allotment in the order of battle was four L. of C. provost companies formed upon an old war establishment. Each company consisted of six sections, commanded by a captain, and having no transport and no signing or other operational equipment.

The Second Front plan called for a minimum of six provost beach units, consisting each of one H.Q., one O.C. Company, two subalterns and four sections, fully mobile and complete with transport, and signing equipment. Apart from the operational role of these units on the beaches, it was never contested that, under conditions of modern warfare, an L. of C. provost company must be as fully officered, self-supporting and mobile as a formation provost company to cope with the disciplinary and traffic control work which would fall to their lot along an extended L. of C.

Towards the end of 1942 1 Corps moved to Scotland to train. In addition to their own normal formations, 1 Corps had the special task of the general training of a number of beach groups on the Ayrshire coast. Half a dozen beach groups were formed and contained all the requisite fighting troops and services, including a beach provost unit of the composition described above. No unit had a more responsible or vital task in the successful development of the assault and the subsequent penetration inland than the provost beach company.

Major F. A. Stanley, then A.P.M., 1 Corps, spent much time and displayed great foresight in supervising the development and training of the provost beach units, and in obtaining authority for the issue of special signing equipment and lamps. Some of these beach provost units were formed from redundant provost companies of disbanded formations; others mainly from recruits coming from Mytchett or Command Training Depots.

Meanwhile other military police units for the Second Front had to be formed, such as a G.H.Q. nine-section provost company and a similar one for Second Army. These companies were formed by taking further redundant provost companies from disbanding divisions and H.Q., British Troops, Northern Ireland.

The important operation of marshalling and embarking the expeditionary force was one of great complexity for the police. It involved the transport of troops and vehicles from all parts of the United Kingdom, their concentration in special areas where they could be finally briefed, the waterproofing of their vehicles and other final preparations. Then they had to be marshalled into boat loads, taken down to ports and "hards" and embarked in small parties at short successive intervals.

The scheme was first considered and put into preliminary shape during the winter of 1942-1943; its improvement and final perfecting remained a commitment of the first importance to D.P.Ms., Command. One further step forward was now obtained by the reappointment of D.A.P.Ms. on the staff of A.P.Ms. Corps.

★   ★   ★   ★   ★

IN North Africa, Sicily and Italy, the enemy was on the run; in Russia, Stalingrad had been relieved, and the Germans were being steadily rolled back; in the Far East the Japanese were beginning to suffer heavy reverses. Full-scale invasion of the United Kingdom by Germany was now out of the question. At most, nuisance raids, possibly on a big scale, might be attempted.

The provost and C.M.P. machine for 21 Army Group still needed much to complete it, but the foundations were all laid and the work went steadily ahead. The V.P. (Overseas) companies were not yet officially authorized, and the L. of C. companies still required their revised war establishment.

On 22nd July, 1943, 21 Army Group was formed under the command of General Sir Bernard Paget, who relinquished command of Home Forces. With him went the bulk of his Home Forces staff. At the War Office Major-General Sir Percy Laurie relinquished his post as Provost Marshal of the United Kingdom on the completion of his three years' service. He was succeeded by Major-General Seymour Mellor, who was at that time Chief Constable of the War Department Constabulary.

Major-General Sir Percy Laurie had presided over the fortunes of the provost service during a period of unprecedented expansion, during which over 32,000 suitable officers and other ranks had to be trained and absorbed into the provost service. The Corps owes Sir Percy Laurie a deep debt of gratitude for the successful achievement of this great undertaking.

With his retirement passed an imposing and lovable figure. He left behind him in the provost service many friends.

Lieut.-Colonel Bassett Wilson, who had been D.P.M., Home Forces, became Provost Marshal, 21 Army Group, with the rank of Colonel; Major F. Stanley, his A.P.M. in Home Forces, became his D.P.M. in 21 Army Group with the rank of Lieutenant-Colonel. Lieut.-Colonel F. C. Drake was already D.P.M., Second Army, and Lieut.-Colonel Ball had been appointed D.P.M. of Canadian

Army. Later in the year Lieut.-Colonel J. N. Cheney, D.P.M., H.Q., B.T.N.I., was appointed D.P.M., L. of C., 21 Army Group.

In July, 1943, shortly after 21 Army Group was formed a big scale invasion exercise, "Jantzen," took place in South Wales; the purpose was to test the whole assault machinery for a landing in force from the sea and the building up and exploitation of a bridgehead and beach maintenance areas and sub-beach areas. It was, in fact, a full-dress rehearsal for the provost beach units who had undergone such long and arduous training in Ayrshire.

In this exercise a testing trial was also made of the use of large numbers of bicycle lamps, with coloured screens, for route and track-lighting. Ultimately, after the L. of C. provost companies had obtained a new war establishment, each beach provost company was authorized to hold, in addition to their normal equipment, 2,000 bicycle lamps and coloured screens.

The principle of including six Vulnerable Point (Overseas) Companies in the order of battle was agreed by War Office towards the middle of 1943. The war establishment for these companies and therefore the official sanction to form and mobilize them did not pass the war establishment committee until February, 1944.

G.H.Q., Home Forces, were, however, fortunately most helpful; and in August, 1943, shortly after the formation of 21 Army Group, these six companies were unofficially formed, concentrated and trained for their new duties by D.P.Ms. of Commands in which they were raised.

They proved a great success; V.P. officers and other ranks were determined to show that older and less physically fit men could do as well as the younger ones; and no one who witnessed their subsequent performance in active service could say that they fell short of their ambition. They were in every way a great credit to the Corps.

In December, 1943, General Montgomery took over command of 21 Army Group from General Paget. Major-General Miles Graham succeeded Major-General Lorie as M.G.A. For four years Major-General Lorie had held the post of M.G.A. successively to South-Eastern Command, Home Forces and 21 Army Group. During all this time, but chiefly during the last two appointments, he was in a unique position to exercise great influence upon the fortunes of the military police. No service ever had a stauncher supporter and friend. He understood to the full the value of a good and efficient provost service to a commander; he also understood military police problems and difficulties, shouldered them, made them his own and fought their battles.

During the summer of 1944 military police were responsible for sealing both the marshalling camps in which the invasion troops were briefed, and the hospitals to which casualties who had been briefed were sent.

The V.P. Wing was responsible for guard duties in "S" Area (Tilbury-Southend), the operational area from which part of the invasion forces actually sailed, and for the two decoy areas "R" and "Q," where dummy landing craft and phantom armies were continually on the move.

It is right that these men who worked in the "dummy" area should be remembered, for there was little satisfaction in their sterile task. Their tact and efficiency deserve full praise, for not only had Germany to be deluded, but our own civilian population as well.

The latter suffered considerable inconvenience from the closing of roads and the stopping of transport services. Despite all these annoyances there was not a single unpleasant incident. Also the perfect harmony in which the V.P. men worked with the civilian police is both noteworthy and praiseworthy.

As General Montgomery and his staff were in charge of the joint planning for both 21 Army Group and the American forces under General Bradley, American staff officers were attached to their opposite numbers in 21 Army Group to ensure proper co-ordination between British and American forces. Two American military police representatives, Lieut.-Colonel Rudolph and Lieut.-Colonel Phillips were accordingly attached to the staff of Provost Marshal, 21 Army Group. When shortly before the beginning of hostilities in June, 1944, they were returned to their own armies, the departure of these two alert and excellent officers was much regretted by the provost staff at H.Q., 21 Army Group.

Colonel Stadtman, Provost Marshal of General Bradley's 12th United States Army Group, was in constant personal touch throughout with Provost Marshal, 21 Army Group, and his staff. His strong, invigorating and lovable personality will never be forgotten by those in 21 Army Group who knew and trusted him.

Only one matter of major importance still remained to be settled. The M.G.A., as a result of experience with Eighth Army, was insistent that the provost service should have its own independent signals. To achieve this end one of the sixteen traffic control companies was re-formed, equipped, and trained by Signals, 21 Army Group, in ground signals duties. The six-section organization was retained, each section being equipped and trained to enable it to work independently, and therefore to be allotted as a self-contained sub-unit to an army, a corps or any other formation or organization as required. This new unit proved of great value.

Special training in disciplinary and traffic control duties was given to T.C. and V.P. Companies respectively to make them interchangeable in battle; an object which was in fact largely attained. With regard to traffic control, the roads at home were too good and the available vehicles too few to provide realistic training; but conditions in Normandy were soon to provide, albeit in a rough school, the means of perfecting their technique.

All troops who were to take part in the initial assault were put through an intensive training upon prepared territory of the dimensions and containing as far as possible similar features of the area in which they would be operating after the assault. Nothing now remained to be done except to wait for D Day and to hope that no vital steps had been missed out either in training or equipment.

In the latter days of May and the early days of June, 21 Army Group was fully mobilized and prepared; "Harlequin" now took place, no longer as an exercise, but this time as the actual operation, and 21 Army Group was duly concentrated and assembled for embarkation. The provost and traffic control arrangements proved first class and worked without a hitch.

An officer of a traffic control company responsible for the control of D Day traffic wrote this account:

"Came D Day and the vehicles, the tanks, jeeps, trucks, bull-dozers, cranes, S.P. guns, all the assorted engines of war, moved forward to their embarkation points. The columns moved endlessly. The nights were filled with the grinding roar of tanks, the squeal of their tracks. the grumble of their engines. The darkness was punctured with the blue flames of their exhaust.

"At all critical points were the traffic control police and their auxiliaries, working all hours, leading convoys, pointing the way, marshalling vehicles, splitting up units into unit craft parties, building up unit craft parties into craft serials, timing them, setting them on their way, calming the agitated, stimulating the laggard, always alert, always present.

"One can see them now, the sergeant with his clip of orders from Movement Control, working in the vehicle parks; the corporal at the telephone in his traffic post, counting the vehicles in each craft serial as it passes his point, endlessly and tirelessly; the officer in charge of marshalling in the embarkation area, ushering the serials into their boxes, holding back the thruster, chasing the laggard, calling each serial forward as the landing craft were made available; the D.R. on his motor cycle, taking orders to a craft serial commander, rounding up a straggler, taking over point duty at a temporarily busy road junction.

"Not a vehicle was lost, not a serial was late, there was never a hold-up nor a delay which could be attributed to the fault of traffic control. By the end of July nearly 30,000 vehicles had passed through the marshalling area. Traffic control had handled them all."

*   *   *   *   *

SO ends the story of a stupendous effort of staff planning, organization and troop training. From the military police point of view, both the operational and disciplinary duties and technique of Provost Traffic Control and Vulnerable Points Wings had been organized and rehearsed in as full detail as could be foreseen, and the whole provost service was now working upon the same lines. Just as there was complete harmony and unity of thought between the three Wings themselves, so was there now full understanding and co-operation between provost and other branches of the staff, and between the military police and the other troops, and our U.S. Allies.

For some eighteen months the task of forming and training this vast Expeditionary Force had been carried out with determination. There had been prunings here, enlargements there, and progressive improvements by trial and error; details of equipment and stores had been worked out to the last ounce, personnel to the last essential man; but there remained a conviction that elasticity had been preserved, and that the mainsprings of this great fighting machine were so well tempered and tightly compressed that, once released, they would carry the British liberating armies irresistibly forward.

CHAPTER V

SECOND WORLD WAR: NORTH AFRICA

B EFORE September, 1939, there were the usual garrison detachments of military police in Cairo, Alexandria, and Moascar, mostly coming under the direct control of the respective Garrison Adjutants.

There was an A.P.M., British Troops Egypt, Major King, and he was responsible for provost work throughout Egypt. The military police in Palestine came directly under War Office, the officer in nominal charge being the Staff Captain "A" of H.Q., Palestine Base.

There had been no possibility of forming Territorial Army companies of C.M.P., as had been done in the United Kingdom. There was approximately one full regular company in Palestine and less than that in Egypt; there was no depot, all the administration being centred in Bab-el-Hadid Barracks in Cairo; there were few facilities for training men: in short, there was practically nothing.

In 1935 a special company had been formed at Mersa Matruh to control the Egyptian-Italian frontier, but they returned home in 1937, leaving some personnel behind in Palestine.

Military police in Egypt and Palestine in pre-war days were always working in close liaison with the respective local police forces. Both the Egyptian and the Palestine Police were mainly officered by British personnel, and a percentage of the senior N.C.Os. of both forces was also of the same nationality. This was naturally of great help and of even greater use after the war started. Several of the civilian police officers had had military police experience during their service in the British Army, and were thus able to appreciate the difficulties peculiar to the C.M.P.; the most notable example was Lewa T. W. Fitzpatrick Pasha, then Commandant of the Suez Canal Police, who always gave ready help to the C.M.P.

At the outbreak of war little change occurred in the C.M.P. in the Middle East. Locally based units provided a few volunteers and a few more trickled out from the United Kingdom. A few more officers joined the Corps, among them Lieut. P. V. Lovell-Payne, who became D.A.P.M. British Troops, Egypt, to Major King in September, 1939. The New Zealand Division brought their own military police with them, thereby nearly doubling provost strength in the Middle East; they co-operated very well indeed.

Towards the end of 1939 it was decided to open a field punishment centre in Egypt. Mersa Matruh was chosen as the site, and Major King was posted to make all preliminary arrangements and to become the first Commandant. These arrangements took the best part of three months, and as he was still officially A.P.M. British Troops, Egypt, and no replacement was made in Cairo, his absence naturally caused a strain on the already slender administrative provost resources in Bab-el-Hadid.

Before the New Year, 1st Cavalry Division arrived in Middle East without any military police, and a company was formed for the division. Soon after this 4th Indian Division arrived in Middle East. It was believed that the division was completely equipped as far as provost was concerned; a rude awakening took place on their arrival when it was found that, while theoretically completely equipped, practically all the personnel were untrained. So the British military police got down to it again, found some space somewhere in Bab-el-Hadid and instituted a series of training courses in all that a military policeman should know.

It was obvious that Italy would soon enter the war, and that the aim of the Axis would be the Suez Canal. So provost were instructed to earmark personnel for a Western Desert Force. Captain Lovell-Payne was A.P.M. designate. By this time a small additional number of reinforcements had arrived from home, a cadre was formed and went into preparatory training at Bab-el-Hadid.

Lieut.-Colonel F. C. Bryant, previously D.P.M., Northern Command, was promoted Colonel soon after his arrival in Middle East and appointed Provost Marshal. Then came reinforcements of officers and N.C.O.s.; but, in spite of this, for the first three years of the war Middle East provost always had the impossible task of trying to get a quart out of a pint pot.

On 10th June, 1940, Italy declared war. The A.P.M. designate of the Western Desert Force had left Cairo on 9th June to visit the provost detachments at El Daba and Mersa Matruh. He arrived at the former place on the 10th, having been delayed in the desert, to find war was declared. He contacted the Provost Marshal by telephone and was instructed to rendezvous with the nucleus of the Western Desert Force, which had left Cairo that morning at Maaten Bagush. On arrival there, the G.O.C. was not entirely pleased to find that his provost force consisted only of the A.P.M. and his driver.

However, a small force of military police arrived at Maaten Bagush the following day ; on this was built the Western Desert Provost Company, always on the job up and down the desert, and also always woefully short of men. It is of interest to note, especially to those who took part in later desert campaigns, that after the first

F

capture of Benghazi, the total strength of military police in the Western Desert was 3 officers and 80 N.C.Os. strung out between Antelat and Sidi Barrani.

The Western Desert Force was composed of 7th Armoured Division and 22nd Guards Brigade (commanded by Brigadier I. D. Erskine, later to become the Provost Marshal,) and 4th Indian Division, with Corps troops. The provost company detached approximately two sections to serve with 7th Armoured Division. The only other military police in the Western Desert were those of 4th Indian Divisional Provost Company, which were not completely trained.

On 10th September, 1940, the Italian Army launched their offensive, which, however, petered out some fifteen miles east of Sidi Barrani in the north and Sidi Omar in the south. During the weeks that followed, the enemy established a series of perimeter camps. In November General Wavell's plans for a British offensive against the Italians matured. The first inkling which the A.P.M. of the Force had of these plans was an instruction to police a certain area of desert where training would take place. An approximate facsimile of the Nebeiwa and Tummar campaigns was marked out on the ground, and the first training exercise took place on the 25th/26th November.

After this was over they were told that the exercise had not been altogether satisfactory and that another exercise would be held at a later date. In the first week of December, provost working both with 7th Armoured Division and H.Q. Western Desert Force moved out to take their respective positions for this exercise which, however, turned out to be the real thing.

On 9th December an attack was made on Nebeiwa, which was a brilliant success, and the first part of the phase of the operation which was to chase the Italians out of Egypt began. The principal work carried out by the military police was track marking, a small amount of traffic control and duties in connection with Ps.W.

By 5th January, Bardia had been captured, and the work of military police entered on a most difficult phase. The A.P.M. was given the job of evacuating Italian Ps.W. from Bardia to Sollum, where they were to be earmarked for Alexandria. They were given specific sailing dates and hours which had to be strictly maintained, and in order, therefore, to get the Ps.W. out of the advanced cages and back to Sollum, continuous convoys had to be arranged.

There was no transport, the distance was sixteen miles, and the majority of Ps.W. were half starved and shell-shocked. The largest number of police N.C.Os. which could be spared for each convoy of 500 prisoners was 5.

Orders were given that the A.P.M. and as many N.C.Os. as

possible should get into Tobruk as soon as possible, and accordingly on 21st January the police followed up the last wave of infantry and arrived on the outskirts about the same time as the final white flag was hoisted. It was decided, however, that Tobruk should be considered an "Australian" town and that control from the point of view of discipline should be carried out by the Australian divisional military police company, with assistance from British provost. On arrival in Tobruk, therefore, the principal work allotted to C.M.P. was in connection with the evacuation of Italian Ps.W.

As the battle receded towards Benghazi a great strain was thrown on provost in the control of traffic. A large portion of the Forces had to be carried over the single coast road, which in many cases had been demolished.

In the meantime, 7th Armoured Division and provost personnel were aiding the advance of the division in the south. It was generally understood that Benghazi would fall early in February, and the A.P.M. and a small party of military police were ordered forward to take part in the entry to the town and endeavour to maintain order. Unfortunately, they had to make a considerable diversion over ground which bogged vehicles over the axle, and it was not until the day after the capture of Benghazi that they arrived in the town, to find the usual state of chaos.

At this period, no form of military control, such as Civil Affairs, existed, and the A.P.M. was entrusted by the Sub-Area Commander with reorganizing the entire police system in Benghazi. For this purpose, a composite civil police force had to be made up from the various bodies which had functioned in the town before its capture. Members of the Carabinieri, national police, Italian African police and municipal police were accordingly welded into a more or less composite force which, on the whole, functioned fairly satisfactorily. Provost shared with the civil police the responsibility for running the fire brigade.

By extremely drastic measures, a reasonable degree of order was restored in the town and looting and drunkenness restricted. An anecdote which gives point to these observations is that the entire stock of a Benghazi brewery was removed and consumed one night by the unit on guard who were responsible for the security of the premises and contents.

On 24th February, 1941, Major Lovell-Payne handed over to Major Bury, late A.P.M., 1st Cavalry Division, and returned to Cairo for a fresh posting.

At the end of July, 1941, Major Bury was posted home at short notice. His handing over to Major A. R. Forbes, who had recently arrived in Middle East as A.P.M., 10 Corps, took place in

Cairo. This entailed for the latter a sudden journey into the "blue."

H.Q., Western Desert Force, was at Maaten Bagush divided into two parts about a mile apart. Rear H.Q. lived and worked in tents dug down in silvery sand and chalk close to a small bay. The A.P.M. was located here. Main H.Q. lived in tents on higher ground, but worked in a network of underground offices which had the advantage of being free from sand-storms.

The general situation was quiet and the 7th Armoured Division was about four miles south of Mersa Matruh and had instructions to avoid contact with the enemy, who were a mile or two west of the Egyptian–Libyan frontier. The Divisional D.A.P.M. was in the process of training his provost company in desert navigation, and he had already evolved the system of track and axis signing which was to stand the test of the final victorious desert operations.

During August there was a show of force by an enemy mechanized column, causing the armoured division to withdraw a few miles, but this served as an excellent exercise for the divisional provost company, who acquitted themselves well. The A.P.M. was visiting the division when the operation started.

The main function of 204 Provost Company at this time was traffic control and enforcement of road discipline on the coast road, also water point duty.

Towards the end of August, 1941, an Army H.Q., soon to be named Eighth Army, was formed in Cairo, and Major Forbes was appointed D.P.M. He was not provided with an Army Provost Company at first, but as a result of several visits and appeals to the P.M., Colonel Bryant, it was agreed that 10 Corps Provost Company would be allotted as soon as it arrived in Middle East.

When this provost company disembarked they were met by an old friend in Corporal Paxton, who had left the Company in United Kingdom a few months before. Paxton was killed later in an air raid on Tobruk, but he had worked wonders towards making the company desert-worthy in a short time.

In September, 1941, Eighth Army H.Q. assumed command in the desert with Advanced H.Q. near railhead at Mischeifa, while Main and Rear occupied the former Western Desert Force camps near Maaten Bagush. For the first few and important weeks Eighth Army was still waiting for a provost company to be allotted. The D.P.M.'s task was therefore a difficult one since Corps and Divisional provost companies, with the exception of the New Zealand and 2nd South African Divisions, were much under establishment. The 204 Provost Company was in the process of becoming 13 Corps Provost Company, but was in fact, together with two sections of the New Zealand Provost Company, trying to fulfil the role of an Army provost company. Major E. W. Hayton was A.P.M. of the New Zealand Division, and his willing co-operation enabled a skeleton provost organization to be established. The 7th Armoured Division Company was fully employed by its own formation, as was the 5th Indian Division Provost Unit, which consisted of a Company H.Q., two British sections, one Sikh and one Mohammedan section. The British other ranks were not members of the C.M.P. and had received scant training.

Railhead Sub-Area Commander had in this early stage a provost officer, Captain Dalrymple, and one section, which was inadequate for the manifold duties, two of which had to take priority over all others, namely track marking and signing. Important duties at water points and prevention of pilfering had to be neglected.

With the arrival of 105 Provost Company it was possible to dispense with the two New Zealand sections and release 204 Provost Company for its correct role.

Sand-storms meant additional work for provost and signal line maintenance parties between railhead and Corps. In their anxiety to keep to the tracks in bad visibility, drivers used to go far too close to track signs and signal poles, usually with unfortunate results.

With the advent of the first offensive by Eighth Army, railhead gradually became a hive of activity. Enemy air attack increased, but the dummy railhead a short distance west of the real one came in for most attention. The dispersal of vehicles was an important function of provost at railhead, forward maintenance centres and all H.Qs. Normally the plan was "one bomb one vehicle," but when space was limited vehicles were parked in twos.

The D.P.M. was for the first twelve months or so located at main Army, but before the El Alamein battle of 1942 it was realized that in an advance he must be farther forward.

Before any appreciable advance could be undertaken it was necessary to bring forward as far as possible the water pipe-line. The work was carried out by Libyan Arab P.W. labour under R.E. supervision. When the date fixed for the first advance was only a fortnight off it was discovered that there were attempts to sabotage the project by blocking the pipe at the most inaccessible places; in addition to which a big petrol fire occurred in the petrol siding on the eastern perimeter of Mersa Matruh. Lieutenant Nicholls and two N.C.Os. of S.I.B. investigated.

After several days and nights of inquiring and observation it was established that the P.W. labour was responsible both for the Mersa Matruh fire and for the destruction by fire of a 10-ton lorry loaded with petrol. Lieutenant Nicholls' recommendation that all P.W. labour should be withdrawn from certain types of work was acted upon immediately and Pioneer labour substituted. With forty-eight hours still to go the final test of the water pipe-line was carried out successfully.

30 Corps H.Q. was located on a track a few miles south-west of Mersa Matruh. Major Kay, 10th Hussars, was appointed A.P.M., but after a few months he went back to his regiment and subsequently commanded it with distinction, for which he was awarded the D.S.O. When the attack started, which had as its primary objective the relief of Tobruk, 13 Corps was on the right near the coast and 30 Corps on the left.

The advance of the Eighth Army was held up soon after crossing the frontier into Libya, and provost detachments at the various gaps in the frontier wire and minefields had a very busy time. After a stalemate of several days, General Auchinleck visited Army Tactical H.Q., located near Ridotta Maddelana. The Army Commander, General Cunningham, who had fought a firm and highly successful campaign against the Italians in Eritrea and elsewhere, was replaced by General Ritchie. After a further struggle some advance was made by 13 Corps, culminating in the heroic battle of Sidi Rezegh, where Brigadier Jock Campbell earned his V.C.

When the advance continued it was soon found necessary by Major Kirk, A.P.M. 13 Corps, and Major Kay, A.P.M. 30 Corps, to institute forward patrols to prevent wanton pilfering of scarce and valuable instruments and fittings from knocked-out armoured fighting vehicles and crashed planes. As a result of this pilfering several tanks had to be evacuated to base workshops for repairs, whereas had they not been interfered with they could have been back in action after a day or two in Army Workshops.

With the relief of Tobruk the provost commitments were considerably increased, especially for the Army Company, since L. of C. had lengthened by some seventy miles and no special L. of C. provost companies were available. The 70th Divisional Provost Company, which had done such valiant work during the siege, was quite rightly withdrawn with the division for a rest and re-fit. Tobruk therefore became the responsibility of 105 Provost Company. A strong detachment was located in one of the few remaining buildings intact overlooking the harbour. Sunken ships were everywhere, navigation even for small ships was hazardous, and nearly all off-loading had to be done by lighter.

All this handling of stores made added opportunities for pilferers. Soon, however, a rigorous system to prevent losses was put into operation, but was not made easy by the frequent bombing raids. Traffic always presented a problem in Tobruk, and vehicles frequently broke down on the twisted gradient above the harbour.

Advanced Army H.Q. was moved into an area midway between Tobruk and El Adem, to a site surrounded on all sides by minefields and an assortment of small miscellaneous explosives and booby traps.

A day or two after the fall of Tobruk the A.P.M. 13 Corps, Major Kirk, was blown up in an air raid in which Corporal Paxton was killed. The A.P.M. was evacuated and he was replaced by Major Vredenburg, who was soon after replaced by Major Blake; and just before the big battle of Knightsbridge, A.P.M. 30 Corps, Major Kay, left to join his regiment and was succeeded by Major Rees-Reynolds.

Plans were made for a further advance westwards and these included extending the railhead to Mekili and marking a track across the desert from Al Adem to Msus. The task of marking this route was given to the D.A.P.M. Army, Captain Cashen, an officer with an almost uncanny knack of finding his way about in the "blue." The day after completing this stupendous task the D.A.P.M. set out over the route and found his way with little difficulty to H.Q. 13 Corps, a trip of some 250 miles over every conceivable type of desert going. A few days later the Afrika Korps started an offensive and advanced along this very route which Captain Cashen had so painstakingly marked the previous week.

By the end of May it was clear that the attack of the Afrika Korps had gained considerable impetus. Main Army H.Q. was at that time at Timimi and, with the evacuation of Benghazi and then of Derna, orders were given at short notice for Main Army to move back once more to Tobruk. The move out of Benghazi by provost was well planned and they left their H.Q. scrupulously clean and tidy. Captain Melville, the D.A.P.M., left a note in German on his desk saying that the C.M.P. had left their accommodation clean and would expect to find it left clean by the Germans when the British took over at a later date.

The first few miles were very difficult indeed, the road narrow, gradients steep and corners sharp. When a vehicle caused an obstruction the C.M.P. put it over the side.

Another small detachment of 105 Provost Company, assisted by a few N.C.Os. of a traffic section, detached from the traffic organization in Cairo, had been controlling the exceedingly steep and hazardous Derna pass. Some drivers could not face the descent and their vehicles were driven down by military police N.C.Os.

Owing to the congested state of the coast road it was decided that Main Army H.Q. should move back to Tobruk across the desert, and the D.P.M., who was then with Rear Army, personally supervised the marking of this track. The task, part of which was carried out after dusk, was completed with half an hour to spare. The provost detachment at Timimi had a colossal task in getting Army H.Q. vehicles on to the track and at the same time keeping the endless procession moving along the coast road. Luckily there was little enemy air activity. Major T. C. Irvine, who was later to become D.P.M., Eighth Army, was at that time attached to Army provost, and the D.P.M. put him in charge of the Timimi detachment. Under his command they did wonderfully well and finally came back as whippers-in to the procession.

While all this was going on to the west, provost were fully employed along the L. of C. Pilfering from trains and at railhead was a problem requiring continuous attention. At Christmas a lorry load of whisky, valued at several hundred pounds, had vanished. The D.P.M. therefore issued instructions for a series of simultaneous raids to be carried out at selected points on receipt of a code message. This system worked well and large quantities of N.A.A.F.I. and other attractive stores were recovered after many hours of search and digging. One rubbish dump at railhead concealed wines, spirits, sweets, canned goods and even tooth-brushes.

It was hoped that once the Afrika Korps had been halted west of Tobruk it would be possible to launch another offensive. In readiness for this eighty Grant tanks—they were looked upon as a match for anything Rommel could produce—arrived from America. Road traffic became heavy all along the coast road and Sollum Hill, with its steep gradients and sharp bends, required rigorous control, especially when tank transporters were ascending it.

Towards the end of May, 1942, Eighth Army was once more prepared to take on the Afrika Korps and the morale of the men was high. The Army commander's plan was to let Rommel attack and then fight him on ground of his own choosing. The general defensive line ran west of Tobruk from the coast to Bir Hakim, where a French Brigade was located. In the centre was the 50th Division, who bore the brunt of the initial attack. The provost company had worked hard to make a first-class H.Q., but within a few hours of the battle starting it had been overrun. 13 Corps H.Q. was soon after the victim of a raiding column, and several members of the Corps provost company became involved in the general melée which resulted in some N.C.Os. being taken prisoner, but for most of them it was only temporary captivity. Enemy air activity increased and raiding columns were increasingly active.

The tank battles which took place in the first week of June resulted in heavy casualties for the Eighth Army's armour, which received rough handling from exceedingly well concealed 88-mm. guns. When it appeared that the battle was going badly preparations were made to bring into operation a plan for further retirement. This required a great effort from provost, and 105 Provost Company, already widely dispersed, was split up into 14 detachments in

DESERT MILITARY POLICE PAINTING FORMATION SIGNS CUT
FROM PETROL TINS

MR. CHURCHILL INSPECTING MILITARY POLICE NEAR TRIPOLI

order to control the coming rearward move. It was, however, watched, sorted out and controlled efficiently. After the battle of Acroma the forward elements of 13 Corps began to retire via the bottle-neck between the Tobruk defences and Knightsbridge, the centre of the battle. The A.P.M. 13 Corps had no time to concentrate any large number of military police to control this narrow defile and progress through it was slow.

There was enough work for at least six provost companies, but only the Army and two Corps companies were available. The D.P.M. was out of touch with both Corps A.P.Ms., but was fortunate in meeting A.P.M. 30 Corps, Major Rees-Reynolds, during a reconnaissance. This meeting enabled a rapid and effective provost plan to be made for the two respective companies. Meanwhile traffic became denser and denser and the task of sorting out desert-worthy from non-desert-worthy vehicles began in earnest. The orders that as much movement as possible was to be carried out at night was not being obeyed. By dark there were few moving vehicles to be seen and this resulted in unnecessary congestion by day.

Up to 20th June a C.M.P. detachment had been provided from British Troops, Egypt, for Mersa Matruh; on being relieved by a section of 105 Provost Company this detachment withdrew to El Daba, once again to be relieved two days later when Daba came within Eighth Army control. During the one night there a special watch had to be kept on the big N.A.A.F.I. road-house, which was well stocked with food and drink, to prevent pilfering and looting. In fact the military police were preserving these good things for the Afrika Korps, who were no doubt extremely grateful.

The stream of traffic along the Alexandria–Mena road seemed never-ending, and every now and again some thoughtless driver would double back in the face of on-coming traffic, with disastrous results as the sand on either side of this road was for the main part the soft, silvery kind in which a vehicle soon gets stuck. When possible the offending driver was ordered to drive into the sand where he ceased to be a nuisance to others for many hours. One slow procession of vehicles, two abreast, was headed by a member of a South African road construction company driving a large motor-roller at about five miles per hour. The D.P.M. saw him, blew his whistle and signalled him to get off the road and let the miles of traffic behind him speed up. He ignored the signals. The D.P.M. drew his pistol. The effect was immediate and the offending roller was soon safely embedded in the soft silvery sand.

During this difficult period D.A.P.M. (Traffic) had been added to the Staff of the D.P.M. Army, and Captain Wedlake-

Lewis, who had been with 105 Provost Company in the United Kingdom, was posted to this appointment.

Once the El Alamein line had been consolidated it seemed that the onrush of the Afrika Korps had been stopped, but there was still a possibility that if a strong armoured column could make its way to Cairo across the desert a further retirement, this time across the Suez Canal into Palestine, would be inevitable. With this in view the D.P.M. was instructed to reconnoitre and sign two routes, both east of the Amariya–Cairo road. This task was carried out within twenty-four hours by Captains Cashen and Mandy, O.C. 105 Provost Company. Fortunately, this measure turned out to be over-insurance. Gradually the situation became more and more static; Rommel had shot his bolt and his L. of C. was nearly at breaking point. By the end of the first week in July it was possible to set up an effective provost plan which worked with great efficiency until the final preparations for a further offensive made a change necessary.

A check post was set up at El Deir coast road about mid-way between Alamein and Amariya. Every vehicle was checked, and personnel travelling eastwards as passengers had to satisfy the military police as to the authority of their journey. Written orders had been given to this post to fire on any person failing to halt when called upon to do so. An officer who had deliberately forced his way through received a bullet in the shoulder, which was followed up on his discharge from hospital by a warning from his Divisional Commander. It was realized that some drivers would try to evade this post, so the area between it and Burg-el-Arab was kept under almost continuous observation, with good results.

One night an Italian Commando party landed about half a mile east of the El Deir post, moved inland and tried to destroy the railway and water pipe-line south of Burg-el-Arab. They made a poor job of it, and the following morning an ammunition train passed safely over the spot where the charge had been laid. No damage was done to the water pipe-line.

One morning an Arab came to 105 Provost Company and indicated that there were some enemy soldiers hiding in an old tumbled-down house about a mile away. Only Captain Mandy, R.S.M. Sims, a driver, one cook and a clerk were available. Captain Mandy and his driver with the Arab went off, followed a few minutes later by the R.S.M., the company clerk and cook. The information proved correct and soon Captain Mandy and his driver found themselves facing twelve Italians armed with tommy-guns and grenades. After a staring match of some seconds, followed by a few words in Italian by Captain Mandy, the party put down their arms and filed out into the open just as the R.S.M. and his party arrived on the scene. The Italian officer said afterwards that the most frightening part of the whole operation was the drive to Provost Company H.Q. with Captain Mandy at the wheel.

During the first year of the Eighth Army's existence numerous V.I.Ps. paid visits, and it fell to the lot of provost to provide escorts and guards. The first of these was the Duke of Gloucester, and the day of his visit to Tobruk was spoilt by one of the worst sand-storms of the year. He had spent the night with his regiment, the 10th Hussars, which was located on the escarpment south of El Adem. It was more by good luck than good management that the D.P.M. Army managed to contact his car and pilot it into Tobruk, where the official programme was abandoned. A short visit was made to the harbour, however, and this was followed by lunch with the Commander of the South African Division.

The visit some weeks later of Field-Marshal Smuts meant last-minute changes in the police arrangements because of poor visibility at the air landing ground intended for his departure. Twenty minutes before he was due to go down Sollum Hill a 15-cwt. truck turned over, completely blocking the road. A passing vehicle tried in vain to move it, and then the provost officer in charge of Sollum Hill collected all available military policemen, who lifted the truck on to its wheels with five minutes to spare.

On 19th January, 1942, the Minister of State, Mr. Oliver Lyttelton, accompanied by Mr. Bullitt, representing the American Government, paid a visit to the Army. On arrival by air at El Adem they were met by Brigadier Martin, Commander 88 Sub-Area, and Brigadier Sir Brian Robertson, D.A. and Q.M.G., Eighth Army. The morning was spent touring Tobruk and in the afternoon a visit was made to Sidi Rezegh, where Brigadier Jock Campbell gave a vivid and detailed account of the battle where the Royal Artillery had fought to the last man and the last round against Rommel's armour. Another visitor was the King of Greece, who came to discuss the employment of a Greek Brigade.

★   ★   ★   ★   ★

IN Africa the military police had undertaken new roles; they had worked side by side with combatant troops, and by their efficient traffic control and discipline helped to produce an orderly retirement to the line of El Alamein. Fighting troops came to take a new and good view of the "Redcaps." Stragglers' posts and information posts were established, manned by two or three military policemen, and the survivors, ranging from single stragglers to brigade columns, passed back to comparative rest and safety behind the wire. Practically all the men who had escaped from Gazala, west of the minefield, many of them wounded, all of them exhausted and without water for days on end, were put on their way by the "Redcaps" manning stragglers' posts.

As long as troops came in, so the posts were kept manned, in places for more than a week, and, as there were no reliefs available, the same men stayed there, living on bully beef, biscuits and water.

★ ★ ★ ★ ★

DURING August, 1942, General Montgomery took over command of Eighth Army, and with his arrival all thought of any further retirement was dismissed. An Australian Division was brought over from Palestine and put into the El Alamein line in the coastal sector. The 51st Highland Division, 44th Division and 8th Armoured Division were all brought up for training and acclimatizing in the desert. As they arrived, selected N.C.Os. of 105 Provost Company were attached to help and advise their Divisional provost companies, a system which paid large dividends. Then Corps H.Q. was re-formed; Major Waters was appointed A.P.M. and by degrees his provost company was trained and brought up to strength. Since this Corps was intended to have under command two armoured divisions, rigorous training was required for the Corps provost company as extreme mobility was the first essential.

In September, 1942, Lieut.-Colonel T. C. Irvine was appointed D.P.M., Eighth Army, to replace Lieut.-Colonel Forbes, shortly to become P.M. Paiforce in the Middle East.

For the actual preparation and preliminaries of training for the El Alamein campaign the following account has been given by Lieut.-Colonel Irvine:

"At the beginning of September I was posted from Deputy Provost Marshal, Ninth Army, to a like appointment in Eighth Army. On reporting, I found that the Army was in process of re-equipment, and it was no secret that we were about to go into battle on a large scale.

"I found my police developed into a force of seventy-three Provost Officers and two thousand and forty-seven rank and file."

At this time the Allied Forces had been driven back to a position around El Alamein. In front of them was the narrow waste known as the Qattara Gap, bounded on the south side by an impassable escarpment and on the north by the sea.

"At a very early stage it became evident that the 'easing' of the Eighth Army fighting troops, their armour and their 'soft' vehicles through this gap was going to be a great task. It also became obvious that a large proportion of the task before the General Staff was a traffic problem, and that therefore the opening stages were to be in the nature of a trial for provost and, in the words of the Army Commander, 'Day One would make or mar the name of provost for ever.'

"We set about preliminary plans without delay, feeling confident, with the large provost personnel at our disposal, that the task would not be beyond our capabilities.

"To proceed with the battle story. A general plan was formed in the terms that provost in conjunction with certain elements of the Chief Engineer's and Chief Signal Officer's organizations should operate the movement through the Qattara Gap up to our minefields, through our minefields and eventually through the German minefields. Provost were to control traffic by diverse means, the Sappers were to grade tracks and clear minefields and Signals were to provide special communication facilities.

"I therefore called a meeting of all A.P.Ms. at Army Headquarters so that I could allot each a task to complete within their Formation Area.

"The enemy, aware that attack was due, was ignorant of the direction from which it was to come and of the forces and strength of armour against them. It was not possible therefore to mark and grade tracks by means of 'graders,' which would be obvious to air reconnaissance. On the other hand, our task was to bring forward on the night of 23rd and 24th October, through an area twenty-six miles in length and four miles in width, the New Zealand Division, the 9th Armoured Brigade and the 1st and 10th British armoured divisions.

"Before this, between D−5 and D−1, provost handled, mostly by night without lights, through the Qattara Gap, the 51st (H) Division, 4th Indian Division, 10 Corps Artillery, 30 Corps Artillery, 'B' Echelon, rations, petrol and ammunition vehicles, for five days.

"Arrangements for D/D+1 were planned as follows:

"It was decided to provide six clearly defined tracks, in addition to the main coastal road, through the corridor of the Qattara Gap. These were christened: Sun, Moon and Star; Bottle, Boat and Hat.

"The general direction was marked by means of cairns of stones painted white on the approach side. In these cairns were placed iron bars surmounted by the silhouette of the insignia of the track name. The average length of these tracks proved to be twenty-six miles.

"The ensuing movements were to be carried out during the full moon period, so the white-faced cairns with their silhouetted sign-tokens were easily visible even to the drivers of tanks. In order, however, that no mistake could possibly be caused through loss of direction, each of these lines of entry was equipped, at regular intervals, with petrol tins containing hurricane lamps, the pattern being stamped out of the tin to display the appropriate insignia. These improvised lamps were manufactured by police N.C.Os. In addition to this, two sections of provost were allotted to each track for point duty, general control and lamp maintenance.

"Communication was established by means of a private telephone exchange, situated in the neighbourhood of El Alamein station. This exchange was linked up with the main exchange and in addition served eighteen telephone posts on the tracks, three to each track, which were manned by 18 officers attached to provost and under command of provost officers. Control was situated at the exchange near Alamein Station, where the A.P.M. 10 Corps was situated and in charge of operations."

Here is a copy of the Routine Log of the night of 22nd/23rd October:

Serial No.	Time	From	Message
1.	1850	G2RA	At 0500 hours D+1 Lt. A.A. Bty, want to get through own minefields by first light. They are under command 30 Corps. It will therefore concern 1 and 10 Armd Div.—High Priority.
2.	1935	Maj. Cashen	Has reports from all stations that all lamps are lit.
3.	1940	APM 1 Armd Div.	4 miles of Moon Track E. of Springbok had not been lit.
4.	1950	APM 10 Corps	Gave Message 3 to Maj. Cashen.
5.		DPM	Rang Rear Army to say that everything was under control.
6.	2050	Lt. Hobbs	Reported that at 2045 he saw 1 Crusader disabled but clear of the track. Dvr. stated he had run into minefield. At 2055 saw APM N.Z. Div. Stated there was another tank in the minefield but the minefield had been lighted.
7.	2055	Cpt. Mandy	Said that Divl. T.C.P. Officer had reported that 10 Armd Div. have already started on Boat Track but had not reached Sydney.
8.	2110	APM 1 Armd Div.	Said that he had found out position of A.A. Bty, who were now in action. They would be allowed to follow through after 2 Armd Bde.
9.	2115	Sgt. Howard (See 6)	3 tanks went on minefield on Bottle track owing to leading tank going 75 yards to the left of entrance. Entrance was lit by red lights and Bottle sign in posn. 2 M.Ps. were on duty. Small damage done. 1 tank still remains in minefield. After about 2 minutes traffic was normal.
10.	2120	APM 10 Armd Div.	Reports that Div. has left assembly area and has not yet reached Star track 2125 hrs.
	2140		BARRAGE COMMENCED.
11.	2156	Maj. Cashen	10 Armd Div on Bottle track halted at Sydney Road starting 8 minutes time.
12.	2203	Maj. Cashen	Head of Moon just passed Sydney Exchange. Head Star half mile away. No sign of Bottle.
13.	2209	Maj. Cashen	First vehicle on Hat track passing Sydney.

Serial No.	Time	From	Message
14.	2210	APM 10 Corps	Phoned G2RA gave message 8.
15.	2222	Maj. Cashen	Serials 1, 2, 3, 4, and 5 have passed Sydney on Hat.
16.	2230	Maj. Cashen	Head of coln. passed Sydney on Sun 2218. All well on Boat and Bottle.
17.	2300	A/Q 10 Armd Div.	Asked A.P.M. to contact L.O., R.E.M.E.
18.	2305	Maj. Cashen (confirmed later)	Star, Boat, Bottle all going O.K. Unconfirmed report 2 bombs on Bombay Road. No damage.
19.	2310	APM rang DDME 10 Corps (See 6)	Said that tank on Bottle track minefield was being passed by 1 Armd Div. who did not wish to waste their recovery on somebody else's vehicle. Tank believed to belong to 9 Armd Bde.
20.	2312	APM rang Boat 2	Asked for grid where tank was disabled.
21.	2322	Maj. Cashen	Sun and Moon everything O.K.
22.	2324	APM 1 Armd Div.	Head 2 Armd Bde. has reached Springbok and is now topping up.
23.	2327	Maj. Cashen (See 6)	Tank is in 2nd Minefield going towards Sydney from Springbok right hand side of track.
24.	2330	APM rang DDME	Gave message 23—Grid 434.
25.	2340	Maj. Cashen (See 18)	120 yds. E. of Bombay Road just about where Bottle turns off 2 small bombs. As far as can be ascertained no damage.
26.	2350	Maj. Cashen	1 Sherman tank 320 yds. W. from Sydney Exchange has broken down, carburettor flooding. Tank belongs to 1 Armd Div. LAD has passed.
27.	2353	APM rang	Regulating H.Q. 1 Armd Div. Gave message 26.
28.	2359	APM rang	Capt. Wedlake-Lewis to enquire how tracks were.
29.	0004	Maj. Barker (See 6)	Bottle track 1st minefield W. from Sydney 15 tanks went over minefield following Sqn. Leader's tank. Last Tank struck a mine. Disabled. No casualties. A Bren Carrier came over and struck another mine. Disabled. No casualties.
30.	0010	Maj. Cashen	Last of 24 Armd Bde. (on Bottle) has passed Sydney.
31.	0019	Maj. Cashen	Hole near Sun 2. He has reported it to DCRE, Col. Shannon.
32.	0030	DPM rang	Col. Graham. All heads of colns. at Springbok on all tracks at 0025 without hitch.
33.	0031	APM rang	DA & QMG 10 Corps and gave message 32.
34.	0040	Maj. Cashen	Honey got stuck in the hole with his 4' x 2' x 12'. Tank is out and DCRE is bringing up 3 vehicles to fill in hole.
35.	0210	Maj. Barker	Boat and Hat started to cross at 0200. 10 Armd Div.
36.	0212	APM rang	Rear 10 Corps and gave message 35.
37.	0215	APM 1 Armd Div.	2 Armd Bde. crossed Springbok 0203.
38.	0218	Lt. Hobs	Reported 2 Armd Bde. moving on Star track.
39.	0219	APM rang	Rear 10 Corps and gave Message 37.
40.	0223	APM rang	Maj. Cashen and gave message 37.
41.	0230	41 R.T.R.	3 miles E. of Springbok, were they to follow on behind or what orders were there. They were referred to 10 Armd Div.

Serial No.	Time	From	Message
42.	0235	APM rang	10 Armd Div. and asked if 41 R.T.R. had contacted them. Answer in the affirmative and matter cleared up.
43.	0247	Maj. Cashen	Sun 2 hole filled in and are filling in a smaller one they found.
44.	0310	Maj. Cashen	Moon and Star now in use. 2 colns. lorried Inf. have crossed Sydney Road. Nothing on any of the others.
45.	0312	APM rang	Rear Corps and gave Message 44.
46.	0321	Maj. Cashen	Sun and Bottle now in use by the colns.
47.	0517	2 K.R.R.	Reported topped up and ready to move on Star track.
48.	0520	APM 10 Armd Div.	10 Armd Div. proceeding to 2nd German minefield and while gaps are being made are deployed. 51 Div. and Australian went straight through. N.Z. went through on the right and were held on the left. South Africans went through on left and were held on right. Routes to first German minefields are marked. From 1st to 2nd are being marked.
49.	0535	DPM rang	Army and gave Message 48.
50.	0537	APM rang	Corps and gave Message 48.
51.	0556	Maj. Cashen	Everything very quiet. Believes there is a lot more to come.
52.	0607	APM rang	Maj. Cashen with regard to marking the one way routes as per Appendix C.O.O. No. 2. Was informed that "A" Ech. were still on all the tracks stationary.
		Echelon B.1.	
53.	0620	DA & QMG 10 Armd Div.	All roads must be kept West bound until he got his B.1. Ech. clear.
54.	0645	Maj. Cashen	Reported concentration of traffic on Star and Moon which he was dispersing.

"From Springbok Road" (continues Lieut.-Colonel Irvine's account) "which incidentally was well up in the 25-pounder Artillery barrage, divisional provost took over. At twilight they lit their appropriate lamps, up to and through gaps in our own minefields; during the barrage they advanced across No Man's Land with their attendant sappers and signalmen, marking and lighting their passage, the signalmen laying their communication lines. On arrival at the enemy minefield the sappers in conjunction with our N.C.Os. selected a suitable location for penetration and commenced to sweep for mines, the policemen and signallers following in their wake. All this time, a barrage, the density of which is now well known, was being operated. The enemy reply was largely directed on no-man's-land and included machine-gun and mortar nests within their own minefield. The latter was unsuspected, and although the barrage to some extent nullified their activities, the 'minefield forces' was suddenly called upon to give battle. In no cases were these developments allowed to hinder the gap makers. . . ."

MR. EDEN SHAKING HANDS WITH A LANCE-CORPORAL OF THE
A.T.S. PROVOST, JUNE, 1944, IN THE MIDDLE EAST

One of the "gap-makers," Lance-Corporal Eeles of 10th Armoured Division, was the military police candidate recommended for immediate reward. He received the Distinguished Conduct Medal. When all his policeman comrades had been either killed or wounded he and two sappers, whose help he enlisted on his own initiative, completed their gap under heavy fire, thus providing the passage for the armour to advance.

From the point at which the armour broke through, tactics assumed a more local atmosphere, the one paramount feature as far as provost were concerned being the continual discovery of unexpected minefields and booby traps. During the period, owing to their successful manipulation of the initial breakthrough, continuous calls upon the military police and sappers were made and responded to.

On the morning of 5th November this message was received in London newspaper offices from Cairo on the Exchange Telegraph tape:

"In one of the recent attacks by General Montgomery's Forces against Rommel's weakening African Army, tanks of a British Armoured Division were led into battle by highly-trained specialists of the Royal Engineers, Royal Corps of Signals and by 'Redcaps' of the Corps of Military Police. This complete reversal of the previously accepted order of battle in which specialists were given a certain amount of protection by combatants in front is inevitable in the type of warfare in which British armour has been engaged.

"In an attack on a position strongly organized for defence against tanks it is essential for the sappers to clear gaps through the enemy minefields. Signallers must be there to establish communications from the front to the rear at the earliest possible moment. 'Redcaps' must be there to mark routes as they are made and control the immense volume of traffic being rushed through gaps in the minefields.

"So brilliantly have these three arms worked in face of fierce enemy fire that the officer commanding the Armoured Division gave them high praise in a special order of the day. 'They marked routes,' he said, 'with the same precision and efficiency as in training schemes in the rear areas.' At intervals along the route 'Redcaps' quickly established inquiry posts where information could be obtained. At every cross-road or bad patch of sand, helmeted policemen were on duty adeptly controlling traffic. It is the first time 'Redcaps' have been front line troops in desert warfare—and they did a grand job."

No more need be said about the actual move. The two divisions were passed through the tracks in roughly six hours, well ahead of time, and reached their battle assembly places at the inter-section

G

of Springbok Road. Few incidents occurred and unit discipline was excellent.

Practically speaking, every desert track was laid and marked by provost throughout the campaign. Seven signs to the mile was the average, and every one was manufactured out of whatever was available (the 4-gallon tin was available in large numbers) with the track sign or number cut in silhouette in the side.

The battle, or series of battles, originated at El Alamein, continued back over the same ground that had been traversed twice before by the original Desert Rats, 7th Armoured Division, and where they went, naturally, provost went too.

Detachments were left at each sizeable town as the advance continued; a number of these were relieved later by N.C.Os. sent up from the Depot in Cairo, so that experienced men could return to their own units with the fighting troops. The old familiar names came once more into the news—Mersa Matruh, Sollum, Capuzzo, Tobruk, Benghazi, Tripoli, and so on. Military police, by a system whereby Army provost personnel were almost up with Divisional provost, were among the first into these historic towns.

As the advance continued, so traffic control on the coast road became more important. The road was practically free from air interference by the enemy, so the deviation tracks (all reconnoitred and marked by military police) had rarely to be used. Before the battle started transport drivers had been well trained in Coast Road Regulations, a code of traffic rules that had been worked out by provost officers in conference.

The first and most important rule was "Do not stop on the road." This was enforced with vigour, and if a vehicle broke down the driver had to stop following or approaching vehicles and either have the break-down towed or pushed off the road.

Another traffic innovation was to establish special vehicle maintenance check posts at various places on the roads. These were manned by an R.A.S.C. officer, a military policeman and a fitter; offenders were brought to these "corrals," the officer and the fitter inspected the vehicle, and a policeman took down details of the offence.

105 Provost Company Headquarters and most of the sections were near Wadi Zemsem, some hundreds of kilometres east of Tripoli, but after several delays involving enemy resistance the company finally arrived on the outskirts of Tripoli, having dropped off light detachments to look after Misurata and Norns.

As dawn was breaking over Tripoli on 23rd January, 1943, the Italian military governor was being awakened by a military police officer and asked to provide a suitable H.Q. for a large force of military police. (He was the same Italian general who later handed over the keys of Tripoli to General Montgomery.) He accompanied the police officer, lighting the way with his torch, to the Carabinieri Barracks and formally handed it over.

★　★　★　★　★

TEN weeks earlier than the incident last recorded, British and American troops under General Eisenhower invaded North Africa and assaulting troops of British First Army landed, together with some L. of C. troops, to open the port of Algiers. They were reinforced four days later on the arrival of the follow-up convoy. This completed the initial phase of the build-up, no further reinforcements being scheduled for ten days.

Lieut.-Colonel Mark Sykes, D.P.M., First Army, and the senior Provost officer of B.N.A.F., landed on 12th November, together with Lieut.-Colonel H. V. McNally, D.P.M., L. of C. By this date the whole of 78th Divisional Provost Company (A.P.M., Major Bennett) were ashore, together with elements of 6th Armoured Division Provost Company and 200 Provost Company.

L. of C. troops disembarking consisted of 227 Provost Company, 3 Company Traffic Control, a Special Investigation Section and elements of 179 (Ports) Provost Company. 1 Base Sub-Area, Algiers, had opened up, and 2 Base Sub-Area, Bougie, began to function the following day.

The 78th Division pushed forward along the coastal road to secure the main objectives of Tunis and Bizerta. A small armoured regimental group moved along the Constantine–Medjez El Bab road farther to the south, whilst parachute landings were made at Souk El Arba and Souk Les Bains (near Tebessa).

As 78th Division and 6th Armoured Division (A.P.M. Major D. E. C. Price) moved forward, 3 and 75 Company (T.C.) were deployed on the rapidly lengthening L. of C., which was restricted to the inner (Algiers–Constantine–Souk Ahras) roads. The build-up continued and by the beginning of December, 6th Armoured Divisional Provost Company, 230 Provost Company, 179 (Ports) Provost Company, were operating as complete units and 101 Provost Company were disembarking. Bone, which had been opened up as the advanced port, was being attacked from the air, through most of the twenty-four hours, which made the disembarkation, entrainment and embussing of personnel and supplies a difficult operation.

Traffic control duties were carried out by provost units both in the forward area and on the L. of C. under extremely difficult conditions. The number of good roads in the country is limited. The main roads are mostly tarred in the centre and with soft verges and become slippery in wet weather. Second-class roads were sometimes well metalled, but more often little more than earthen tracks. After a few hours' rain many so-called roads became largely impassable for the movement of M.T. columns, while in dry weather the surface deteriorated rapidly. Hundreds of wadis were crossed by small road bridges, most of which were insufficiently strong to carry the heavier military loads and lent themselves to single demolitions. Thus many diversionary tracks had to be made.

Maintenance of supplies in the forward area entailed constant forethought and improvisation because of the state of the roads and restricted railway facilities. The problem was made more difficult by the fact that the enemy then had air superiority and vehicle road movement had mainly to be confined to the hours of darkness. Under these most difficult and dangerous conditions the outstanding feature was the coolness, initiative, imagination and resourcefulness displayed by the military policeman, whether he belonged to the Provost or Traffic Control Wings.

Military policemen in units on the lines of communication were called upon to undertake tasks which were bereft of glamour, but were a most important contribution in supporting the main operational effort.

The potency of the local wine which the troops thought they could drink like their native beer caused a great deal of drunkenness and disorderliness. To these were added the temptations of the Casbah of Algiers and the less desirable quarters of other base towns, such as Bone, Bougie, Setif and Constantine. This created a problem which taxed to the limit the resources of the restricted number of military police available.

As the troops became acclimatized and control of cafes, restaurants and undesirable establishments was tightened up, conditions became easier. 227 and 230 Provost Companies, although hard worked, profited by their experience, which stood them in good stead later in the campaign.

The initial landings were unopposed, but a good deal of disorganization occurred and useful experience was gained for the planning and executing of the invasions of Sicily and Italy. It was found that much of the signing equipment could be dispensed with —the maximum use being made of local resources.

During the advance of the 78th Divisional Provost Company it was found that when crossing country it was impossible for motorcyclists to keep up with their sections. An establishment of three jeeps, two 15-cwt. trucks and five motor-cycles per section was introduced and motor-cycle combinations were discarded. It was soon found that wireless trucks were essential to control the movement of large columns of transport.

Towards the end of February, Eighth Army, which had captured Tripoli on 23rd January and had been advancing north-west

in the face of a series of Axis rearguard positions, made contact
with the enemy on the outposts of the Mareth Line. H.Q., 18
Army Group, was now formed under General Alexander to co-
ordinate the action of both First and Eighth Armies. No
representative of the provost service served on the staff of H.Q., 18
Army Group—Lieut.-Colonel Sykes who sometime earlier had been
appointed D.P.M., Allied Force H.Q., with Lieut.-Colonel Paton-
Walsh, his successor as D.P.M., First Army, controlling the operation of provost units in the field.

Provost continued to sign, patrol and control the Eighth Army
which had developed into a great mechanized war machine.
Dusty tracks, bad roads, the constant overpowering smell of oil
and petrol; eyes full of grit, lungs full of sand and choking white
dust; the ever-present risk of being crushed under a tank or a
five-tonner, a bulldozer, or guns; all this had become part and
parcel of the military policeman's life. Night and day troops
and vehicles moved incessantly on through Gabes to Sfax and
Sousse, nearer and nearer to Tunis, the town coveted by the
Army in the east as much as by the Army in the west.

It was at this stage that the D.P.M., Eighth Army (Lieut.-Colonel
J. Archer-Burton), accompanied by Captain Joslin, made the link-
up with First Army. They arrived to find the D.P.M., First Army,
Lieut.-Colonel Paton-Walsh, deep in conference, the subject of
which, it was gathered, was the policing of Tunis. Offers of police
assistance for Tunis were made on both sides by both D.P.Ms.
and the provost stage generally set for the coming assault and disin-
tegration of the German Army.

On 22nd April the final assault began; by 8th May, First and
Eighth Armies had broken through to Tunis and Bizerta had fallen
to the Americans; on 12th May von Arnim surrendered and the
Axis lost their last remaining foothold in Africa.

*   *   *   *   *

EVENTS of 1943 and 1944 in Egypt were Mr. Winston
Churchill's visits. Military police were naturally entrusted
with his safety and each visit went off without incident. The
responsibility of guarding him was a heavy and difficult one;
it was even more difficult with Mr. Churchill than with other
notables, for he was not content unless he saw everything himself,
and he had no thought for the safety of his own skin.

In April, 1944, came the incidents leading up to the mutiny of
Greek troops in the vicinity of Alexandria. They are described by
Lieut.-Colonel Whitehead, D.P.M., 16 Area, and they show the
diversity of military police duties in an emergency.

On 1st April, 1944, orders were received from G.H.Q. for the arrest of Mr. Karayanis, President of the Greek Merchant Seamen's Union, because of his subversive work with soldiers of the 2nd Greek Field Regiment. Four Egyptian policemen who were sent to make the arrest were met by twenty Greeks, mostly armed, and the attempt was discontinued.

Information was received on the following day that he was in his office in Place Ismail, surrounded by 180 of his supporters. It was, therefore, decided to arrest him by a show of force, using the 7th Battalion Rifle Brigade. The arrest was made the following afternoon, 6th April, according to plan. A.A. and Q.M.G., 16 Area, D.P.M., 16 Area, accompanied by six N.C.Os. of the military police known to be good pistol shots, entered Karayanis's office with two officers from G.H.Q. to act as interpreters. Jays Pasha, Assistant Commandant Alexandria Civil Police, with whom Karayanis was on friendly terms, had entered five minutes previously to speak to him, and the party met with no resistance, but Karayanis refused to leave his office or his supporters, who were calm but appeared to be determined to resist if any demands were made to remove him by force. It had been arranged with 7th Battalion Rifle Brigade to double into the square and surround the building if fire had been opened on the police party or if the arrest had not been accomplished within three minutes of the police entry. As Karayanis had become very truculent, argumentative and dramatic, it was necessary for the Rifle Brigade's plan to be carried out.

He was invited to look from his window and see that resistance was useless. He did so and was then quickly removed to a waiting motor-car with twenty of his supporters. The arrest fully justified the use of troops in support of the police and undoubtedly avoided bloodshed.

In the meantime, it had been reported that the feeling in 1st Greek Brigade, encamped at Burg-el-Arab, was quiet and that neither they nor the Commanding Officer anticipated trouble. However, at 6.0 a.m. on 6th April, the duty officer, 16 Area, received a message that revolt had broken out in the 1st Greek Brigade. The entire camp was picqueted and the approach to the camp strategically defended by armed revolutionaries. The Brigade Commandant, Brigadier Papas, had been put under close arrest, shots had been fired and the commander of a Light A.A. Battery had been killed.

On 7th April, Brigadier-General Beaumont Nesbitt, accompanied by the Area Commander, 16 Area, D.P.M., 16 Area, and other officers, proceeded to the H.Q. 1st Greek Brigade and presented the Commandant with a written order demanding, in the

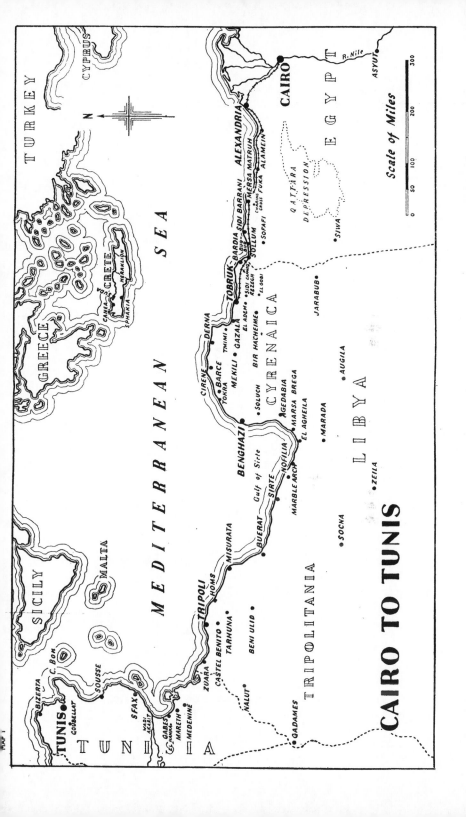

CAIRO TO TUNIS

name of the Commander-in-Chief, that the Brigade should lay down its arms. *En route*, Second-in-Command Armoured Brigade recognized Major Malgaris, one of the leaders of the revolt, and he was placed under arrest. Shortly after this, Major Abotzoglou, another ringleader, was also arrested. An Anti-Tank Battery had seen the arrest of Abotzoglou and Malgaris and formed up with arms which were trained on the British party.

The two prisoners were quickly driven off by the police and got through without incident. The Greek revolutionaries surrounded the British officers at H.Q. and took up firing positions in slit trenches. This was taken as a signal to cancel the plan to disarm the Brigade and the deputation withdrew. It was then proposed to cut off all supplies to the Greek Brigade and to establish police check posts on all roads leading to Burg-el-Arab and to institute police motor patrols in the desert.

The Greek Naval Prison, the Greek Cadet School and the Greek Naval Recruiting Office were then occupied by armed revolutionaries. These buildings, which were situated in the town, were surrounded by British troops, assisted by military policemen, to prevent dislocation of traffic and the formation of crowds.

All lorries reaching Amiriya from Cairo or Alexandria were thoroughly searched for food and petrol and all supplies suspected to be destined for the Greeks were stopped.

On 11th April an ultimatum was sent to the Greek Forces demanding the laying down of arms. A P.W. cage was opened at the old Field Punishment Centre, Amiriya, under D.P.M., 16 Area. H.Q., 9th Armoured Brigade, proceeded with plans for operations against the Greeks in the event of the ultimatum not being complied with.

On 17th April ten men escaped from the provost unit of the 1st Greek Brigade and arrived in the British lines. They gave the information that the unit was commanded by one of the leading mutineers. They also stated that in the event of an attack, British troops would not be fired on, but this statement was doubted.

On 21st April the occupants of Zizinia Naval Barracks surrendered.

Orders were received on 23rd April that the ultimatum would expire on the 24th. At 4.20 a.m. the 1st Greek Brigade surrendered. They agreed to move out of their lines unarmed in their own transport at 10.0 a.m. Disarmament was complete by 6.0 p.m. Our casualties, one officer killed; enemy casualties, nil.

1,200 Greek mutineers were put into a cage at Agami which already held 1,350 naval mutineers. Later that day plans were made for the arrest of the three known ringleaders. This was done by a trick. The cage had been divided into two halves by a strong barbed wire fence with a gate at one end. The prisoners were put in one half. They were then filed in single file in batches of ten across the emptied compound on the pretence of drawing blankets. As blankets were drawn they were then shepherded up to the far end of the compound, far away from the entrance. A member of the British Liaison Unit, who knew the three ringleaders, was sitting in the back of a covered truck watching for them as they passed from one compound to another.

As each ringleader was indicated to a waiting policeman, he was seized as he bent down to take up his blankets and rushed quickly to a cell. All were successfully arrested.

*   *   *   *   *

B EFORE the incidents just described, preparations had to be made for the invasion of Sicily, and for this purpose Malta was organized as one of the jumping off places.

105 Provost Company was ordered to Malta with five sections, including stores and vehicles. The rear party composed of an officer and two sections; two sections still remained in Cairo. They were to remain behind with vehicles and stores and ultimately join the company when it finally arrived in Sicily.

Lieut.-Colonel Philip Waters, Scots Guards, D.P.M., Malta, greeted the company on arrival, and it soon settled down to duty helping the existing Malta Provost Company.

Soon troops began to arrive and D Day for Sicily loomed near. It is interesting to record that the company commander had five sections with him in Malta, two sections in Cairo, and two sections still in Tripoli with all company stores and transport.

On D+1 the sections of the company arrived in Syracuse, Sicily, and by D+3 the company was again complete, including the transport and the Cairo sections.

*   *   *   *   *

N OT only was the North African campaign the turning point of the war; it was also the turning point in the employment of military police.

The B.E.F. campaign in Belgium and at Dunkirk had already shown that the "Redcaps" could no longer be regarded as "base troops" who never came under fire and always lived in comfort. El Alamein and the subsequent operations in North Africa confirmed this claim.

The message from Cairo to the London newspapers after El Alamein had reported "The 'Redcaps' are front-line soldiers *now*" —and front-line soldiers they were to remain.

CHAPTER VI

SECOND WORLD WAR: ITALY

ON the night of 9th July, 1943, the airborne operation planned against Sicily was launched. The landings were widely dispersed on account of bad weather conditions, inexperience in routing and faulty navigation. The objectives (the canal bridge at Ponte Grande south of Syracuse and the high ground six miles from Gela) were reached by small parties.

The bridge at Ponte Grande was held until the following afternoon, when the enemy regained control of it. However, the 5th Division arrived and recaptured it before it could be demolished.

The seaborne landings went according to plan, except for a delay in the arrival of landing craft (tanks) caused by a cross-swell. The assaults were virtually unopposed and only coastal units were encountered. Surprise had been achieved in spite of the employment of large forces. The only serious counter-attack came from the Hermann Goering Division with tanks at Gela and was repulsed.

The Americans had landed at Palermo in the north-west, and the objective, Messina, in the north-east point of Sicily became the target of a two-pronged drive. After a bitter battle for Catania the army pressed on through Acirelae and Taormina, and finally arrived with the Americans at devastated Messina. It was during this campaign that Provost Eighth Army had its first taste of blown-up passes, blown bridges and the necessity, always urgent, of finding diversions and policing them.

Towns such as Syracuse and Augusta, Catania, Acirelae, Taormina and Messina, all had permanent detachments of military police drawn from one or more of the following units: Army, 13 Corps, 30 Corps, 505 and 501 Provost Companies.

The three beaches selected for the landing in Italy were between Reggio and Gallico, a small town about ten miles north of Reggio. The main road there runs very close to the shore and it was realized that there would be difficulty in finding space for beach dumps and depots. Had the landing been contested this would have indeed been the case.

After heavy bombardment the assault was made in the early hours of 3rd September, 1943. Resistance was negligible and the main hindrance to the advance proved to be extensive demolitions on all roads. 5th Division advanced up the main west coast road while the Canadian Division took to the hills, crossed the toe and reached the coast on the east side. During this period the main provost problem was moving large numbers of vehicles over roads where many bridges had been blown.

It was not long before the Army provost companies were fully deployed on the road behind 13 Corps, and by 15th September Army provost were deployed from Reggio to Belvedere on the west coast road and across to Nicastra via Catenzaro to Crotone on the east coast. Apart from two days' rain in the hills above Reggio which hindered the Canadian Division, the weather was good and the diversions through river beds held firm. By this time the 2nd Parachute Brigade had landed in the Taranto area and arrangements were being made for the 78th Division (A.P.M. Major G. White) to cross from Sicily to Reggio, move by road to Crotone and then by L.C.T. to Taranto, as it was thought that the route Crotone–Taranto would not be available for large-scale moves for some time.

This plan was cancelled and it was decided that 78th Division should go the whole way by road. It therefore became necessary for the 105 Provost Company to be switched from the west coast road behind 13 Corps to cover the Crotone–Taranto stretch, thus relieving 78th Divisional Provost Company of any commitments behind their forward Divisional Concentration Area. The gap behind 13 Corps on the west coast road was not filled. By this time supplies were reaching Corps through L.C.T. to Sapri, thus the L. of C. was quiet with practically no maintenance traffic and the Corps had completed its move up.

505 Provost Company was sent to Bari from Crotone and the detachment of 181 Ports Company to Taranto, a very busy port. 505 Provost Company arrived at Bari on 26th September well ahead of the main influx of troops, which did not take place until some days later. One section was sent to Brindisi, which was to open shortly as a port.

On 24th September, 8th Indian Division and H.Q. 5 Corps disembarked at Taranto. 101 (5 Corps) Provost Company was only three sections strong; the remaining six sections were not to arrive for some weeks. While in this area 5 Corps (101) Provost Company, 8th Indian Divisional Provost Company and 2nd Parachute Brigade Provost Company assisted with police duties in Taranto, which was full of troops of all nationalities. There was considerable trouble in the early stages of occupation as large numbers of unemployed Italian naval ratings wandered round the town all day.

Three companies, 43 and 49 Traffic Control and 105 Provost Company, were committed on road to Reggio–Taranto, and the 505 Provost Company to Bari and Brindisi. Ahead, the 78th Division was advancing. A gap therefore existed which had to be filled. At the time it did not seem possible to remove police from the L. of C. and arrangements were made to call forward 51st (H) Divisional Provost Company from Sicily to control the road to Reggio–Nicastro; their arrival would thus release 105 Provost Company to work forward of Taranto. The projected move of the 200 Provost Company from Sicily to the mainland was now cancelled. It had been anticipated that this company would fulfil a large part of No. 2 District's commitments in the heel area of Bari, Brindisi and Taranto. As a consequence, Army could not anticipate an early release from that area, as a port provost company, a traffic control company and an L. of C. provost company called for by No. 2 District from North Africa were not likely to arrive before mid-October at the earliest. The Army provost now was therefore stretched to the limit over both Army and No. 2 District, L. of C., commitments.

Senior provost appointments in the Italian campaign were complicated by the succession of Headquarters which sprang up in the theatre, lived for a few months and then died.

In October, 1943, A.F.H.Q., Advance Administrative Echelon, was formed and moved into Italy, with Lieut.-Colonel McNally as D.P.M. and forward representative of Lieut.-Colonel Mark Sykes, D.P.M., A.F.H.Q., which was still operating from North Africa.

In March, 1944, H.Q. Allied Armies in Italy (A.A.I.) was formed, with Colonel A. R. Rees-Reynolds as P.M., and A.F.H.Q., Advance Administrative Echelon, disappeared. A little later A.F.H.Q. moved into Italy with Colonel Mark Sykes, who himself had been upgraded earlier to Provost Marshal. This parallel system had its obvious drawbacks, and in December, 1944, H.Q. A.A.I. was in its turn abolished; Colonel Sykes (who two months later was to become Provost Marshal, India) going home and being succeeded as P.M. A.F.H.Q. by Colonel Rees-Reynolds, who was himself followed in the same post by Colonel McNally in June, 1945.

By 24th October the 8th Indian Division had moved north of Foggia and concentrated in the Ururi area. A.P.M. Indian Division had only three sections of British police in a six-section company, and the quality of those three sections was not good. They consisted chiefly of transfers from British troops in the Division and had undergone a short course at the C.M.P. Depot, Almaza. The Indian Division axis presented great difficulties through breaking weather. A section of 105 Provost Company was sent to assist temporarily. This section operated with 8th Indian Division for a period of about ten days until the balance of 5 Corps Provost Company arrived. During this move in appalling weather on a breaking road the A.P.M. was killed when the jeep in which he was patrolling slid over a precipice.

The arrival of 230 L. of C. Provost Company for No. 2 District enabled 509 Provost Company to move forward and take over behind 13 Corps on the Campobasso Road and release 34 Brick Provost Unit from Brindisi. This latter unit was dispatched to Termoli to assist 5 Corps until the Termoli area became the Army Roadhead, where the unit would be in a position to take over roadhead duties.

The position in Army area was now eased considerably, although at the same time the plans for the crossing of the Sangro made it obvious that 43 Traffic Control Company would shortly be required in Army area. The Divisional and Corps companies were by now fully employed in moving traffic over bad roads and diversions rendered much worse on account of heavy rains. The task of the Army companies at this period was less exacting, as the road up to Termoli was good tarmac with only a few blown bridges. North of Termoli the road deteriorated rapidly.

During this period the concentration of New Zealand Division in the area Lucera started. Its axis was to be Ururi–Aquaviva–Carunchio; it was to operate directly under Army, therefore it was decided to put the 105 Provost Company in direct support of the New Zealand Division. As the New Zealanders had previously known 105 Provost Company during the advance from Alamein to Enfidaville, this arrangement proved most satisfactory.

The stretch of road between Termoli and Vasto was only thirty miles long, and proved to be one of the worst so far encountered; it included two miles of one-way road and nine single Bailey bridges, amongst them the Trigno river crossing, all of which were difficult bottlenecks.

At this time Army provost were responsible for the L. of C. from Barletta and Canosa forward to Vasto and Campobasso, approximately 210 road miles.

The landing on the Anzio beach-head took place on 22nd January, 1944. 1st Division landed on the north of Anzio town at first light, three provost sections in the lead with the assault brigade. A.P.M. (Major G. Sharpe) with two more sections landed shortly after, followed by the rest of the company. Apart from some shelling and dive-bombing of the landing-craft, the operation was unopposed and roads, report centres, traffic posts were quickly organized and manned. In the meantime, U.S. troops had taken the town.

In the Anzio beach-head a little incident occurred between a sailor and a military policeman. The sailor never forgot it and when this history was being written he sent this note:

"I believe that the date of the occurrence was February, 1944, and the scene was the town of Anzio, in Italy. At this period a beach-head had been established around Nettuno and conditions were quite 'rough.' Sea-going convoys arriving regularly from Naples were shepherded into the small harbour by means of a special Royal Navy wireless procedure, of which I was a small 'cog.'

"It was from one of these vessels that I was put ashore to assist in the shore-based control station.

"Imagine my surprise when after experiencing frequent German field-gun and aircraft actions, I stepped on to dry land to find a very spruce looking 'Redcap' standing near by.

"In absolute contrast to everyone else, this man was in regulation uniform and freshly shaved. Seeing me, he said, 'Have you a tin of boot polish to spare, Jack?' Of all the things I had expected to hear in Anzio, a request of this description was most certainly the farthest removed.

"My admiration for the man persuaded me there and then to search for and find a tin of polish in my kit-bag. I hadn't been ashore many hours before I discovered that this 'keep smart' campaign was the watchword of all the 'Redcaps' present.

"Two years later I was the 1st Lieutenant of a Fleet Minesweeper and I recall on many occasions using this example to inspire the odd liberty man who failed to pass the routine inspection before going ashore.

"I am now back to my civilian job, a police constable, and I must confess that even here I have found it necessary to quote this incident to a 'scruffy' youngster with whom I had 'words'."

However, the advance to Rome was not to be. The Germans threw in everything they had to force the attack back into the sea, and for four months 1st Division fought and lived in the narrow beach-head, taking everything that the enemy could throw or drop. The functions of provost during this period were not pleasant. Life was only possible underground, but the control of the two roads and many tracks up to the forward positions was of first importance, and in performing these duties the "Redcap" was much exposed.

There were many police casualties at the notorious Flyover Bridge and at the various nodal track-junctions. No part of the beach-head was immune from shelling and low-flying attacks by enemy aircraft day and night. Despite the use of smoke to screen activity, the enemy had little difficulty in seeing every move from his outpost in the Alban Hills overlooking our positions.

On 14th February, 56th Division arrived and with them Lieut.-Colonel H. V. McNally, D.P.M. A.F.H.Q., Advance Administration Echelon, on a visit.

Thursday, 16th March, was a bleak day for 1st Division Provost Company. The company had six casualties in the Divisional H.Q. Section following an air attack in the small hours. In addition, shelling had set off a large ammunition dump from which flying lumps of metal caused great unpleasantness on the main axis-road and a sticky job to control.

An appreciation of the work done by provost in the beach-head was given by the G.O.C. 1st Division, in the following terms: ". . . the conspicuous success and efficiency of 1st Division provost. I am not piling it on when I say that I look on them and shall always, I trust, do so as one of the best organizations I know. In every branch of their activity they have won a reputation second to none. . . ."

The period 21st November–31st January was a time which saw the Sangro crossed and Ortona captured. Preparations were made for further advance, but they were cancelled owing to the main effort swinging to the west coast. Then came a period of reorganization in which 1 Canadian Corps and 2 Polish Corps joined the Army. It was a period notable for the sudden switching of formations and much traffic control experience was gained.

The plan was that after the initial onslaught had been carried through, Corps R.E. would throw Bailey bridges across the Sangro river by the demolished main road bridge. The Bailey bridge subsequently built proved to be one of the longest ever built in the field. The stream at this point, under normal conditions, only occupies a fraction of the whole river bed, most of which is shingle. Another lighter bridge was to be made upstream by the Paglieta crossing. In addition there were certain fording places where tanks and tracked vehicles could cross. The state of the weather was of the highest importance in this operation.

The provost plan was that 5 Corps provost (A.P.M. Major R. A. Leeson) would be responsible for the crossings in the main road bridge area to enable the 78th Division provost companies to concentrate on duties forward of the river, as it was anticipated that proper traffic control would be of the highest importance so long as the crossings were within range of the enemy guns. As far as the 8th Indian Division provost companies were concerned it was found essential for British sections to handle the divisional crossings, and it was necessary for 5 Corps to assist the divisional provost with duties well within the divisional area.

About 28th November the 78th Division were relieved by 1st Canadian Division, which had been under command 13 Corps (A.P.M. Lieut.-Colonel G. C. White) in the sector north-west of Campobasso. The plan was that the Canadian Division should move in Brigade Groups via Termoli, stage Petacciato area and move from Petacciato to the north of the Sangro on the following day. This move started on 30th November. There was heavy rain during the night and the Canadian Brigade Group staying the night at Patacciato took most of the following day to move out of the staging area. The vehicles brought mud on to the road in great quantities; this made conditions on this road difficult for several weeks. The 78th Division moving back was staged on the side road at Ururi. The change-over was complicated by the Sangro bridges once again being "out" for a certain period of twenty-four hours. This caused great congestion on the road north of Vasto, and had not air cover been complete the consequences might have been serious.

Adverse weather continued; this slowed down the speed of the advance and conditions were made difficult along the whole road from Termoli northwards. It was not until about 20th December that Ortona was entered, nearly a month after the crossing of the Sangro, and fighting went on over Christmas. 505 Provost Company entered Ortona on the heels of the leading troops and made preliminary reconnaissances for circuits, dock routes etc. for it was intended to use the port facilities, such as they were, as soon after capture as possible. The 505 Provost Company detachment, however, after five days was ordered to withdraw as a result of enemy shelling and counter-attack. Because of bad weather it was necessary to give as much assistance to Corps provost as possible, and Army provost had relieved Corps in Vasto by 5th December and were deployed up to the Sangro by mid-December.

Throughout this period appalling weather continued. From Termoli forward the main road was covered in mud brought on to it by tanks and vehicles moving in and out of leaguer, and the result was that every slight incline or cambered curve became a source of danger. One stretch of road between S. Salvo and Vasto became particularly notorious. It was an uphill stretch with several corners steeply cambered. It was narrow and the verges were soft and dropped into ditches. In dry weather the stretch would give very little trouble except during darkness. At night vehicles frequently slid into the ditch. Half an hour's drizzle, however, would convert this stretch of road into a trap, especially for vehicles with only two-wheel drive. It was normal to see as many as fifteen vehicles ditched within one particular stretch not 100 yards long.

Possibly the worst day on this road was Christmas Eve. Rain in the afternoon of the previous day had delayed traffic throughout Army area, and in particular a platoon of Diesel lorries. Those struck the bad patch about 8 p.m. and were still there at dawn on Christmas Eve. These vehicles had only two-wheel drive and the road surface and camber were such that these rather unwieldy trucks could get no grip at all. Eventually they were dragged clear by caterpillar tractors. In the meantime a normal day's traffic piled up on either side of the bad patch. At 6 p.m. there were vehicles on the road which had not moved two miles in twelve hours. About 8 p.m. heavy rain, which had held off all day, began to fall. This removed the greasiness from the road surface and in three hours the road was clear.

During this period it was essential for provost officers and senior N.C.Os. to be on the road almost continuously. Provost company commanders were averaging less than four hours' sleep per night for over a fortnight. In the traffic control companies where the physical standard of the rank and file was low the strain on the officers and N.C.Os. was most marked.

The month of February, 1944, found the Army playing a holding and very static role for the first time since October, 1942. Operational moves were few; the 78th Division moved from the Casoli area back and to the Fifth (American) Army front, and moves forward were mostly of those Canadian units for 5th Canadian Armoured Division and 1 Canadian Corps. At the beginning of the month 1 Canadian Corps relieved 5 Corps on the coastal sector, and 3rd Canadian Provost Company took over the commitments of 101 Provost Company, with the exception of the Sangro bridges, which became an Army provost responsibility. Traffic control became a matter of daily routine, and this period was a breathing space in which plans could be made for the future.

The month closed with the news that a vast regrouping of the armies in Italy was about to take place. The Eighth Army was to take over a new sector west of the Apennines and would assume an offensive role in the spring. Early March saw arrangements made for this regrouping.

For provost, it was largely a question of arranging which Army provost units should go with Army, and which should remain. It was decided that 105 Provost Company, 505 Provost Company, 43 Traffic Control Company and the Eighth Army S.I.B. should accompany the Army, and that 506 Provost Company and 77 Traffic Control Company should come under command when the Army took over the Cassino sector. It was agreed that 509 Provost Company and 49 Traffic Control Company should remain on the east coast under No. 2 District (D.P.M., Lieut.-Colonel N. M. Blair) and 5 Corps respectively.

It was also necessary to make arrangements to replace American provost by Eighth Army provost in the towns and villages and along the roads in an area running from the Volturno river in the south to Cassino in the north, and bounded on the west by the main Rome road, and in the east by the Apennines.

This was by no means a simple undertaking, and the matter was further complicated by the fact that for security reasons the

MILITARY POLICE SEARCH FOR SNIPERS IN A DESERTED
HOUSE IN ITALY

use of the Army shield on signboards was prohibited until the actual day of the take-over. No start could therefore be made on the actual marking of routes, report centres or information posts, etc.

As the various routes, Depot area, etc., were decided on, the boards were painted for erection when the time came. For the short stretch of road north of Capua which was common to Fifth and Eighth Armies large boards—"No Halting," "No Double-banking," and such slogans—were prepared with both Fifth and Eighth Army shields painted in the upper corner.

Contact with the Provost Marshal, Fifth Army, was made very early on. From the start close liaison with U.S. provost was maintained and with excellent results. It was realized from the word "Go" that the Eighth Army provost would be gaining new experiences. Whereas before the Eighth Army had always been cut off by desert or mountain ranges from other Allied forces and generally at great distances from base, now for the first time they would be working alongside another Allied Army, and rear Army boundary would be only a matter of twenty miles from the great port and military base of Naples (A.P.M., Major W. M. J. Carruthers).

It was first thought that the take-over from American provost would be on or about 13th March, but it did not actually take place until over ten days later. The arrangements were complete by the earlier date, but in view of the delay in the Army take-over a gradual thinning out of American provost was arranged in certain areas where Army troops were concentrating, although the main highway was not taken over until 23rd March.

Section tasks had been worked out in detail and sections had moved out to their locations some days in advance. The signboards for the various routes, report centres, railhead and depot areas were distributed among the sections ready for erection. All N.C.Os. had thus had time to become acquainted with the area. This was most important as conditions were very different in a number of ways. In place of the Termoli–Vasto road, which was little better than a farm track, there was Highway 6—the main road from Naples to Rome. This was a three- or four-lane route along which traffic could move at 30-40 m.p.h. Whereas there had been no area between Termoli and the Sangro (fifty miles), where large convoys could halt clear of the road, convoy dispersal areas now presented much less difficulty.

The weather was improving daily. During the preliminary reconnaissance of the new Army area it was obvious that good communications would be required for traffic control. It was therefore necessary for Signals to provide communications. Three focal points would have to be linked to Army H.Q. These were:

H

The Army Report Centre at Triflisco Bridge, a Traffic Control point at the point where the road from Naples forked into Highway 6 leading to Cassino and Highway 7 leading to Rome, and a Report Centre just south of Vairano.

The advantages of the rapid and reliable communications thus placed at provost disposal were immediately apparent. A similar system worked satisfactorily in 13 Corps area. Strict control in this area was particularly necessary as on either side of Highway 6 from Vairano north to Cassino, depots, installations, and camps were located practically the whole way.

At this time another Signals section was formed, this time from traffic control personnel working under Signals direction. The plan was that this section would provide communications along Highway 6 from Cassino forward as necessary. This section would lay a line which would be available to Divisional provost and later to Corps and Army.

On the road in the Capua area joint control by U.S. provost and C.M.P. was maintained—U.S. and British military police, side by side in the same vehicles, on speed traps, checks and road patrols. This proved most effective.

In view of the later date of the take-over most Fifth Army units had moved out of the Army area. These moves were in consequence largely handled by U.S. police. A large contingent of the French Expeditionary Corps, however, remained and did not move out of the sector until the take-over.

In conclusion, the period covered saw no rapid movement similar to the advance from Reggio. For all ranks C.M.P. throughout the Army it was, however, a great period of activity; as a result many valuable lessons were learned.

From 1st to 10th May final regrouping of the Army prior to the battle continued; six Divisional moves took place to and from the front line. The 78th Division pulled out of the "Inferno" valley on handing over to the Poles. The Canadian Corps placed at the disposal of Army a large proportion of their provost resources to assist in the control of traffic on Highway 6.

During the fortnight prior to the opening of the offensive, Army provost handled on an average eleven thousand vehicles daily on Highway 6 alone. Constant watch by police mobile patrols, the use of loud-speaker apparatus, observation aircraft, and first-class police communications made this possible. A ruthless check on "swanners" was enforced; a number of "pull in" areas were established along the main routes into which police signalled suspected vehicles. Offenders were impounded or turned back.

Large warning notices in English, Polish, French and Italian were prominently displayed on the principal routes. Recovery facilities were located with C.M.P. and traffic control posts, and regular use was made of light aircraft.

Immediately before the battle, 6th (British) Armoured Division moved from Piedmonte into the forward area. The armour was moved at night by a tank track which had been constructed parallel to Highway 6.

No lights were permitted on tanks; the track was lit and the armour was escorted by C.M.P. in jeeps.

During the period of heavy tank transporter moves by night which followed, loud-speaker equipment was found to be of the greatest value in passing instructions to tank crews and transporter drivers above the noise of the engines.

At 11 p.m. on 11th May the offensive opened. By 15th May the Canadian Corps was preparing to deploy in the Liri valley on the left of 13 Corps. The 1st Canadian Infantry Division was the first to move forward into the valley and was directed on Pontecorvo. On Highway 6 Mount Cassino proved once again a formidable obstacle and it was reduced only after great efforts by the Polish Corps on the right flank. From then onwards the pursuit became very rapid and the chief obstacle was the limitations imposed on road capacity by damage to bridges, craters and major demolitions. It became necessary to limit the size of the force engaged, and accordingly after the capture of Frosinone the Canadian Corps moved back into the Vairano area, where it could be maintained from Naples. The Polish Corps, too, was detached from the army and moved over to the Adriatic sector, where it took over from 5 Corps after a short period of rest in the Campobasso area. 10 Corps with the New Zealand Division took over from Polish Corps responsibility for the right flank of the army.

The chief work of the police during this period was the control of heavy road traffic, including some large tank transporter moves. The rapidity of the advance made it necessary for reserve tanks, and in fact whole armoured brigades, to be moved on transporters rather than on their tracks. This was both on account of track mileage and also the damage the roads would have suffered.

Rome fell to troops of the American Fifth Army on 4th June. All the bridges in the city were left intact, although the bridges upstream from the city had been blown. Eighth Army was still operating on a two-Corps basis, and the main army axis followed the 13 Corps route up Route 6 to Rome and thence via Route 3 towards Civita Castellana. The 10 Corps axis ran parallel to this on the east, crossing the Tiber by Bailey bridges, and thence by side roads in the direction of Tornia and Perugia.

Route marking in a town the size of Rome presented certain difficulties and great credit was due to Lieut.-Colonel G. White, the newly-appointed D.P.M. Rome and his A.P.M., Major R. A. Whitby for the excellent traffic and route signing organization which they built up. It was thought at first that there might be considerable traffic blocks in the city, but this was not the case, probably on account of the great width of the principal thoroughfares.

The South African Division was the first division to pass through Rome, followed by the 78th Division. The pursuit continued rapidly until Civita Castellana was reached, where the bridges over a large gorge had been demolished. Demolitions and breaking weather slowed down the subsequent rate of advance considerably.

By this time preparations were in hand for entry into Florence, which was to be a Welfare Centre for the Army; but, in point of fact, progress proved to be much slower than had been expected on account of considerable stiffer opposition, many demolitions and rain.

During this period the principal work of the police again was the handling of traffic on inadequate and overtaxed roads. There was little serious crime committed, but in the investigation of the few serious cases which occurred the S.I.B. had success.

During the period 24th–29th July provost arrangements were made in connection with the three-day visit of the King. Military police enforced a "stay-in-doors" order on civilians throughout areas visited and cleared the roads of all traffic. The visit passed without incident.

The provost plan for the army's entry into the city of Florence was completed by 30th June. It was estimated that the headquarters of the 105 and 506 Provost Companies, plus twelve sections, a detachment of the Special Investigation Branch, and a detachment of C.M.P. Wireless and Signal Sections would be available to form a powerful police force (Proforce), under the supervision of D.A.P.M. 71 Garrison. The Chief Engineer attached carpenters to the 105 Provost Company to build the required sign boards, pointsmen stands, axis signs, etc., and six 3-ton vehicles were made available for the carriage of C.M.P. additional equipment.

Police arrangements were complete and a representative detachment of Proforce moved forward to 13 Corps area and thence to the New Zealand sector; as the battle progressed slowly, the Proforce recce unit switched to the 6th South African Armoured Division area when a break-through appeared imminent. The battle for Florence, however, proved a bitterly contested struggle, and it was not until the morning of 4th August that a detachment of Proforce entered Florence South with the South African tanks, established itself, and was operating by 2.0 p.m. At this time the enemy was holding in strength the north bank of the River Arno, and German fighting patrols crossed to the south bank nightly.

When the police entered Florence "mob rule" existed. Street fighting flared up in the neighbourhood day and night; unorganized groups of armed partisans picqueted the town. It seemed that at any time during the early stages of occupation they could have taken complete control. The military police could have done little to prevent it.

The events during the first seven days of the occupation are recorded here by extracts from the daily occurrence book of the provost officer in charge.

"*6th August,* 1944.

"Between noon and 3 p.m. intermittent sniping and small-arms fire took place in the Piazza Tossa, which resulted in the death and wounding of Italian civilians.

"Partisans have been prominent again today. Parades have been held. At about 2 p.m. a large armed body of partisans were seen to infiltrate into position on the British held bank of the Arno.

"Further shelling by the enemy has just commenced—8 p.m.

"During the night much sniping took place in the streets on the south bank of the river. Intermittent enemy shelling took place and this was countered by our own barrage. Curfew was enforced with the assistance of the loud-speaker jeep and all streets were cleared by 9.15 p.m.

"*7th August.*

"Sniping took place during the morning which resulted in a number of civilian casualties.

"Combined patrols of British and Canadian police are working satisfactorily. On orders received from the Garrison Commander, both British and American flags were removed from the entrance to the H.Q., the entrance being under enemy observation.

"Patrols were withdrawn on the instructions of the Garrison Commander in view of the night's operations on this side of the river. Five snipers were killed.

"*8th August.*

"At 3 a.m. 8th August, 1944, half the detachment stood fully armed in readiness for a local operation at 4 a.m. The plan was for large bodies of organized local partisans, together with Canadian troops, to enter the area between this H.Q. and the River Arno to silence the enemy snipers. The operation did not go according to plan; the partisans began operations five hours before the prearranged time, thus the element of surprise was lost. During the early hours of the morning street fighting broke out between partisans and Fascists. Intermittent counter battery shelling continued till first light.

"*9th August.*

"Infantry personnel attached to this H.Q. have been reinforced. It has been decided to establish listening posts in the grounds here; this will prove an added precaution in case the enemy repeats his operation of two nights ago, when a patrol from the north side of the Arno succeeded in penetrating our defences in some depth on this side of the river. This patrol was not observed until it reached the main Piazza.

"At about 11 a.m., representatives of the Gaumont British Film Unit took photographs of N.C.Os. on duty at the information posts and check points.

"At about noon a civilian was shot dead whilst passing our check post at the Main Archway, and at about 6 p.m. another civilian was shot dead whilst passing our check post.

"*11th August.*

"Heavy street fighting commenced this evening and lasted about thirty minutes. After the battle had stopped, a large mob of semi-hysterical civilians accompanied the victorious partisans who were escorting their prisoners up the main street. The prisoners were alleged to have fired on women and children the previous day. The shouting and actions of the mob were very heated. The partisans, brandishing loaded automatic weapons and carrying yards of belt ammunition together with a miscellaneous assortment of pistols, knives and grenades, accompanied by the mob, arrived at this H.Q. The heat and excitement of the crowd necessitated immediate and stern action to prevent the whole affair turning into a riot. The prisoners were taken from the partisans, the leaders of which were quickly disarmed by the Carabinieri.

"*12th August.*

"The check posts on the entrance to the town were supplemented with additional personnel, to cope with the expected rush of sightseers. A further check was established on the Vittoria bridge and ford, where many civilians were stopped who were endeavouring to cross the river. This movement of civilians was controlled and none was allowed to cross. A further seven check points were established to prevent any movement from the north to the south banks or vice versa."

Before the entry into Florence, the decision had been taken to transfer the bulk of British and Canadian forces to the east coast, where the 2 Polish Corps had captured Ancona and thus provided a base for large-scale operations against the eastern portion of the Gothic Line.

The switch was to be executed under conditions of the greatest secrecy and as rapidly as possible so as to lose as little of the remaining fine campaigning weather. 13 Corps was to pass to command of Fifth Army and continue operations in the Florence sector. Little information was to hand about conditions on the east coast, and accordingly an army reconnaissance left for Ancona on 6th August.

No. 1 District, which had been in Foligno, now took over responsibility for Army tasks in the area west of (inclusive) Foligno–Perugia. It was agreed that a proportion of Army military police should be left with No. 1 District until required by Army as No. 1 District Provost resources were strictly limited.

For the move from Foligno to the east coast two routes were available, both starting from Foligno itself—a northern route via Route 3 to Fassato, thence via Route 76 to Jesi and the coast; and a southern one via Route 77 through Folentino and Macerata, joining the coast at Porto Recanati, thence by-passing Ancona to Jesi. The main coast road through Ancona could not be used as it was already carrying very heavy port clearance and Polish Corps traffic.

The period of heaviest movement was over by 22nd August although considerable transporter and other moves continued for a period of fourteen days or more, and by the 24th August the Army Commander, in an address at Jesi, was able to announce that the Eighth Army, with Polish Corps on the right, Canadian troops in the centre, and 5 Corps on the left, was about to attack the Gothic Line positions in the Adriatic Sector.

The attack on the Gothic Line was based on the employment of three Corps—Polish Corps on the coastal strip, 1 Canadian Corps in the centre and 5 Corps on the left flank. Except for the main coastal road there were no good axes of advance, and sappers supporting the advance of 5 Corps and Canadian Corps were obliged to bulldoze tracks across country to link available side roads and lanes. These latter were generally one-way with numerous craters and blown bridges. There is no need to emphasize the effect of rain upon such tracks. The marking of these tracks was done by Corps R.E. in conjunction with military police. It was undoubtedly a success and proved that the lesson of the Liri valley had been well learned.

During this period Divisional and Corps provost were hard at work on the roads and tracks available for the advance. Behind them Army provost were deploying up the main coast road. By

4th September Army provost were responsible for the main Army axis up to and including Pesaro.

1st (British) Armoured Division moved from south of Ancona to under command 5 Corps during this period. 43rd Indian Infantry Brigade, with an Indian provost section attached, was included in this reorganized division. A point to off-load the transporters was found in the Mondolfo area, and the weather remained dry during the move. This was most fortunate as an all-weather tank transporter turn-round was not available in the area.

A traffic census held at Mondolfo revealed that during 6th September, 10,723 vehicles passed a point.

By now the weather had definitely deteriorated. This made progress most difficult. Resistance was stiff, particularly on the 5 Corps sector, where Coriano and the neighbouring features were the scene of heavy fighting. The nature of the country forbade any advance on other sectors until this feature was cleared. During this period the Greek Mountain Brigade took over the coastal sector in the Riccione area and were among the first troops into Rimini, having taken part in the hard fighting which took place around the airfield south of the town. Rimini itself was entered on the 20th September, nearly a month after the battle had started. As Army roadhead No. 6 was to be established in the Rimini area, the town was an Army objective and a detachment of 505 Provost Company entered the town.

It soon became apparent that German resistance remained as stiff as ever and that there was to be no general withdrawal in spite of the fact that the Gothic Line had been overrun in the Adriatic coastal sector. The town of Rimini was considerably damaged and was still within range of enemy shell fire for some days after its capture. This prevented the immediate establishment of the new roadhead, and as a result the work of the Army police during the first few days of occupation was largely a matter of anti-looting patrols.

In the spring of 1945 the advance was resumed, and had been carried well past Bologna and Ravenna into the valley of the Po when the collapse of Germany in May brought fighting to an end.

★   ★   ★   ★   ★

ONCE the Army had been moved to the east coast, the main burden of provost work fell on Divisional and Corps companies: companies who were faced with the task of moving their formations over inadequate roads and tracks never intended for traffic heavier than farm carts.

These roads deteriorate rapidly and frequently wear out while still in constant use. When weather is dry a perpetual dust cloud covers them, and in the wet the numerous diversions and quagmires frequently become impassable. Much hard work fell upon those engaged in traffic control duties and a high standard was demanded of all ranks to alleviate the cramping effects imposed by such conditions upon an army in the field.

Not so long after troops entered Italy it became evident that larger and bolder signs were necessary. Most of the "fighting roads" were narrow and more one-way circuits were needed—particularly in the mountains in the centre of Italy where passes were inadequate and in no state to stand up to the strain of the great volume of heavy traffic which had to pass and re-pass. Provost made reconnaissance and one-way circuits, provided signs and controlled traffic, constantly patrolling over the glaring white chalk dust which composes the surface of southern Italian roads.

From Reggio Calabria onwards poured the huge mechanized fighting machine. Taranto–Bari–Molfetta–Barletta on the east coast, then slightly inland to Foggia–San Severo. All these towns had to be permanently policed. Companies were ordered up posthaste to release Corps and Army companies, badly needed forward: a mad scramble to cross the Sangro before the floods and the arrival of winter.

The never-ending duties of the "Redcap" can never be better illustrated than during the hand-over of one provost company to another. Provost went down to the Sangro in force, but winter arrived first and the Army stopped. The rains and mud came, and Eighth Army provost had its first taste of mud, to which they quickly adapted themselves.

During the last stages leading up to the Sangro it was a common occurrence for units to become split up for two or more days, owing to rivers suddenly becoming torrents and washing away hastily constructed Bailey bridges. The company commander of 105 Provost Company, with an officer and three of the company, went on ahead during one move to find a company location. Having crossed one river, accommodation was fixed up, and as it was getting late and there were no signs of the rest of the company the party went back, to find the river a raging torrent and the unit gazing blankly from the other side. The company eventually joined after a two days' detour.

When it was decided to reduce Cassino many were the details which had to be worked out. Many hundreds of tanks had to be got up. The road surfaces had to be repaired and kept for tyred vehicles. This meant that from about twelve miles south of Cassino tanks were unloaded and were routed up to their starting points across country tracks. Many heavy and light guns, tractors, trailers, bulldozers and vehicles of all descriptions had to pass up and through provost-controlled roads and tracks.

For seven days and nights before the battle traffic control, L. of C., Army and Corps provost companies worked practically without sleep on the roads and tracks, pushing through and guiding this mass of armour and vehicles up to the start line of Cassino. All this went on without a single hitch.

The divisions, particularly infantry, sat up on the heights overlooking Cassino, solving their own particular problems. Their provost company learning the orders of march, signed their sectors and lighted their routes at night.

One provost subaltern of the 4th British Division marking routes on the other side of the river in the heat of battle, found himself facing a body of disordered British infantry who had lost their officers and N.C.Os. He rallied them and led them triumphantly back to battle. For this he was awarded the M.C.

As summer arrived, so also did the dust: dust that raised a tell-tale cloud and brought the enemy shells down on the offending vehicle. Police were told to erect 5 m.p.h. signs from a certain rear boundary to as far forward as a vehicle could penetrate, and that this was to continue so long as it was summer and there was dust. This was not so easy as may be imagined as boundaries changed from day to day and sometimes within an hour or so. The rear boundary had to be constantly revised and kept up to date as, it will be appreciated, vehicles travelling at 5 m.p.h. unnecessarily would have the effect of slowing down to a degree the operations.

The campaign in Italy taught the military police much about the control of bridges, one-way diversions, ferrys, timing and routing of convoys, the value of wireless and the all-important need for keeping things moving all the time.

The operational problems were always severe and testing, and the maintenance of close liaison with the U.S. military police was a constant task in itself.

Much credit for the successful achievement of these tasks must go to Colonel Mark Sykes, Provost Marshal, A.F.H.Q., Colonel Rees-Reynolds, Provost Marshal, Allied Armies in Italy, and afterwards Provost Marshal, A.F.H.Q., in relief of Colonel Sykes, to Colonel McNally who was senior provost officer in Italy from October, 1943 to November, 1944 and succeeded Colonel Rees-Reynolds as P.M., A.F.H.Q., in June, 1945, and to Lieut.-Colonel Archer Burton, D.P.M. Eighth Army, but the excellent results were in the main achieved by the work of all provost officers and military policemen in the Mediterranean Theatre.

MAP 2

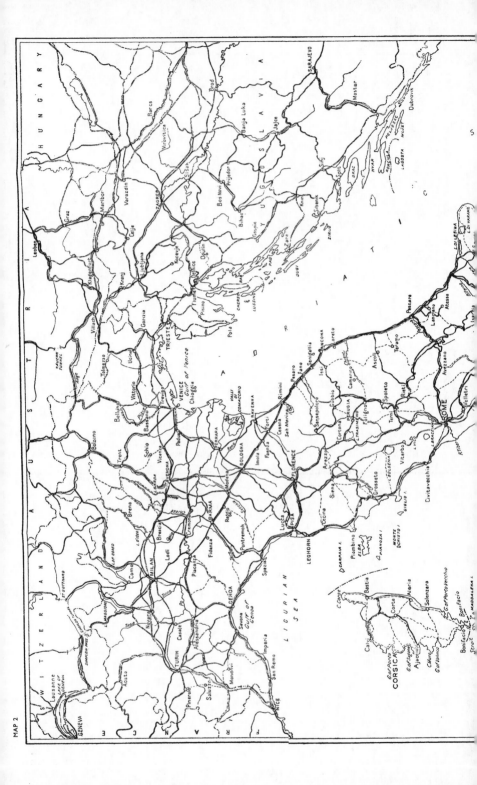

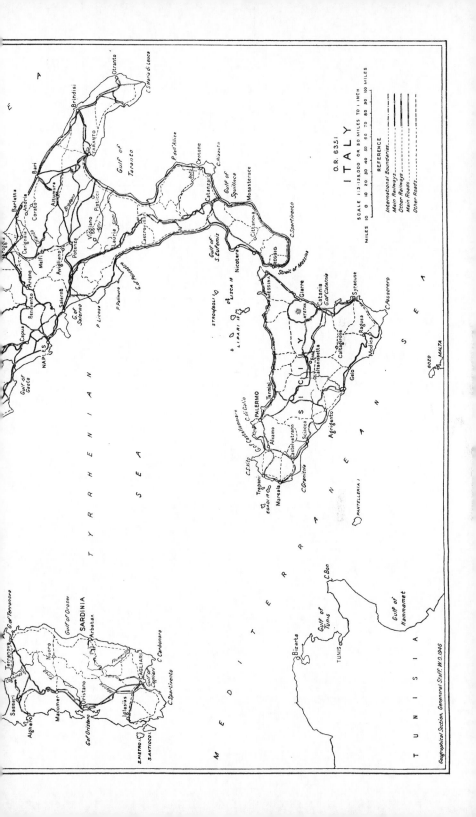

O.R. 6351

ITALY

SCALE 1:3·125,000 OR 50 MILES TO 1 INCH

MILES 10 0 10 20 30 40 50 60 70 80 90 100 MILES

REFERENCE

International Boundaries......
Main Railways...............
Other Railways..............
Main Roads..................
Other Roads.................

Geographical Section, General Staff. M.D.1946.

M OST of the military police who took part in the North African Campaign had gone on to Italy, but some of them had returned to England, in certain cases as complete units, in others as individual drafts. These were absorbed into the force which was being built up in the U.K. for the Second Front. They were of great value because of their unique battle experience.

CHAPTER VII

SECOND WORLD WAR: NORTH-WEST EUROPE

A T 8 a.m. on 6th June, 1944, the assault on Europe by 21 Army Group, with 12 U.S. Army Group on its right, both under the command of Field-Marshal Montgomery, began on the Normandy beaches. At 8 a.m. on 5th May, 1945, eleven months later, the cease-fire sounded upon the unconditional surrender to Field-Marshal Montgomery of all German forces opposing 21 Army Group.

In those eleven months British forces had assaulted and breached the Atlantic wall in Normandy; built a large artificial harbour at Arromanches, which at its peak handled over 10,000 tons a day; landed and enabled to circulate between 6th June and 31st July, in a bridgehead no larger than the Isle of Wight, 631,000 men, 153,000 vehicles and 689,000 tons of stores; and had stocked and operated the rear maintenance area in the neighbourhood of Bayeux. Our forces had, after bitter and prolonged fighting, broken out of the bridgehead and advanced 400 miles to Brussels and Antwerp in just over a week; had opened and operated the port of Antwerp and eight other Channel and North Sea ports, the advance base and fifteen army roadheads. They also opened and ran a leave centre in Brussels during the winter months, catering continually for 10,000 men on short leave.

They helped to defeat the large-scale German counter-attack against the U.S. forces in the Ardennes, pushed the German armies, in truly appalling conditions of thaw and flood, from between the Maas and the Rhine; and finally, in another rapid fighting advance of nearly 400 miles in just over four weeks, battled their way across the Rhine and chased the German armies out of the Ruhr and over the Elbe. Hamburg fell without a fight and on 5th May the war in Europe was over.

The average strength of the British Army in North-West Europe throughout this eleven months' campaign was approximately one million. The armies were in action practically without respite, had fought their way from the beaches of Normandy to the shores of the Baltic, and, together with the U.S. armies, had liberated France, Belgium, Holland and Luxembourg and had overrun and subdued about half Germany.

The principal provost officers in 21 Army Group on D Day were:

H.Q. 21 Army Group		P.M., Colonel Bassett Wilson
		D.P.M., Lieut.-Colonel F. A. Stanley
2nd Army ...	...	D.P.M., Lieut.-Colonel F. C. Drake
Canadian Army	...	D.P.M., Lieut.-Colonel G. Ball
H.Q. L. of C.	...	D.P.M., Lieut.-Colonel J. N. Cheney
1 Corps ...	...	A.P.M., Major P. Godfrey-Faussett
8 Corps ...	...	A.P.M., Lieut.-Colonel P. M. Fitzgerald
12 Corps ...	...	A.P.M., Major R. A. Guild
30 Corps ...	...	A.P.M., Lieut.-Colonel D. W. L. Melville
11 L. of C. Area	...	A.P.M., Major S. F. Crozier
12 L. of C. Area	...	A.P.M., Major Peterkin

It is worth noting that the experienced commanders of 8 and 30 Corps, Lieut.-General O'Connor and Lieut.-General Horrocks, had both given the local ranks of Lieutenant-Colonel to their A.P.Ms.

In accordance with the *Common Doctrine*, P.M. 21 Army Group and D.P.Ms. Armies and L. of C. all had upon their staffs an A.P.M. and D.A.P.M. (Traffic Control).

On the P.M's. staff was also a D.A.P.M. A.T.S. and a D.A.P.M. Provost (Canadian). Captain Wilson filled the latter appointment with great tact and judgment, and kept an excellent personal liaison between the office of the P.M. and Lieut.-Colonel Ball.

On D Day, outside the formation and L. of C. provost companies, thirty in all, there were fifteen traffic control companies, one signal company, eight vulnerable point companies, five S.I.B. sections and one ports company.

It had been appreciated during the planning stages that additional resources would be needed as the campaign progressed, and vigorous steps were being taken by Provost Marshal, War Office, to raise further ports companies, S.I.B. sections and vulnerable point (overseas) companies. War Office had already promised to release four further traffic control companies after embarkation. One complete provost section, commanded by Lieutenant Hills, served throughout the campaign as personal bodyguard to the Commander-in-Chief, Field-Marshal Montgomery.

The operational side throughout the campaign never ceased to be fierce and formidable. At times provost had to contend with conditions of appalling congestion, as in the Normandy bridge-head and also in the forward areas in Belgium and Holland, when on several occasions corps and sometimes four or five divisions at a time were re-grouping, and army roadheads were stocking against the clock in an acutely restricted area on inadequate and crumbling roads. At other times armies, corps and divisions shot forward in pursuit of the enemy extremely fast; Second Army, during the dash to Belgium and Holland, covered nearly 400 miles in a week without a halt. These headlong and explosive expansions put upon provost strains and stresses which, though different, were no less violent than those which that elastic and long-suffering service had previously undergone from the abnormal crowding and compression in the beach-head.

In the course of these whirlwind operations the fighting formations were continuously moved and shepherded in and out of battle and over minefields and bridges by their own provost companies. They fought their way across the Seine, the Somme, the intricate river and canal system in the Low Countries, the Maas, the Rhine, the Weser and the Elbe; content to leave, with the confidence which springs from past experience, the subsequent control of the numerous bridges, bottle-necks, roads and defiles over which they had passed in the safe hands of the military police of the higher formations following in their wake.

The administrative achievement presented a hardly less striking picture; during this period the Beach Groups formed after the initial assault on the beaches merged swiftly into three beach sub-areas, an L. of C. sub-area and a garrison, all under command of 11 L. of C. Area, which had landed on D+1 to conduct the flow of men and material across the beaches. These formations took charge of the Mulberry (artificial) harbour at Arromanches, Port En Bessin and the rear maintenance area. Fifteen army roadheads, a number of administrative "cushions," and innumerable corps forward maintenance areas were formed; the advance base at Antwerp and eight other ports were opened and operated; all of these closely packed administrative areas contained dumps and depots of every kind of vehicle and stores. None of these administrative areas either could or was expected to function without meticulous traffic control arrangements provided by the military police.

Field-Marshal Montgomery, in his book "Normandy to the Baltic," says that in Normandy there were four "outstanding administrative problems." Of these, the first arose from bad weather; the remaining three arose from the difficulty of "expanding the major maintenance installations rapidly from the beaches into the confined area of the bridgehead; from the great traffic congestion within the bridgehead; and from the sudden change from intensive short range operations to the fast moving battle up to the Seine and beyond."

It is an interesting reflection that of these four major administrative problems, three were all problems in which the provost service was of paramount importance.

This is perhaps the most convenient place to note some important appointments and upgradings of provost officers during the campaign:

Provost Company Commanders were given the staff appointments of D.A.P.Ms.

An A.P.M. (S.I.B.) was added to the staff of P.M. 21 Army Group. Major G. Pollard was appointed. This was an essential appointment.

A staff Lieutenant (Provost) was added to the staff of each A.P.M. L. of C. area.

A D.P.M. (Paris) was appointed with an A.P.M. and D.A.P.M. on his staff. The D.P.M. was Lieut.-Colonel Diggle.

In February, 1945, a pool of four D.A.P.Ms. (Traffic Control) was authorized; they were for allotment by the P.M. as required. Normally one was allotted to each L. of C. area whose A.P.M. was in urgent need of extra help for the traffic problems; the other two performed different tasks such as, for example, D.A.P.M. to the "Bank Control" organization which was an *ad hoc* body created for regulating the intricate control of the Rhine assault crossing.

A large number of new L. of C. sub-areas and garrisons were created, necessitating the appointment of new D.A.P.Ms. and staff Lieutenants. This was in the early part of 1945.

On 17th March, 1945, P.M. 21 Army Group was upgraded to Brigadier, and D.P.Ms. 21 Army Group and Second Army to full Colonel.

At about the same time A.P.Ms. corps districts (for controlling the corps areas in Germany) were upgraded to D.P.Ms. (Lieutenant-Colonels).

Many new appointments were also made in the latter days of the campaign of additional provost staff officers of varying grades for the new duties which would arise when hostilities ended.

Mention should also be made of Captain A. de Callatay, a Belgian liaison officer attached to the staff of Provost Marshal 21 Army Group. He carried out his duties with admirable tact and efficiency.

The constant help of the Provost Marshal, War Office, Major-General J. Seymour Mellor, and his staff, and in particular of his D.P.M., Colonel C. T. O'Callaghan, in raising, training, and sending out the many reinforcements and new units required for the British Liberation Army, enabled an extremely high standard to be maintained throughout; a standard which reflected great credit upon the Depot at Mytchett.

During the eleven months of the campaign new and additional units totalling five traffic control companies, eight vulnerable point (overseas) companies, two ports companies, eight S.I.B.

sections and eight new type vulnerable point companies for static duties in the L. of C. were raised by the activities of the Provost Marshal, War Office, and his staff, and added to 21 Army Group.

Further reinforcements came from Italy in 1945 in the shape of one provost and one traffic control company (British), and two provost and one traffic control companies (Canadian).

A new L. of C. provost company was authorized by H.Q. 21 Army Group and was composed of R.A. sergeants who were surplus as a result of disbanding artillery units. This company was formed in January, 1945, and was trained at a 21 Army Group provost school set up a little earlier to train a number of Belgian and Dutch traffic control and provost companies for duty with 21 Army Group. This sergeants' company was specially trained for arresting war criminals and "rough-house" work in Germany.

In all seven Belgian and Dutch provost and traffic control companies were formed towards the end of 1944 and early 1945, clothed, equipped and trained by the provost service, 21 Army Group; these companies became part of 21 Army Group resources and did good work alongside our companies.

A number of Pioneers were attached to Second Army provost resources. This was the result of private arrangements between the D.P.M. and D.D.L., Second Army (Colonel De Pass). Twenty pioneers were attached to each of the four traffic control companies which served with Second Army throughout the campaign. All these men were volunteers and had the option, which few exercised, of returning to Pioneer companies if they wished; they were given special traffic control courses at Louvain and became proficient. At the end of war some applied for transfer to the C.M.P.

The total provost strength with 21 Army Group grew from 6,648 on D Day to 10,294 at the end of the war.

The traffic control and vulnerable point companies and S.I.B. sections were under control of Provost Marshal, 21 Army Group, for allotment between Armies and L. of C. as the situation required. The L. of C. was always and inevitably the milch-cow. There were many occasions when Lieut.-Colonel Cheney, the D.P.M., L. of C., was called upon to give up to armies, traffic control and vulnerable point companies of which he had vital need for his own swiftly expanding duties. His invariable and instant co-operation, often to his own disadvantage, deserves a special tribute in this history.

A feature of modern warfare is the constant regrouping, at high speed and usually under cover of night, of divisions and corps in the forward areas. Sometimes complete corps would slide-slip, sometimes four or five divisions would be simultaneously reshuffling. These moves usually took place very quickly and across other corps

MILITARY POLICE FIXING A HUGE SIGN IN BERLIN

or army areas; available lateral roads were always scarce, on several occasions a single axis route having to be used for a whole movement.

This was a constantly recurring type of operation in which the military police arrangements, requiring the most meticulous traffic control to ensure success, had frequently to be laid on and perfected within a few hours' notice. Lieut.-Colonel Drake, D.P.M. Second Army, co-ordinated these moves with unfailing skill.

Throughout the campaign, divisional provost companies were comparatively little concerned with discipline; they had, of course, their normal disciplinary duties within their formations, but their chief work was the carrying out of their operational functions. There was a certain amount of looting with the suppression of which divisional provost became involved; another practice with which they at times had to deal started in the early days in Normandy and continued more or less throughout. This was the tendency of local inhabitants to make against British troops false claims for looting and damage actually suffered at the hands of the retreating enemy. The cure was for provost or S.I.B., accompanied by an officer of Claims and Hirings, to enter towns and villages hard on the heels of the forward fighting troops; this party would note the condition of property, etc., and, where necessary, take signed statements from local inhabitants. These statements, often taken under fire, were usually accurate, and prevented the later invention of "second thoughts."

Owing to a vast circulation of traffic there were throughout the campaign innumerable blocks and jams. Most of the blocks were caused by stupidity or by the disobedience of traffic rules by a single driver; double-banking, over-taking and cutting-in, and unnecessary halts without pulling clear of the road were the most common causes. Officers were too often offenders.

Perhaps the most practical executive remedy was found by Second Army. Instead of multiplying road patrols, which were seldom in the right place at the crucial time and often got blocked themselves, pairs of police motor-cyclists were stationed at busy cross-roads, bottle-necks, etc. The instant a block occurred they rode down the road, found the source of the trouble, and usually within a minute or two movement began again. It was also found necessary early in the campaign to publish a special order dealing with double-banking and over-taking, stating by whom and under what conditions it would be permissible, and formulating a method of signing certain specially restricted areas in which it would be formally forbidden for everyone save the Commander-in-Chief and Army Commanders. This order also worked well in practice.

I

On one occasion, shortly after the initial break-out from the bridgehead, a bad traffic block occurred on the Caen–Lisieux road; fighting was still going on ahead and the road was being heavily shelled. An R.A.F. officer who was watching it told Provost Marshal, 21 Army Group, later, that it gave him a sense of unreality and security to see in the middle of the shelling and confusion, two "Redcaps" at a cross-roads sorting out and controlling the movement with the same efficiency and nonchalance as a couple of policemen controlling a massed exodus from London on a summer bank holiday.

Stencil sign plates, though quite good for a first and temporary layout, were found to be unsuitable for a permanent system; and therefore the practice of erecting large permanent wooden road signs was adopted without delay. Unfortunately, every unit in 21 Army Group considered that they should have some of their own; this in a surprisingly short time led to a competitive inter-unit contest for better, or anyhow bigger, signs than anyone else. The cross-roads became plastered with batteries of wooden hoardings each masking the other. In addition to this, C.M.P. companies began to adopt different styles of official signs, and it was clear that it was time to co-ordinate and regulate the whole question. It was therefore ordered that all military police signs would be in white lettering on black boards, and that only the military police were entitled to use this type of sign.

This meant that whenever a driver saw a black sign with white lettering he knew it was an official police sign. The order which dealt with this also covered the question of individual unit signs in general and conferred upon the provost service full powers to deal with them so that they caused no furthur obstruction.

Night lighting of traffic signs was always a difficulty, but it was found that in many French and Belgian urban areas excellent lighting arrangements for traffic signs could be made by using the local electricity resources, and this method was adopted in many places with good results.

The system of C.M.P. information posts was put into operation from the beginning of the campaign, and thereafter steadily developed. The practice was to site the information posts at focal points near an important cross-roads or in a town with as big a "pull in" as possible so that inquirers could park clear of the traffic stream. These information posts were further sited upon an organized general layout, arranged to cover at reasonable intervals the whole road net-work for which the police were responsible. The posts gave information of the locations of H.Qs., units, installations, where drinking water could be obtained, petrol points, fire service, medical officers, etc., and road information of all kinds. In addition to the above, they furnished in towns, information as to parking facilities, places of entertainment, baths, N.A.A.F.I., shopping facilities and so on.

Up to 31st March, 1945, 370 military police information posts were opened and manned by the C.M.P. The following are the numbers of the average daily inquiries recorded at a few important posts:

Bayeux	...	...	...	...	400 per day
Antwerp	...	...	...	...	200 per day
Brussels (Gare Du Nord)	...		...	1,750 per day
Brussels (Avenue Louise)	...		...	500 per day
Osnabruck	...	...	...	...	1,600 per day

The rear maintenance area, the advance base, and the large number of ports, army roadheads, forward maintenance areas, etc., opened up and operated during the campaign have already been mentioned. Many of these were of great size and complexity. Each had to be reconnoitred, circuited, signed and controlled by the C.M.P.; furnished with information centres, and with harbouring areas and signals communications between C.M.P. and the local H.Q. so as to facilitate the harbouring of convoys or vehicles which could not for the moment be accepted; calling them forward, and later clearing them from the area, in accordance with the needs and the orders of the installation authorities.

The signing of all such areas after the end of July was carried out with coloured commodity signs which were easy for drivers to follow. Armies found in practice that a roadhead supplying three corps required one complete traffic control company. A single roadhead required about 2,000 signs, and inasmuch as the next roadhead would open before the one in the rear was closed these 2,000 signs had to be duplicated and held in reserve ready for the next jump forward.

In all towns of any size it was necessary for the police to organize and control official car parks. The first of these was set up in the main square of Bayeux and, as the advance progressed, car parks controlled by C.M.P. became a common feature in all towns. Theft of army cars and vehicles in Belgium became so troublesome that the orders regarding stationary army vehicles were tightened, and the official car parks in Brussels were run by military police upon a tally system which was virtually thief-proof. This system was successful, the losses of vehicles which had been parked in the Brussels car parks being reduced from what threatened to become a crippling figure to a practically negligible quantity.

The main through routes were numbered 200, 210, 230 and 240; they all started from Normandy and ran across France through

Belgium and into Holland; routes 200 and 240 continued across Germany to the Danish border and the Elbe respectively; and a fifth route, 250, starting from Antwerp, cut south-east across 230 and 240 and eventually found its way via Aachen and Cologne to Hanover and Brunswick. There were, of course, many lateral routes which, with the routes mentioned above, were all signed and controlled throughout their length by the military police.

These main through routes, which were subsequently developed under the Army Group numbers given above, were in the first instance laid out and signed by military police of the advancing armies. During the pursuit to Brussels the whole maintenance traffic between the rear maintenance area in Normandy and Brussels moved up one road and down another. It was a very considerable feat for army military police therefore to ensure the arrival of convoys on time after so long a distance. Operational traffic was as far as possible kept to a third route. In order to ensure continuity to convoy drivers, Second Army traffic control companies signed these through-routes S.A. 26 and S.A. 27; the Canadian Army adopted a similar system, using the maple leaf for their road designation.

The following statistics are complete up to 31st March, 1945, a few days after the crossing of the Rhine; they are, therefore, exclusive of the campaign in Germany:

(i) Approximate total mileage signposted by C.M.P. in the British sector   4,000

(ii) Approximate total number of C.M.P. road signs erected   141,800

(iii) Number of towns where local electrical resources were used for night lighting of C.M.P. signs   ...   35

Equipment and mechanical transport of C.M.P. units and the military police service in general in most respects proved adequate. For this the greatest credit is due to Lieut.-Colonel Stanley, whose resourcefulness never failed.

There were, however, two serious deficiencies which no amount of pressure and effort were ever able to rectify.

The first was the absence of a 3-ton lorry on the War Establishment of traffic control companies; this meant that traffic control companies were incapable of moving their H.Q. and company stores without either a shuttle service of section trucks or borrowing a lorry. The other serious deficiency was the lack of reasonable transport for S.I.B. personnel.

Besides this both provost and traffic control companies were obliged throughout the campaign to carry large quantities of essential signing equipment and signs which required two or three additional 3-ton lorries per company. In practice "Q" services of

21 Army Group, army or lower formations always supplied the answer; but this was an unnecessarily burdensome method in the case of the 3-tonner for traffic control companies and in the case of cars for S.I.B. sections.

Periodical inspections of the mechanical transport of all units were made by R.E.M.E. Almost without exception the reports on military police units were first class; in several cases the unit being described as a "model unit."

In the early invasion days, Second Army, following the custom introduced by the Eighth Army in the desert days, ordered the whitening of all C.M.P. webbing equipment. This was done to enable military policemen on point duty to be readily distinguished, and thereby not only help the road users and add to the authority of the police, but also to protect the pointsman standing in the middle of the whirling traffic. The red bands on steel helmets and M.P. armlets were, in the Normandy dust and at night, very hard to pick out. The white equipment provided the answer. This change which proved such a success in the Mediterranean Theatre was equally successful in N.W. Europe and it was made the official dress for the whole of the military police, and its use by any other troops was prohibited.

12 Traffic Control Company, commanded with ability by Captain Barford, had been converted into a signals company, equipped throughout as such, and was given a thorough, although speedy, training in the United Kingdom by 21 Army Group Signals. It was composed of the usual traffic control H.Q. and six sections, each of which were organized and equipped as independently operating and self-supporting sections.

In principle, company H.Q. and one section were retained by P.M. 21 Army Group and utilized for many different tasks; the remaining five sections were usually farmed out to armies and corps, who without exception found their services invaluable.

The detachments of A.T.S. provost, under Junior Commander Buckle, were most useful and worked efficiently; not only with the A.T.S., but also in the special task, for which they were often in demand, of searching women suspects, displaced persons, etc. They also did valuable work at information centres.

The constant liaison with the large number of staff branches and services with whom provost were continuously dealing was, on all levels and with all branches, excellent. On the operational side the complete understanding between provost and "Q" (M.) was remarkable. Although provost is basically a branch of the "A" staff, it was ever since the publication of the *Common Doctrine*, accepted as the executive service of "Q" (M.) branch on the roads.

A tribute should be paid to the A.P.Ms., Traffic Control. Major

Low, A.P.M., Traffic Control, 21 Army Group, who had throughout the important duty of keeping himself constantly primed by "Q" (M.), 21 Army Group, as to present plans and future projects, and of maintaining the closest liaison between provost and 21 Army Group armies, and L. of C. He carried out this difficult task with unerring tact and skill. Major Buist, Major Swinden, and Major Steward, A.P.Ms. (Traffic Control) of Second Army, 1st Canadian Army and L. of C. had corresponding duties with their own formations, and in each case performed these duties admirably.

In North-West Europe provost dealt direct with the civil police. In Belgium and Holland particularly, indigenous informers made a habit of coming direct to the S.I.B. and of short-circuiting their own police. Many cases were brought to light and dealt with in this way. The French gendarmerie were inclined to rely too much upon support from the British police. The Belgian police were more active, and indeed highly co-operative. The principle difficulty in Belgium arose through the civil prisons becoming so overcrowded that they were unable to accommodate the increasing number of applicants for admission. In Holland the civil police were less helpful; in Germany they appeared to wish to help, but felt themselves gravely handicapped by being disarmed.

Just like the civil police, the civil population in the various countries varied greatly. In Normandy the natural dourness of the people made relations sometimes uneasy; nor could they be expected to enjoy the sight of Caen and many other towns being progressively destroyed by Allied bombers, but on the whole they made the best of this and were friendly and often helpful.

The Belgians, on the other hand, gave us from first to last the warmest and most spirited welcome imaginable. They had never lost their morale during the German occupation, and from the moment our troops first crossed the Franco-Belgian frontier, the Belgians seemed unable to do enough for our aid and comfort. The Dutch were more phlegmatic and far less demonstrative; but underneath their aloof aspect there lay a deep and often warm-hearted appreciation.

But although the superficial relations between the indigenous population and the liberating armies were pleasant, there were frequent troubles. No sooner were the Germans ejected from these countries, in which food, clothing, coal and other bare necessities of life had been progressively dwindling, than the friendly Allied armies poured in, bringing with them thousands of tons of these commodities; many of which, stacked in enormous dumps over the countryside or passing slowly over the railway in open trucks, became accessible to those who were prepared to take the risk of discovery. Youths of eighteen had been boys of thirteen or fourteen when the war started; and, during those four or five years so important to the formation of character, sabotage of the German war machine, pilferage of rations, clothing, cars and accessories, had been for them a patriotic virtue and an act of heroism. It was hardly to be expected that young men of that age could, in a night, suddenly realize that what had been heroic and even encouraged by the British Government on Monday became on Tuesday a serious crime for which they would be severely punished.

On the whole, the relationship between the British and the United States armies was excellent. Both British and United States troops recognized the essential differences in each other's methods and points of view, and it was only on rare occasions that such differences produced incidents.

This is perhaps the best place to mention a joint conference of senior provost officers of 12 United States Army Group and 21 Army Group which was held at Liege on 15th November, 1944. P.Ms. and all D.P.Ms., A.P.Ms. (Traffic Control) and their United States equivalents attended; the meeting was intended to be a direct successor to the series of similar provost meetings held in the United Kingdom before D Day by Provost Marshal, 21 Army Group.

The Liege meeting was held under the chairmanship of Colonel Stadtman, P.M. 12 United States Army Group. It began with a full review of the experiences and technical methods of military police in each Army Group during the campaign, after which followed a detailed discussion on future plans.

Every aspect of military police work was touched upon and resulted in the exchange of many useful practical points. The meeting was a great success both technically and internationally.

The need for military police to have great flexibility and the ability to switch at a moment's notice from operational to disciplinary duties or vice versa can rarely have been more forcibly illustrated than in this campaign. During the periods when operational duties were paramount, it was "all hands to the pump," provost, traffic control and vulnerable points alike. At other times, particularly between September, 1944, and March, 1945, when the relatively static conditions were a fertile ground for theft, racketeering, absenteeism and so on, the greater proportion of provost resources behind corps areas were plunged into a hard struggle to control crime and to maintain discipline.

In the provost service disciplinary duties always become more complex and more onerous in a theatre of war than elsewhere. Opportunities for looting multiply; crimes of violence tend to increase; pilfering and racketeering reach a huge scale; absenteeism is enlarged. Provost and the S.I.B. become intimately concerned with civilian offenders; and the checking of crime is essential not only to prevent loss of money to the nation and the lowering of army morale, but also to mitigate the direct menace to the success of operations caused by big losses of stores, equipment and supplies, vital for the need of the fighting troops.

In the early days in Normandy there were already signs, though at that time slight and undeveloped, of many of these evils. During the winter of 1944/45 they came to full fruition; and in the case of pilfering, black market activities and currency offences, reached really serious dimensions. Huge losses occurred in cigarettes, petrol, foodstuffs, clothing, blankets and motor vehicles, particularly in ports and depot areas, and in the course of road, rail and barge transit. These losses, although to some extent due to direct theft by civilians, were probably in the main a result of collaboration between a few unscrupulous soldiers and officers and highly qualified civilian thieves and receivers. Apart from "property" offences, there was little grave crime; cases of murder, rape, assault and looting were few. This type of offence tended to increase during active battle conditions and to die down in the more static times.

Army discipline was good. There was little drunkenness, although this may have been partly because of the shortage of liquor in the early days and to its high price later. Serious trouble, however, did arise during the winter from the sale to troops of poisonous liquor produced in illicit stills. Vigorous steps had to be taken in conjunction with the civil police and the Customs and Excise authorities to stamp this out. With regard to dress and general turnout there was a shaky start in the bridgehead; some of the seasoned veterans from the Desert army appeared to think that their just reputation for initiative and toughness and their magnificent fighting qualities needed enhancing, either by wearing strange and gaudy garments of a high and varied colour-value, or by appearing in a studied state of decay. For a short while some of the other troops of 21 Army Group showed signs of yielding to this seduction; but this phase soon passed, nor did it ever affect the high morale of the troops as a whole. In regard to discipline generally, and in particular to the question of dress, saluting and behaviour in public, always closely and interestedly watched and assessed by the indigenous population, it was noticeable that in many units the enforcement of order was far too much left to the military police.

Too many officers would pass a slovenly soldier or one who failed to salute, and take no action. Probably this failure on the part of some officers was due to the reflection that a desperate war was on, the men had been fighting hard, and that they ought not to bother

SEARCHING A GERMAN PRISONER

S.S. HAUPTSTURM-FUEHRER J. KRAMER, "THE BEAST OF
BELSEN," AND HIS MILITARY POLICE ESCORT

to dress themselves up and exchange the normal courtesies while enjoying a few hours' relaxation in a friendly town.

Of absentees and deserters the numbers indeed at times reached high figures. In most cases men were absent because of boredom and family troubles.

Before the big operation in the early part of 1945 to clear the country between the Maas and the Rhine, one of the corps commanders had the nature and importance of the coming engagement made known to every soldier. Corps H.Q. anticipated a sharp increase in absence as a result; but in fact nothing of the kind took place. Throughout the campaign absence reached its highest points during the quieter rather than during the more active periods. In previous wars absentees usually gave themselves up after a week or two from shortage of funds; in this campaign, by dint of periodical pilfering of army stores and subsequent sales to civilians at fantastic prices, large numbers of absentees were enabled to maintain themselves in hiding indefinitely. This added greatly to the difficulties of apprehension and caused an abnormal growth in the numbers of absentees.

The following totals of charges preferred by C.M.P. are of interest:

Drunkenness	1,092
Looting	72
Theft and Improper Possession	1,249
Absence	10,363
Improperly dressed	2,792
Vehicle offences of all kinds	6,409

36,366 charges in all were preferred by the military police during the whole of the campaign up to 31st March.

*   *   *   *   *

THE invasion started in the small hours of the morning of 6th June; gliders, followed by parachute brigades, of 6th Airborne Division dropping at 2.0 a.m. astride the Orne, on the east side of which they established a small bridgehead. The assault on the beaches began a few hours later, at 7.25 a.m., with the landing of the 50th Division under 30 Corps on the right and the 3rd Canadian Division and 3rd British Division under 1 Corps on the left.

Parachute detachments of 6th Airborne Divisional Provost Company, commanded by Captain Thompson, who was awarded the M.C. for his work during the first two days, were actually the first provost to land on the Continent. They were quickly followed by military police of all three wings; many of them were landed with the sea-borne assault troops on the first and second tides of D Day.

These military police units comprised:

(1) The provost companies of the 50th Division, 3rd Canadian Division and 3rd British Division, whose task was to regulate and control the traffic of the assault and follow-up brigades.

(2) 240, 241, 242, 243, 244, and 245 Beach Provost Companies and the bulk of 73 Traffic Control Company, who were responsible for traffic control and route and circuit signing in the beach, transit and assembly areas. With them were the majority of two vulnerable point companies for guarding P.W., detaining suspect civilians, and constructing cages.

(3) 102 and 113 Provost Companies, whose primary task was the control of the areas between the beaches and the forward divisions.

Captain Pearson, commanding 241 Beach Provost Company, gained an M.C., and 244 Beach Provost Company, officer commanding Captain Ellesmore, was warmly praised by Lieut.-Colonel Tapps, who commanded No. 8 Beach Group.

245 Provost Company, commanded by Captain John Corbett, were held up by stiff German resistance. They assaulted a German strongpoint and, although casualties were sustained, succeeded in establishing their position. Captain Corbett, later to become Deputy Provost Marshal of Berlin, was awarded the O.B.E.

The allotment of provost resources would have been sufficient had it landed according to plan; but, owing to the rough sea conditions and the failure of the Rhino ferries, only Divisional and Corps provost companies arrived on time. During the first two days there were not enough provost, therefore, to give adequate control to the assembly areas or the narrow exits from the beaches. By D+2, however, more provost had landed; and, by D+3, although the volume of traffic was steadily increasing, the routes and circuits within the beach maintenance area were working satisfactorily. By D+5, 11 L. of C. area, which had arrived on D+1, took command of all beach troops, thus relieving Corps of that responsibility.

By 14th June, 1 and 30 Corps with three divisions each, the six beach provost companies, 247 L. of C. Provost Company, four traffic control companies, Second Army provost companies, three vulnerable point companies, one S.I.B., and four sections of 185 Ports Provost Company were all ashore. Brigadier O. Wales, commanding 4 L. of C. sub-area, in charge of the Mulberry and

Port En Bessin, and always one of the staunchest supporters of the military police in their disciplinary duties, was particularly complimentary about the work of his D.A.P.M., Captain Baker, and 247 L. of C. Provost Company, officer commanding Captain Price.

By 24th June 8 Corps with two divisions and 12 Corps with three divisions, four more traffic control companies, two more vulnerable point companies and two sections of the C.M.P. signals company had also come across; and, to complete the provost build-up, by 25th July practically the whole of the military police resources had reached the theatre of war.

The bridgehead quickly assumed a shape and size which did not alter greatly during the first fifty days. It was, during this period, about twenty miles broad by an average depth of twelve miles; the whole area being much the same size as the Isle of Wight.

But within this minute space, during a period of seven weeks, a great military effort developed. On D Day alone, 59,900 troops, 8,900 vehicles and 1,900 tons of stores were landed on the beaches; a week later these totals reached 326,000 troops, 54,000 vehicles and 104,000 tons of stores; by D+50 there were in the bridgehead no fewer than 631,000 troops, 153,000 vehicles and 689,000 tons of stores, not including 68,000 tons of bulk petrol. Of these stores a small proportion only came in through the Mulberry during these first weeks; the greater part was landed, over the open beaches; from there, and from the Mulberry, troops, vehicles and stores had to be concentrated inland into their appropriate depot and installation areas.

Prisoners in large quantities kept coming in and had to be taken to cages near the beaches, run and manned by vulnerable points companies and handed over by them to police escorts from the United Kingdom, who operated a shuttle service across the Channel.

The original plan had counted upon the early capture of Caen and the speedy development of the rear maintenance area between Bayeux and Caen. Caen, however, did not fall until 7th July, and the adjacent suburb of Vaucelles remained in enemy hands until 20th July. Nevertheless, throughout the first seven weeks a daily average of 3,000 vehicles and 14,000 tons of stores kept pouring into the bridgehead. It was, therefore, impossible to postpone the development of the rear maintenance area. The altered tactical conditions, however, made it necessary to change the layout and shift the main weight north-westwards; this meant that Bayeux, instead of being clear of the depot areas, now became surrounded by main depots on all sides; a feature which greatly aggravated the traffic problem, Bayeux being a maze of bottle-necks and sharp corners and narrow streets.

Meanwhile two army roadheads had been formed; on 20th

July, H.Q. 21 Army Group assumed administrative control of the theatre, and these two later roadheads became known as R.M.A. East and R.M.A. West and later merged into the final R.M.A. Despite the Caen difficulty, by 25th July the new R.M.A. was fully organized and stocked and contained reserves more than sufficient to support the break-out from the bridgehead.

While this administrative activity was in full swing the forward troops were engaged in a series of battles. The forward limits of the more southerly depot areas were within three or four miles of the front line; and the constant tactical moves and regrouping of division and corps had to be largely carried out in and through the depot areas, which themselves were surging incessantly with administration movements on a constantly growing scale. The road system which had to support all this movement was scanty; the Bayeux–Caen road alone had any claim to first-class status, and that only by comparison with the rest, which were no more than lightly surfaced agricultural lanes, the margins of which crumbled and disintegrated.

Tanks played havoc with these by-ways, and Second Army swiftly organized a system of cross-country tank-tracks, which were reconnoitred by traffic control companies with R.A.C. assistance, signed and lamped for night moves. Four hundred minefield lamps per traffic control company were issued for this purpose, and a floating reserve of 3,000 was held by provost for replacements.

During these first seven weeks a number of major re-groupings occurred; at the end of June, Second Army regrouped to launch 1, 8 and 30 Corps into the final battle for Caen; in the middle of July, Canadian Corps became operational, and a further regrouping took place. Between 15th and 18th July the whole of 8 Corps, with three complete armoured divisions, was passed right across 1 Corps area and over the Orne bridges, moving all day and night over four routes; a difficult move only made possible by the closest co-operation between Major Godfrey-Faussett and Lieut.-Colonel Fitzgerald (A.P.Ms. 1 and 8 Corps). At the end of July, Lieut.-Colonel Drake, D.P.M. Second Army, had to complete the move of four armoured divisions, one tank brigade, 1 Army Group, R.A. and corps troops, 16,500 vehicles, right across the bridgehead on two routes, within thirty-six hours from the time he received the order.

On yet another occasion 10,000 vehicles, including two armoured divisions, were at short notice switched from Caen to the right of the line, and had to be passed by the C.M.P. through the narrow and torturous streets of Bayeux in forty-eight hours. Only by the closest traffic control on the part of provost could these vital operational moves and the incessant movement of administrative vehicles and stores be kept under control and up to time.

Every road in this small bridgehead was full. Provost and "Q" (M.) made a joint air reconnaissance shortly after the capture of Caen to observe the road traffic generally, and that passing through Caen in particular. Apart from the endless convoys on the roads, it was impossible to detect a single field in the whole area not occupied by troops, vehicles or dumps. The roads, moreover, began quickly to break up, and repairs were almost impossible owing to the persistent traffic.

It became urgently necessary to take all possible steps to alleviate the congestion, and a number of methods were adopted. Two of these, the tank tracks and the police motor-cyclists at cross-roads, etc., have already been mentioned; a third was the speedy construction by sappers of a large circular dirt track around Bayeux, which was followed soon after by a metalled inner circular road, built by connecting suitable sections of existing roads with a few specially constructed connecting links. As soon as these were in use the situation improved, no through traffic being permitted to traverse Bayeux. After the capture of Caen a similar circular road was constructed to by-pass this town, and a number of smaller but useful by-passes and roundabouts were also built and helped the situation enormously.

Another important step was the evening-up of the load on the roads by Movement Control orders, which confined operational moves to night and administrative moves to day. Before this was done the policy was to accept all-comers at all times; this resulted in most moves taking place simultaneously during hours of daylight, and the roads being nearly empty during the few hours of darkness.

A traffic census taken at a number of the worst points during the height of the congestion will illustrate the strain thrown upon individual pointsmen. At one period in Second Army area 305,276 vehicles were counted on the roads in seven days, a daily average of 43,600 vehicles. The peak day gave 49,396 vehicles, of which 18,836 were counted at the Tierceville cross-roads; giving an overall average of nearly 800 vehicles per hour, or one vehicle every four and a half seconds. The peak hour on this day was 922 vehicles, rather more than one vehicle every four seconds.

The military police put their backs into their work and succeeded in establishing during these first weeks a relationship of trust and confidence between themselves and the rest of the army which was never subsequently impaired; they worked until they were ready to drop, but they never lost their poise.

Towards the end of July the question of additional provost resources became an urgent one. Provost 21 Army Group were watching the situation very closely and were throughout in almost daily touch with the War Office. It was clear that as soon as the break-out occurred traffic control resources would be insufficient; also that, with the anticipated capture of new ports, additional ports provost companies and S.I.B. must be provided. On 6th July the first request for the urgent provision of six further vulnerable point (overseas) companies was put forward; towards the end of the same month two more ports provost companies and four S.I.B. sections were asked for. A request was also made for a thousand C.M.P. vulnerable point personnel, not trained or organized for mobile work, but for ordinary vulnerable point work on the L. of C.

By the end of August the break-out was complete, and the German armies, shattered in the "Falaise pocket," were in full retreat; the British and American forces were rushing forward in pursuit at tremendous speed; both our armies were over the Seine and 30 Corps was actually crossing the Somme.

Both armies had to be reinforced with additional traffic control companies to maintain their swiftly stretching communications and to control the army roadheads and "cushions." During the twelve days between 25th August and 6th September, five new army roadheads and "cushions" were opened by Canadian Army and three by Second Army. The Seine and other river crossings required close traffic control; all the permanent bridges were down and all crossings were on improvized structures. As usual, provost and traffic control reinforcements to armies had to come from L. of C. resources; which at this time could ill be spared as the L. of C. was continually having to absorb fresh areas of country in order to relieve armies from having to look too far over their shoulders.

At the end of August, in addition to the resources already asked for, a further demand to War Office was made for four additional traffic control companies. Six vulnerable point (overseas) companies were already formed and had received some training; a new ports provost company had been formed exclusively of sergeants from disbanded gunner regiments, and a second similar company would follow soon afterwards; several more S.I.B. sections were being formed, and six new type vulnerable point companies would be formed for static duties on the L. of C.

Within a few days the first of the new vulnerable point (overseas) companies was already in the theatre and at work. To give them the quickest and best operational training, they were at first split into half companies; each half company being attached to a C.M.P. (T.C.) company for work alongside of them and under their direction on the L. of C.

This method proved successful; the new companies picked up the work in a very short while and were soon able to take over their own sectors. On 17th September, only ten days after the War Office conference, Provost Marshal 21 Army Group and D.P.M. L. of C. were on their way together up to Brussels; on crossing the Seine at Vernon they found some of the new vulnerable points men (who had only been in the country forty-eight hours) controlling the bridge crossing with complete efficiency; and, what was even more astonishing in the case of completely unseasoned troops, these men had a full and accurate knowledge of road directions, distances, locations, etc.

Both traffic control and vulnerable points companies put up a first-rate show throughout the campaign; but nothing that they did deserves more praise than the speed and accuracy with which, during this headlong pursuit, they controlled the vital main supply routes, bridges, depot and dump areas.

On the staff side, Lieut.-Colonels Drake, Ball and Cheney and Majors Buist, Swinden and Steward, their A.P.Ms. (Traffic Control), kept their organizations intact, their links unbroken, and the whole traffic system covered and mutually supporting, throughout that rocket-like advance over four main routes of nearly 4,000 miles each; a feat for which great credit is due to them.

Meanwhile, 1st Canadian Army had the task of clearing the coastal belt; this meant a rather slower advance, as they had to contain, and later reduce, German garrisons who still held on to Le Havre, Dieppe, Boulogne, Calais and Ostend. The last of these ports to fall was Calais, which was captured on 30th September. Meanwhile Le Havre, which fell to 1 Corps, was handed over to the American armies for use by them as a port. A cross-traffic problem arose. The American supply routes which ran from Le Havre across our main L. of C. were called "The White Ball Routes." 101 Traffic Control Company (Captain Papworth) and United States military police detachments were jointly responsible for the cross-traffic control at all intersecting points.

The C.M.P. signals sections attached to army and corps did good work in maintaining the provost communications; but, in the case of corps, movement and altered provost layouts often went too fast for them to do much more than connect the A.P.M's. office with provost company H.Q.; but this, which was always the first priority, was valuable.

During the dash from Normandy to Belgium the army and corps route-notations already mentioned came into regular use. "Club" route, the main 30 Corps axis-route, was actually marked from Bayeux to a few miles short of Arnhem by Sergeant Chalk and a detachment from 113 Provost Company. 59th Division had, a little earlier, been disbanded for reasons of manpower, and the divisional provost company became an L. of C. provost company, which was a most welcome addition to the L. of C. provost force.

After the capture of Brussels and Antwerp there was a short breathing space while armies, corps and divisions curled up their tails, sorted out their resources, overhauled their M.T. and built up reserves of signing equipment, etc. All the time the L. of C. was steadily coming up, and in relieving armies of much territory was adding greatly to their own burden.

The operation to seize a bridgehead over the Rhine at Arnhem was now to be launched. 1st British Airborne Division and two American Airborne Divisions, with 30 Corps in charge of ground operations, were responsible for the attempt which succeeded at Nijmegen, but, after bad weather conditions, failed in spite of much heroism to achieve full success at Arnhem. The provost problem which Lieut.-Colonel Melville had to tackle was one of great difficulty. 30 Corps moved up with Guards Armoured Division, 43rd Division and 52nd Division under command; 101 U.S. Airborne Division came under command later. The control of the operational traffic, including the airborne tail, was the task of 30 Corps Provost.

In the course of this move approximately 20,000 vehicles had to be moved across Holland on a single-axis route, supplemented, in places only, by a subsidiary route; but wherever these two routes joined, as they frequently did, a troublesome bottle-neck was produced. The whole essence of success lay in the combination of an efficient traffic control system and good march discipline. Traffic control was exercised by three regulating H.Qs., each of which controlled three traffic control posts with wireless communications between the posts and regulating H.Qs.

There were also static posts with provost detachments located along the main axis, who were responsible for mobile traffic control and the general policing of the road. The static posts were in charge of Lieut.-Colonel Oxley, and the whole traffic layout was under the joint control of this officer and Lieut.-Colonel Melville, A.P.M. 30 Corps. The arrangements proved excellent and the move took place without undue trouble.

113 Provost Company did some fighting on their own during this action; one detachment at St. Oedenrode was in action on 18th September against German snipers; and the following day in action again, together with American Airborne troops, repelling a German attempt to break through. In this case an Irish Guards tank which had lost its officer was commanded throughout by Lieutenant Smith of 113 Provost Company. The Guards Armoured

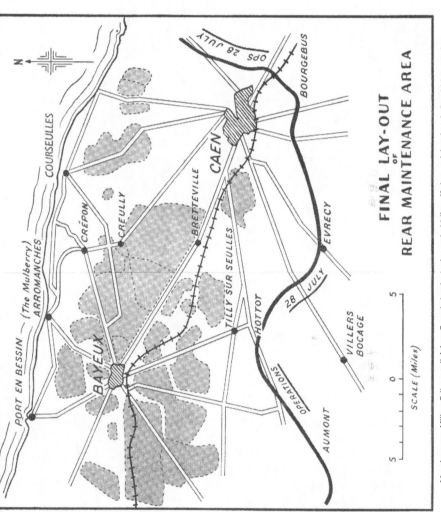

FINAL LAY-OUT
OF
REAR MAINTENANCE AREA

More than 1,000 Military Police controlled the traffic on the invasion beaches, at the Mulberry Harbour, and throughout the Rear Maintenance Area

Divisional Provost Company was mixed up in the fighting around Nijmegen, and actually established traffic control over the bridge whilst the action was still in progress. This was, incidentally, another occasion where a section from the traffic control company did splendid work in action; this time in maintaining line communications across the bridge, for the most part under heavy fire.

A lance-corporal from 113 Provost Company came across a strong party of Germans in a wood near the main road. He reported this to a nearby American unit. The American officer divided his men into two and said, "You take half and go up one side; I will take half and go up the other." The military policeman pointed out there was an officer present as well as several other sergeants in his half, but was told by the American officer, "That's O.K., boy; they'll follow you!" After a short bout of woodland fighting the situation was cleared and the policeman returned his "half" to its rightful owner and went about his duty.

Field-Marshal Montgomery now decided that before further advances could be attempted the port of Antwerp must first be cleared and brought into operation. This task, therefore, became the first priority. It was carried out by 1st Canadian Army with 2 Canadian Corps on the left and 1 British Corps on the right. Major Godfrey-Faussett, A.P.M. 1 Corps, was in this operation, as indeed throughout the campaign, a tower of strength and quiet determination. The operations started on 27th September and were completed by 8th November. 2 Canadian Corps cleared the Scheldt and the islands of Walcheren and South Beveland, whilst 1 Corps moved up towards the line Tilburg–Bergen-op-Zoom, and, on the right, 8 and 30 Corps worked eastwards. By early December the enemy had been completely cleared from the south and west of the Maas.

Lieut.-Colonel Fitzgerald and Lieut.-Colonel Melville, the A.P.Ms. of 8 and 30 Corps, were both splendid examples of operationally minded fighting provost officers; but both of them knew well how and when to stiffen disciplinary control.

On 13th December regrouping began for the next task of pushing the enemy east of the Rhine. 30 Corps were withdrawn into reserve to make preparations, the H.Q. moving to Bextel to plan the forthcoming operation. This was a curious move, as, for security reasons, all signs on men and vehicles were removed, nor were any signs allowed on the road; so that on this occasion 113 Provost Company had to be strung out over 100 miles of route to act as human signposts. But on 16th December the great German counter-offensive in the Ardennes was launched and the operation had to be postponed.

*   *   *   *   *

K

D URING the past three months there had been much administrative activity in France and Belgium. For the first few
days after the relief of Brussels there was throughout Belgium an air of festivity. The friendly and high-spirited Belgians
lavished upon our troops a prodigal hospitality; nor was there any
mistaking the genuineness of their kindness and deep feeling. The
conduct of the British troops was a lasting credit to the army and
the nation, nor was this unappreciated by the Belgians.

A report received from the Chief of Civil Police in Antwerp
gives the Belgian view of our police : "The turn-out and bearing
of 244 Provost Company is wonderful, was an expression often heard
in connection with the military police in Belgium. What impressed
the people of the town mostly was the fact that, after more than
three months' fighting and rapid advance across France into
Belgium, the military police were on duty in the town right away
with their boots and equipment polished and their trousers pressed;
and they were most polite to the civil population."

Provost Marshal 21 Army Group had already made the acquaint-
ance in Normandy of General Ganshoff, who, immediately after
the liberation of Belgium, was appointed Auditeur-General to the
Belgian Government; a position which put him in virtual control
of all civil police and gendarmerie forces. This contact was renewed
at once in Brussels with the greatest cordiality. Both the municipal
police and the gendarmerie worked with us in close and effective
co-operation. General Dethise, Commandant of the Belgian gendarmerie, attached to Provost Marshal 21 Army Group and
D.P.M. Second Army detachments of picked Belgian gendarmes
to work under British orders.

By the end of November the port of Antwerp was opened and
cleared, the first convoy actually berthing on 28th November.
The Mulberry was closed about the same time and the rear
maintenance area gradually faded out of the picture. The ports of
Dieppe, Le Treport, Boulogne, Calais and Ghent all came into
operation at different times. Meanwhile the L. of C. underwent a
series of reorganizations, gradually curling up its tail until, on
15th February, 1945, its rear limits were the south-west boundary
of the Somme Department, whence it stretched forward as far as
the Belgium–Dutch frontier, with an "island" surrounding the
rear maintenance area and the port of Caen still under its control.
By late September the military population in the rear maintenance
area alone still totalled 100,000; and at the end of Oc tober the
L. of C. ration strength amounted to 450,000 including R·A.F. and
prisoner-of-war personnel. To assist the growing commitments
of the L. of C. 16 L. of C. Sub-Area was formed, and 11 Garrison
was converted into 9 L. of C. Sub-Area, Captain Wood and Captain

SECOND WORLD WAR: NORTH-WEST EUROPE

Willey being appointed their respective D.A.P.Ms. Captain Wood, and later his successor, Captain Byerley, handled with skill and firmness the particularly difficult traffic and disciplinary problems of the port of Ghent. Major Clitheroe-Smith was appointed A.P.M. of Brussels.

The L. of C. was divided throughout into two areas: No. 11 L. of C. Area was the most experienced administrative formation in this theatre. It had landed in the beach-head on D+1 and had been responsible for every phase of the administrative build-up in the beach-head and across the whole of France during the break-through. Its commander, Brigadier R. H. R. Parminter, always gave his support to his provost staff. No military police officer ever went to him and came away without assistance.

The A.P.M. of this H.Q. had to deal with troublesome disciplinary problems both on the beach-head and in the larger administrative areas which were later formed. He was at one time in control of military police in Holland, Belgium and Northern France. Later into the theatre came 12 L. of C. Area (A.P.M., Major Peterkin), who took over the area from 11 L. of C. as the latter formation moved forward.

Major Peterkin's good police work, vigilance and determination earned the fullest confidence of his commander.

Meanwhile, the stocking of the advance base was proceeding at full speed. The advance base was roughly rectangular in shape, with Ostend, Antwerp, Turnhout its northern limit and Tournai, Hal, Hasselt its southern limit; it covered an area about 100 miles wide by 50 miles deep. It was signed, circuited, controlled and policed throughout by the L. of C. provost service. Antwerp was a port for joint use by British and American forces. It was planned to handle up to 40,000 tons per day, the British share being 17,550. A combined British and American staff was set up to plan the clearance of the port, and its results were contained in a document known as "The Charter of Antwerp," which outlined the traffic control arrangements necessary for dealing with the difficult cross-traffic problems.

The deep-water berths, which alone could take the United States liberty ships, were all in the northern part of the port. All United States commodities had to be taken to the south or south-west of Belgium; therefore, every single United States lorry and convoy was bound to cut directly across British clearance routes.

The solution adopted was, in the first place, to keep United States vehicles clear of the British dock area by the use of a circular route running through the east and south suburbs of Antwerp, whence they broke off on to their main administrative routes towards Malines, Brussels and Louvain. All intersections were permanently manned (as had been done so successfully before on the Le Havre–Paris corridor) by joint British and United States military police. The method worked without a hitch or a suspicion of an incident. Colonel Dubois, at this time the United States Provost Marshal of Channel Base Section, was most co-operative and helpful in organizing this arrangement.

In Antwerp every type of C.M.P. unit was represented, the whole being organized and controlled by A.P.M. 7 Base Sub-Area, Major C. Cowie.

A traffic office was established in the port, with Lieutenant Lewis Parker (from 6 Traffic Control Company) as traffic control liaison officer; four major traffic posts were set up, each with a R.E.M.E. reconnaissance squad, first-aid appliances and a direct telephone to H.Q. 73 Traffic Control Company from this H.Q.; another direct line ran to Lieutenant Lewis Parker in the Traffic Office, and he again had a direct line to Major Cowie. Civilian traffic on main routes was only permitted at 50 kilometres per hour and no halts were allowed. The eight Belgian gendarmes were chiefly engaged as mobile patrols to enforce this order, which was designed to prevent slow civilian traffic from hampering the free flow of military vehicles. All signs were in two languages. Information centres were established, one being a joint British and United States post.

Antwerp quickly became the most unhealthy place behind the front line. An incessant stream of V1 and V2 missiles were rained upon it; for weeks they came in at the rate of one every half-hour by day and night. The target area was small, and, progressively, much damage and loss of life was caused. As the bombs continued throughout the night no real rest was possible and the whole Antwerp garrison went through a severe strain. The provost service suffered many casualties. Major Mason was seriously wounded and four policemen were killed when a V2 bomb demolished the H.Q. of 185 Ports Provost Company. Major Mason had done good work, and was greatly missed.

On 27th November a V2 fell at midday just outside the C.M.P. Information Post in the Keyserlei, the main street of Antwerp, N.C.Os. of 244 Provost Company and 602 Vulnerable Points Company were on duty at the post; two were killed—one was never found—and eight were wounded; many civilians were also hurt in this incident. M. de Potter, the chief of Antwerp police, wrote: "Belgian civilians and civilian services were most impressed by the kind and efficient organization provided at the incident and the civil police are most grateful for the assistance which the military police gave."

A special system was instituted for dealing with bomb incidents with the minimum delay. Each of the four traffic control posts took a compass bearing of the smoke rising from bomb incidents and telephoned it immediately to Company H.Q. who promptly plotted the bearings and located the incident; the special "incident" squad which was always standing by then went straight off to the trouble. Thanks to these arrangements, no main routes in Antwerp were out of use for more than thirty-five minutes; and in each case a diversion was working within fifteen minutes of the incident.

185 Ports Provost Company was no less busy. The perimeter of the dock area had to be closely controlled and the large number of civilian dockers carefully checked and supervised to prevent pilfering. Ships were watched during unloading, and personnel of the company undertook the duties of river police and manned fast launches and visited barges in the harbour and up the river. Many arrests were made of enemy agents and local collaborators.

The S.I.B. had as usual far more work than they could hope to cope with, and Captain Purslow and 81 S.I.S. did a particularly good job in Antwerp.

On 21st March, Major Cowie became A.P.M. 12 L. of C. area in succession to Major Peterkin. Major Cowie had won the M.B.E. during the landing in Normandy as A.P.M. 3rd Division; as A.P.M. 7 Base Sub-Area he had also gained the high esteem of his commander, Brigadier McMicking. He was succeeded as A.P.M. at Antwerp by Major L. Wood, whose good work at Ghent has already been mentioned, and who particularly directed his attention to stopping abuses in some officers' messes where he found that the inmates were living on a scale which was more lavish than rations or normal officers' incomes would warrant.

A day or two before Major Mason was wounded he organized an evening entertainment at which 185 Ports Provost Company were hosts, and many of the local civilian police and gendarmes were guests. The Provost Marshal attended the function, and made a short speech partly in English and partly in French; it must have been a success, as he was congratulated afterwards by a Belgian guest upon having such an excellent knowledge of Flemish.

Before the end of October three more traffic control companies, all the six new vulnerable points (overseas) companies, and two ports provost (sergeants) companies and several additional S.I.S. sections had arrived in the theatre and helped to ease the provost burden. The two ports provost (sergeants) companies took charge of the ports of Boulogne and Calais.

The more the advance base, the army roadheads and other dumps and depots grew, the greater became the amount of crime and racketeering. Many civilians were arrested for tapping the petrol pipe lines and a great many others for improper possession of W.D. stores. The crossing of the Franco-Belgian frontier was followed by an outbreak of illegal dealings in the currencies of the two countries, and also by considerable smuggling of tobacco, cosmetics and liquor.

Soldiers were concerned chiefly in thefts of foodstuffs, petrol, vehicles, cigarettes, clothing and blankets which ultimately found their way into the civilian black market; the blankets often re-appearing in the form of modish and attractive ladies' overcoats. On the one hand, the local population was suffering from a great scarcity of coal, clothing and food—in fact, all the necessities of life, on the other, the British soldier lacked the means to pay the high prices charged for luxury goods such as scent, films, jewellery, watches, etc. These two cravings came together for comfort, and produced, with great ease, the illegitimate offsprings of racketeering and pilfering. The official rate of exchange being about half the current market value put an added temptation in the way of the British soldier to lend himself to these illicit dealings.

Major Pollard, A.P.M. S.I.B., had a task of especial difficulty, and one which called not only for unassailable integrity and a first-rate technical knowledge of criminal investigation, but for organizing powers and foresight of a high order. It was fortunate for 21 Army Group that he possessed these qualities, as well as an unfailing tact and ability to deal with senior officers.

The provost service and S.I.B. were in daily touch with both French and Belgian civil police, and a large number of arrests were made. Civilian cases were dealt with by the civil courts and a large number of convictions were recorded; unfortunately, as already mentioned, convictions failed to have the desired effect because most of the civil prisons were soon filled, and fines alone were little or no deterrent. A somewhat Gilbertian situation arose in Belgium. Many civilians were sentenced to imprisonment and then sent home; having been told by the Judge that as soon as there was a vacancy for them in prison, they would be notified.

In Brussels frequent joint checks were held by provost and the civil police or gendarmerie; at each check post provost investigating all army vehicles, the civil police handling civilian vehicles. Many civilian users of W.D. petrol and other offenders were thus caught.

Army areas had similar problems to contend with which they tackled with the same vigour as provost in the L. of C. Major Keighley, A.P.M. Second Army, under Lieut.-Colonel Drake, was particularly responsible for the disciplinary side of provost in Second Army. His drive and imperturbability were of the highest value in suppressing crime and maintaining discipline.

In Brussels there was a short-leave scheme on a large scale. Thirty clubs and canteens and several hotels were set up to cater for 10,000 British and Canadian troops at a time; a much smaller quota was entitled to go to Paris for the same purpose. The period was at first two days, which was subsequently enlarged to three. At the same time a similar short-leave scheme was operated for American troops, their Brussels quota being even larger than the British.

By the end of April, 460,000 officers and men, British and Canadian alone, had visited Brussels and Paris on short privilege leave.

Provost, of course, had a major commitment with all the problems attendant on setting up a leave centre in a large city, such as controlling clubs and cafes, countering black market activities, currency offences, apprehending absentees, and checking and investigating thefts of W.D. vehicles, which were now becoming serious.

Major Clitherow-Smith, A.P.M. Brussels, had a difficult and thankless task, but he did it with success. The civil police in Brussels and indeed throughout Belgium were co-operative in closing cafes and night clubs where regulations were broken or where improper prices were being charged.

The general co-ordination of the administrative side of the provost service, the S.I.B., and the over-all supervision of the Brussels problems were mainly the work of Lieut.-Colonel Stanley, D.P.M. 21 Army Group.

*　　*　　*　　*　　*

THE approach of winter produced a new problem. The bad conditions of the roads led to much apprehension as to the effects of snow, frost and thaw. A winter roads maintenance plan and thaw plan were made. Many thousands of special signs had to be made and a strict system of traffic control was necessary to put them into effect. All these signs had to be erected by provost well ahead of the earliest time they would be needed, the signs themselves being kept covered until required. The provost service had barely completed these arrangements when, early in December, hard frosts followed by snow occurred.

Roads were ice-bound when on 16th December the Germans struck hard and unexpectedly at 1st American Army in the Ardennes. Surprise was complete, and in conditions of thick mist a partial break-through was quickly achieved and the Meuse was threatened. 1st and 9th American Armies were, for tactical reasons, placed under Field-Marshal Montgomery, who immediately moved 30 Corps south, to concentrate in the area Louvain–Hasselt and subsequently to operate with 1st American Army, south and east of the Meuse.

Three features of the reinforcing "side-slip" of 30 Corps, and the subsequent operations are of especial interest. The first feature was a first-class object lesson of what happens at a bottle-neck

(a) When formations decide to move without previously notifying either the movement control staff or Provost;

(b) When Movement Control puts a greater traffic load on the roads than they can carry; and

(c) If Provost fails to appreciate accurately the probable danger spots and has insufficient resources at those points.

Two brigades, independently and without notification, decided to move simultaneously through Louvain, the busy junction of five important main routes; they, of course, interlocked and for some while there was a momentous jam. The situation was energetically handled by the police, and eventually all was sorted out; it was estimated that during the first day of this move 40,000 vehicles were cleared around Louvain by the police and the British and American armies.

The second interesting point was that most of the big and particularly tricky regrouping or reinforcing moves of the campaign were, to some extent, foreseen; consequently the movement control and the traffic control arrangements had not much but some time for preparation. On this occasion, however, the move was unforeseen, sudden, and of an emergency nature; and although rectified in a comparatively short time, mistakes were made on all sides which had not occurred on other occasions.

The third point was the close co-operation between British and American military police. To ensure quick news and liaison on higher levels between American and British provost, Lieutenant Blenkharn of 120 Provost Company was sent to American H.Q. ADSEC to act as British provost liaison officer, and an American provost liaison officer was similarly attached to A.P.M. 30 Corps. Lieutenant Blenkharn, who was later awarded the American Bronze Star for his work, sent in frequent and good reports which on more than one occasion contained material of general interest to H.Q. 21 Army Group and not merely to provost.

Captain Lee, then R.S.M., 51st Highland Divisional Provost Company, gained an M.C. for his gallantry in reconnoitring under fire forward routes, studded with mines and concealed by the snow in the Ardennes.

By 14th January the German counter-attack had failed. 1st Canadian Army with 30 Corps under command were now able to stage the next operation to expel the Germans from between the

Meuse and the Rhine. 30 Corps had been built up to a huge strength of seven divisions, three independent armoured brigades, most of 79th Armoured Division, and five A.G.R.As.; the total strength of 1st Canadian Army being nearly half a million men.

The concentration was complicated and produced a hard traffic control problem for provost, ending with a troublesome move into Nijmegen bridgehead through the bottleneck of the Grave and Mook bridges. The minutely organized control laid on by Lieut.-Colonel Ball, D.P.M. 1st Canadian Army, and Lieut.-Colonel Melville worked well and the military police did a magnificent signing job. Four traffic control companies, reinforced by 150 Gunners, were used in this operation, which started on 8th February and was completed by 10th March, by which time 1st Canadian Army had driven the Germans behind the Rhine as far south as Wesel, the good work having been continued with equal success by 9th American Army as far up the Rhine as Dusseldorf.

During this operation the traffic conditions in the zone were appalling. The joint effects of melting snow and disintegrating roads, coupled with much organized flooding by the Germans, made all kinds of progress on the roads a nightmare. Many policemen worked up to their waists in water for hours at a stretch. Despite all difficulties, vehicles were kept upon the roads and the objectives were attained. The obstacle of the Rhine alone remained to be crossed before our forces would overrun Germany.

During this period of abnormally difficult road conditions, the Second Army normal provost telephone layout was greatly developed by the ingenuity of the Traffic Control Signals Company. On one occasion a unit on the move was breaking wireless silence. Provost were told to find the unit and stop it. By means of the military police telephone system the unit was traced and action taken within ten minutes of receiving the order.

Prisoners of war were a weighty and constant problem, but the vulnerable point police handled this task well ; to give one instance, 1 Corps closed their cage (on moving into the Rhineland) with a record of 32,000 prisoners and only two escapes. Men from 603 Vulnerable Point Company were in charge of this cage.

The seven Belgian and Dutch provost and traffic control companies were now almost ready for active employment. They were all formed, equipped and trained by 21 Army Group officers and N.C.Os. Lieutenant Douglas played an important part in connection with the Belgian companies; he was a good French linguist and performed a difficult task well. Some of the Belgian companies went through a further course of instruction at the C.M.P. school, now formed upon an official War Establishment, with Major Thrussel (who had done good work previously as D.A.P.M. (T.C.) 21 Army Group), as its commandant.

Lieut.-Colonel Melville, A.P.M. 30 Corps, whose H.Q. had had in some ways the most gruelling and unrelenting time of all Corps H.Qs., was sent temporarily as A.P.M. to Lieut.-Colonel Diggle in Paris for a short rest; his place as A.P.M. 30 Corps being taken by Major Innes, previously A.P.M. Guards (Armoured) Division. Needless to say, the C.M.P. contingent in Paris, under the wise and seasoned leadership of Lieut.-Colonel Diggle, was taken to the hearts of the Parisians; and, working in complete harmony with the U.S. Army authorities, they furnished a fine example of well-disciplined and helpful military police.

It was clear in the very early days of 1945 that the S.I.B. were so busy in investigating past crimes that there was a danger of losing the value of these highly trained detectives in tracking down the more serious leakage and vulnerable spots in the army supply machine.

One S.I.B. section was accordingly taken off all routine work; the section itself was forbidden to involve itself in following up individual cases, and was ordered to concentrate exclusively on observing and investigating the movement of pilferable stores, in the course of transit from the docks to depots, and from depots on to the forward areas, whether by road or rail; they were also instructed to make reports and suggestions for tightening up control.

This section carried out a close investigation on these lines with the wholehearted co-operation of all the supply services. A number of points of interest emerged, but two things stood out in sharp relief. The first was that the check and tally system of the various supply services contained a troublesome gap between the dockside and the depots; this arose mainly from the essential operational necessity for the quickest possible clearance from the docks, coupled with an accelerated turn-round of lorries to enable them to compete with the pace. After much discussion it was decided that this gap must, for operational reasons, be accepted, although much leakage certainly occurred during this stage of transit. The second point was the serious amount of pilfering caused by absentees still in the theatre.

The resources of the provost service were never sufficient to organize constant searches of French and Belgian towns for absentees and deserters. The hospitality and credulity of civilians made it easy for absentees to go into safe hiding and they became experts in forging false passes and documents. A vigorous attack was, however, made by military police on this problem in February; a large-scale check (organized as a secret operation)

MAP 4

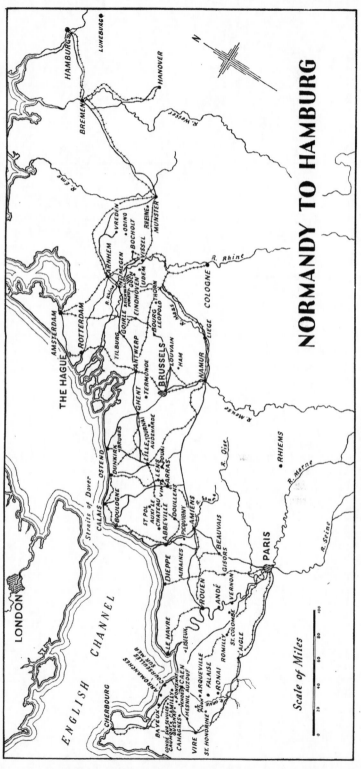

NORMANDY TO HAMBURG

From Normandy to Germany military police signed and controlled the roads. A military driver could travel, from Arromanches to Hamburg without a map or a question.

was carried out over forty-eight hours; all local leave was stopped for this period, and for twenty-four hours, all ranks throughout the whole L. of C. were confined to their unit lines or billets, save the minimum of officers or O.Rs. who were obliged to go out on duty, and they had to be provided with a special duty order.

It was a drastic measure, but it produced a successful result. Road checks were operated all over Belgium and north-eastern France; cafes, hotels, and suspected areas were raided. Every officer and man in the provost service took part, and the civil police co-operated as it gave them an opportunity to find some of their own "wanted" persons. At the end of forty-eight hours, over 450 absentees, many of them long-timers had been collected.

The final round was now about to begin. Second Army was to assault in the area Xanten–Rees, with 9th U.S. Army on their right crossing farther south near Rhinesberg. 1st Canadian Army on the left were to make feint attacks along the lower reaches of the river; 6th Airborne Division and two United States Airborne Divisions were to drop east of the river to seize tactical points; a considerable naval force was included to negotiate some of the craft required in the actual crossing.

During the week preceding 23rd March, the date of the assault on the Rhine, moves by road in Second Army area totalled over 32,000 wheeled vehicles, 662 tanks and no less than 4,050 tank transporters, three corps had been concentrated, while over 130,000 tons of stores in addition to ordinary maintenance requirements had been moved into No. 10 Army roadhead, formed between the Meuse and the Rhine.

In all, 70,000 vehicles moved under strict control in sixteen days. The following are figures of Second Army movements between 1st and 31st March:

Total numbers of vehicles in timed convoys   97,557

Total convoys dealt with   774

Total number of tank transporters routed ...   9,653

The operation itself was timed to take place at night, zero hour being 9 p.m. on 23rd March. An elaborate and most carefully signed and controlled scheme had therefore to be produced to ensure the parallel lines and successive waves of the hundreds of river-crossing craft, dukws, amphibious tanks, etc., taking to the water at the right spots.

12 Corps were given the task of working out the method of control and this was fully rehearsed by Major Guild, A.P.M. 12 Corps, before the assault began. The special organization called "Bank Control" was set up for the purpose, the commander of "Bank Control" having a complete system of check-posts and

controllers so that he knew at any moment where different waves of the assaulting craft had got to, and by which he could control their movements. The traffic signing and control was entrusted to 101 Traffic Control Company, Captain Papworth, and 22 Traffic Control Company, Captain Taylor. Elements of both these companies crossed the river with the first assaulting waves, and immediately set up traffic control on pre-arranged lines on the farther bank.

Only a few words can be said regarding the final pursuit and mopping-up operations.

Second Army Provost adopted a traffic control system similar to the one they had employed during the dash from Normandy to Belgium; but this time they were better off as they had an extra traffic control company under command. All necessary signs had been prepared in advance and it had been agreed with the staff that only one forward and one return route (240 and 250) would be used for maintenance.

As a result of careful deployment, the end of hostilities found Second Army with one company still in reserve and ready for use beyond the Elbe if required. One of the principal troubles was the hordes of Ps.W. to round up and handle and the endless stream of dreary columns of displaced persons of all nationalities moving apparently aimlessly in all directions.

Between 1st and 31st March alone, the Ps.W. came in at an average rate of 10,000 per day. After active operations were over, 21 Army Group alone took into captivity in the space of a few days more than two million German troops.

The advance proceeded fast; the Elbe was reached, Hamburg and Kiel occupied, and our troops reached the Danish border and the shores of the Baltic. On 5th May all German armies still opposing 21 Army Group surrendered formally at Luneburg Heath. The C.M.P. provost detachment which had accompanied the C.-in-C.'s tactical H.Q. throughout the campaign conducted the German delegation to Field-Marshal Montgomery to ask for peace.

To end this chapter, here are the words of Field-Marshal Montgomery when he spoke to the military police in Paris: "The battle of Normandy and the subsequent battles would never have been won but for the work and co-operation of provost on the traffic routes."

CHAPTER VIII

SECOND WORLD WAR: THE FAR EAST

India

IN September, 1939, there were no members of the Corps of Military Police in India. Police duties, which were confined to disciplinary foot patrols in the chief garrison towns, were carried out by regimental and garrison police. But as the war developed it became apparent, first that large numbers of new troops would have to be raised and trained, and later that India must be put in a state of defence against Japanese invasion, and organized as a main base for our own offensive operations in the Far East.

In November, 1940, it was decided that divisional provost units should be raised and trained in India with an up-to-date knowledge of provost duties in the field.

An officer was therefore sent to the Middle East for one month to study the latest ideas in training. Major W. H. R. Dutton, M.C., 13th Frontier Force Rifles, was the officer selected. On his return to India in February, 1941, he began touring formations and commands, and in June, 1941, the first D.A.P.Ms.' course was held at Mashobra, near Simla.

The term "provost" was applied to the personnel of all units thus raised between November, 1940, and August, 1942. It was not until the latter date that the Corps of Military Police (India) was formed and many of the provost personnel were posted, in the case of British and Gurkha other ranks, and transferred, in the case of Indian other ranks, to the Corps. The first static provost unit to be formed in India was the Bombay Provost Unit.

In May, 1941, the first field formation provost unit, comprising one British and one Indian section, was raised for 2nd Armoured Brigade. By July of that year an Indian Basic Provost Unit Establishment had been evolved. This allowed for a mixed headquarters and a varying number of British and Indian or Gurkha sections.

As the army in India expanded, the need for a fully trained and capable body of military police, on the lines of that existing in the United Kingdom and Middle East, became apparent. In the first instance, except for the Bombay Provost Unit, all units raised were for formations to be sent to the Middle and Far Eastern theatres for an operational role. Later provost units were raised for static and L. of C. duties in India, in order to maintain the discipline of the greatly increased army in India and to control the movements of troops by road and rail.

One important commitment was the policing of the Assam supply route to Burma from railhead to Dimapur, through Kohima to Imphal and Tiddim. For this purpose additional provost units had to be raised.

When offensive operations against Burma, the Andeman Islands, and Malaya were contemplated, beach provost units had to be provided. At the same time the importance of India as a base increased considerably, resulting in a heavy demand for vulnerable point units for the docks at Bombay, Calcutta, Vizagapatam, Madras and Karachi. At the same time a request was sent to the War Office for four companies of Military Police for normal disciplinary and traffic control duties at those ports. This demand was met and their arrival eased the provost situation generally.

The appointment of Provost Marshal (India), with rank of Brigadier, was sanctioned on 27th February, 1943, but Colonel A. R. Forbes, formerly Provost Marshal, Paiforce, was not appointed Provost Marshal in India until July of that year.

On his arrival in India he found the provost position unsatisfactory, because:

(a) The early intakes into "Provost" and C.M.P. (Indian) were, for the most part, men for whom their parent units had little or no use. The consequences were serious and the army in India knew that it had military police who could not be relied upon.

(b) Provost officers were, with few exceptions, badly chosen and both administration of provost units and supervision of duties was of a low standard.

(c) The attitude of the people of India generally towards any form of police was one of suspicion and resentfulness.

(d) Up to July, 1943, there had been no real head of the Provost service.

To improve these defects was an uphill task, but not too much for the new Provost Marshal.

The military police in India had a wide measure of responsibility in connection with bounds and price control. Their supervision benefited troops and ensured that hotels, restaurants and cafes, open to them, were maintained up to reasonable standards of cleanliness.

The best example of this was the placing out of bounds to all ranks, for meals, an hotel in Calcutta. Before the medical service would allow it to be placed "in bounds" again the owners had to rebuild the kitchens at a cost of Rs.24,000.

A MILITARY POLICEMAN CHECKS THE PASSES OF WRENS IN
KANDY, CEYLON

Another important duty was the enforcement of anti-malarial orders. Here again, as a result of provost suggestions, an anti-malarial curfew was introduced in many large towns by varying means, which included mobile patrols displaying large warning notices, sounding of sirens, ringing of bells at railway stations and the display of slides in cinemas.

The smuggling of arms, ammunition and explosives into towns and villages by Indian troops returning from operational and training areas was rife. The civil police became alarmed.

Searches of personnel and baggage were carried out at certain main railway junctions and, at Lahore in particular, recoveries were considerable. On many occasions valuable medical and mechanical transport stores were discovered as well as arms, ammunition and explosives. A few instances of smuggling large quantities of opium also came to light.

Mechanization of the army in India was very rapid, whereas the standard of driving was low and pedestrians exceedingly unimaginative and careless. The combination of these factors resulted in a high accident rate which caused the concentration of the inadequate provost resources in and around the main towns.

The Indian railways were working to the maximum capacity and it was seldom that a third-class compartment contained less than three times the number of persons it was designed to carry. The crowds on the platforms at most of the main junctions were, at times, almost impenetrable, and little effort was made by civilians to cut down their travelling, which appeared to be one of the national sports (especially travelling without a ticket). The work of provost at railway stations, in helping troops on their way, was extensive and important.

The control of ports embraced the normal duties, gate checks, control of traffic, prevention of pilfering and supervision of embarkations and disembarkations. In all cases, however, the control was shared with the civil port and harbour police and at Calcutta with American provost.

In addition to duties within India, provost personnel had to be trained and provided for army, corps, divisions and independent brigade and beach maintenance units. The last named were trained at the Combined Training Centre, Mahd Island, near Bombay, under a specially qualified A.P.M., Major D. L. Hunt.

It was not until 1943 that formation commanders in India began to understand and appreciate the organization and functions of the provost.

Many commanders still retained their conception of the "Red-cap" as he was largely looked upon in the First World War, and it was a long time before they realized that, in this war, it was not possible for him to move his formation without the active support of his provost.

In 1945 Brigadier Sykes succeeded Brigadier Forbes as Provost Marshal, India.

★   ★   ★   ★   ★

Singapore

THE story of Singapore is not so much a story of what provost did, but of what it suffered. It is the story of death and disease on the up-country roads and railway, built at the expense of many lives. Beri-beri, diarrhoea, cholera, malaria and ulcers claimed over fifty men from a divisional provost company forced to act as coolie labour for the Japanese.

The 18th Division left Great Britain on 30th October, 1941, was at sea when Japan came into the war and within a few weeks was in Japanese hands almost to a man. A handful escaped. Of those for whom there was no escape a remarkable story is in existence. Written in a hand-made, rudely bound volume on the back of Malayan prison documents by the C.Q.M.S. of the Divisional Provost Company, this narrative, from which the following summary is made, traces the history of the Company from its formation in June, 1940, to September, 1944, when liberation was not far away.

The document has little to say of provost activities prior to the surrender, except that the main tasks were dock and town duties, control of traffic to the Nee Soon dump and maintenance of a control point on the Jahore Causeway until it was breached on 30th January. But from other sources it is known that as a result of the frequent air raids provost had a difficult task to prevent looting.

After the breaching of the Causeway the beleaguered Singapore garrison experienced almost incessant raids and shelling. The Japanese dropped leaflets calling on Lieut.-General Percival to "give up the meaningless and desperate resistance." Should he fail to do so, the Nippon Army High Commander added, "I shall be obliged, though reluctantly through humanitarian considerations, to order my Army to make an annihilatory attack on Singapore." Five days later, having explained to all ranks the shortage of petrol, food, ammunition and water, Lieut.-General Percival surrendered.

The 18th Divisional Provost Company, less a small party which escaped, soon found itself imprisoned on Singapore Island. It was not long before tinned food brought into camp by the British began to run short, and soon meals were of rice and a watery stew made from leaves picked round the camp. Later Red Cross supplies improved the diet and prisoners received pay, though a fortnight's pay would buy little more than a bag of peanuts.

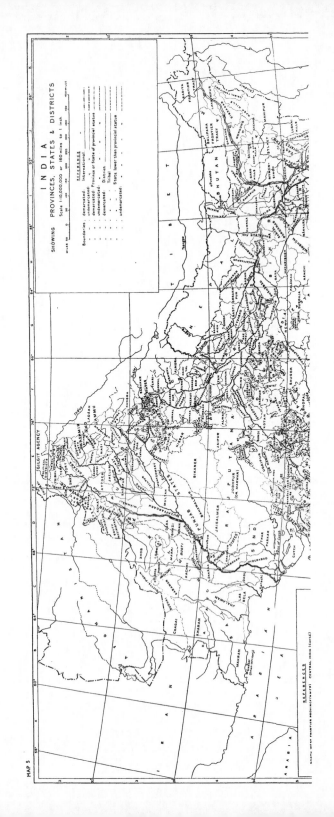

MAP 5

INDIA

SHOWING PROVINCES, STATES & DISTRICTS

Scale 1:10,000,000 or 160 miles to 1 inch.

REFERENCE

Boundaries: demarcated: International
undemarcated: "
demarcated: Province or State of provincial status
undemarcated: "
demarcated: District.
Tribal.
undemarcated: "
State lower than provincial status

Geographical Section, General Staff (No.) 1947. G.R. 6420.

After several escape attempts (four would-be escapees were shot in the presence of British officers) general reprisals took the form of concentrating 15,200 Ps.W. in an area of 8.6 acres, which allowed each man 2.74 square yards of living space. Latrines and cook-houses were adjacent and, in order to prevent a serious outbreak of dysentery, the senior British officer was obliged to order all ranks to sign a document in which they undertook not to try to escape. Prisoners were then allowed to return to their respective areas.

Practically all members of the provost company, less those in hospital or in a very poor state of health, were sent "up country" in April, 1943, most of them to their death. The journey was completed in lorries, by rail and on foot. In a series of gruelling night marches these men covered 193 miles in nineteen nights, including five rest nights. They carried all their belongings, suffered considerably from dysentery, and trudged most of the way through a torrent of rain along tracks ankle deep in mud. Japanese guards had little or no consideration for the prisoners, and when two men failed to move off after a halt their officer was held responsible and had his face severely slapped.

At one rest camp *en route* another officer was beaten up, his bamboo shelter pulled down and his belongings scattered because he refused to "sell" his silver propelling pencil to a Japanese guard.

The diary goes on: "Terrific downpour of rain just as we were about to leave. Us and all our belongings soaked. It rained nearly all the way on the march and we had to wade through mud and water in some places. In spite of this, the spirit of the men did not flag and songs like 'Tipperary' and 'Pack up your troubles' were sung. . . ."

But eventually the 193-mile journey to Sonkrai was completed, and within forty-eight hours large working parties for road and rail construction were demanded. Owing to chills, dysentery and exhaustion, it was found almost impossible to produce the full numbers, for few were capable of working from 8.30 a.m. until 7.0 p.m. with a one-hour break. Work was very heavy—quarrying, tree-felling, bridge-building and cutting drains, this latter entailing standing in water for hours on end. Diarrhœa cases increased alarmingly and were herded into one hut, fever cases, cholera carriers and fit men also being segregated.

Japanese brutality took the form of beating weary prisoners with sticks, kicking on the shin and, after men had been knocked insensible, kicking them when on the ground.

About mid-June, 1942, there was an increase in the incidence of malaria; also swelling of the legs, thighs, face and testicles—all

L

symptoms of beri-beri, due to undernourishment on a rice diet. The ration situation grew serious and meals were cut to two a day except for working parties, who had three. Deaths from cerebral malaria began to occur and there were non-fatal cases of smallpox. On one occasion roll call lasted two and a half hours because, owing to prisoners being too weak to stand any length of time, Japanese guards were unable to take an accurate count.

On 1st July, 1942, the Japanese demanded 165 men for a working party, but owing to sickness only 130 men were available out of a camp strength of 1,600. The Japanese threatened to collect hospital cases and, in fact, men with fever, external ulcers, dysentery and even ulcerated stomachs had to be turned out to saw trees, carry granite and heavy logs. Many had no boots. Treatment was callous in the extreme, and one man had a crowbar thrust into his stomach, causing him to vomit and collapse in exhaustion.

Gone, now, was that "Pack up your troubles" spirit of the march to Sonkrai; it had been completely crushed. Says the diary: "They had lost what spirit they had and their reaction to orders was very slow indeed. There was a vacant look and lost expression on their faces. . . . There was no time for the washing of either body or clothing except at night. . . . When working they were treated little better than animals and certainly it could hardly be wondered at that they lost their individuality. . . ."

On 5th July seven officers and one other rank escaped—an unpopular event amongst fellow prisoners as reprisals were feared. The senior officer left in camp was held responsible, sentenced to be shot, reprieved, and warned if there were any further escapes sentence would be carried out. There were no meals for thirty-six hours. All ranks were warned that anyone seen attempting to escape would be shot and that if any man made good his escape the whole camp would be shot.

Sixteen days after the escape the diary records receipt of news that all escapees had been caught in a village near Moulmein and were being brought back to the camp, some dead.

The diary continues: "The Japanese Commander came round the hospital. One patient did not answer his name and as a result was beaten up. He died in the middle of the punishment. Our M.O. was told the patients were being treated too kindly and that more men must be found for the road."

A cholera epidemic swept through the camp and in two months, of 305 victims admitted to hospital, 213 died.

The narrative concludes: "Of 'F' Party, of which the provost company was a part, 63 per cent. deaths were suffered, the company losing 70 per cent. The highest loss was that of the Beds and Herts, who lost 83 per cent."

Burma

THE percentage of military police employed in South-East Asia Command was exceedingly small. Total forces employed was 757,023 of whom only 4,089 were police; but in April, 1945, there was a general increase in provost sections throughout Allied Land Forces, South-East Asia. Establishments were increased from two British and four Indian sections to three British and six Indian sections.

The provost service in this theatre developed from fairly small beginnings, for as Fourteenth Army advanced into Burma and, later, into Malaya, new areas and sub-areas were created, all requiring provost units. Apart from normal wastage and replacements for repatriates, strictly operational demands did not greatly increase, though it was realized throughout that provost resources available for operational formations were inadequate.

Provost in India and Burma was an innovation and provost officers frequently found themselves disagreeing with staff officers about the employment of military policemen. This was particularly true of new units. For instance, in May, 1944, when the A.P.M. 1 Corps arrived, he found that he was expected to run a good mess and generally do as he was told. He could not expect to be consulted. The A.P.M. did not have a typewriter in his office, and it was considered that he did not require one. On the other hand, the 25th Indian Division were very "Pro minded" and well trained.

At this period Corps H.Q. had a D.A.A.G. (Traffic), and this officer was virtually the A.P.M. as far as operations went. Corps provost were expected to guard Corps H.Q., act as orderlies, and guard and escort Ps.W. All this took time to change.

Towards the end of March, 1944, at the time of Major-General Wingate's death in an air crash, it was decided just before Imphal was surrounded, that Advanced H.Q., 3rd Indian Division, should evacuate to Sylhet. The war at Imphal was not actually the problem of the Special Force, their task being 200 to 300 miles inside Central Burma behind the Japs then threatening Imphal.

The provost store and some of the motor-cycles and N.C.Os. were flown out; the remainder of the Company escorted the road convoys to Sylhet. Soon after this, the Manipur road was blocked by the Japanese and Imphal was cut off.

A sub-section of provost was established at Comilla airstrip, and three N.C.Os. were flown into the stronghold of Imphal. Their duties were control of M.T. and ambulances and their parking on strip, assisting in checking and collecting arms, etc., assisting in evacuation of wounded from ambulance planes, animal management, assisting in deplaning, guiding to concentration areas of animals, collection and guiding fit personnel by M.T. to camp, reporting number of arrivals, sick, wounded and fit, to the staff officer on duty.

Supply-dropping sorties by Dakota aircraft departed from the rear main strips usually between 6.0 a.m. and 7.0 a.m. daily. These planes taxied from their revetments on to the runway and thence to the main strip.

As the runways were always crowded with vehicles of all kinds it called for high-pressure traffic control on the part of the police. In the course of the operations many planes were damaged through vehicles failing to give way. Indian drivers proved the biggest source of trouble; they usually took fright on seeing a plane approaching and stopped. Usually the military police had to take charge and remove them. In one instance an Indian driver tried to drive under the wing of a plane. The hood of his vehicle was ripped off and the aircraft was put out of action for several days.

No. 3 Air Base was established at Dinjan during May, as it was still more suitably situated for the operations then being undertaken with General Stilwell, and for the withdrawal of our troops when their part had been played in these operations. Six N.C.Os. were all that could be provided at first, but later another six were dispatched.

When the decision to fight was taken the front line was approximately thirty miles from Imphal. The main provost task was therefore traffic control, which divided into two main phases: (i) To evacuate all "soft troops" (i.e., not required for immediate operations) on both roads into the Imphal plain, and to evacuate all supplies and equipment from roadheads and forward roadheads into Imphal. (ii) To evacuate all "soft troops" from Imphal to Base at Dimapur.

Numbers involved on the Tamu road were approximately 20,000 "soft troops." Enemy did not cut this road until much later.

Main convoy timings were adhered to so that Corps third-line transport could reach roadheads to evacuate supplies and personnel. Special timings were given from Regulating H.Q.

In these circumstances, stragglers and information posts established by the police could not operate successfully when most required. It must be remembered, too, that most of the Corps police were cut off down the Tiddim Road with 17th Division or were in process of being relieved by 20th Division on the Tamu road.

All units returning to Imphal, whether from the Tamu or Tiddim roads, together with sixty units from Kanglatongbi, had to be met and given their new locations.

A decision was taken at very short notice to evacuate Kanglatongbi. Police in this area were not told of the evacuation until

AN INDIAN MILITARY POLICEMAN QUESTIONS A SOLDIER
ABOUT HIS PASS

after it had begun. Not only were sixty units sent off, but vast quantities of petrol, ammunition, and ordnance stores from the depots had to be brought in. An order of march was given by the Administration Commandant, Kanglatongbi, but this was not adhered to. The enemy was already in Depot area, and the road was being mortared. Units got out as soon as they could. So great was the volume of traffic that vehicles were nose to tail all the way from Kanglatongbi to Imphal. An A.P.M. with service representatives were sent to meet the units and give destinations. Units were found mixed in different lorries. To explain the location of a destination to Indian soldiers took time and patience. Meanwhile, the rear of the column was being mortared. The only practical solution was to allow the transport access to the marshalling area and the rest camp.

The volume of traffic in Imphal itself increased enormously during this period. The main two-way road down the middle was drenched with vehicles from dawn to dusk. There was no question of dispersing, as vehicles had to reach their destinations, and there was not enough road space. There was no question of police control allowing only certain vehicles on to the road, for all vehicles had assumed operational importance, and in any case no police were available.

M.T. discipline deteriorated greatly, but the police did good work in keeping the traffic on the move. There was one big bottle-neck just south of the Imphal airstrip, where a narrow road turned east into Corps H.Q., and another road turned west into the R.A.F. area. The A.P.M. asked for a roundabout to be built. This was refused on camouflage grounds. The A.P.M.'s request was sanctioned one week later—one week too late.

There were complaints at this time that insufficient military police motor-cycle patrols were on duty. The A.P.M. was told to put all unit motor-cycles in a pool to be used by any military policemen at any time of day. The A.P.M. did not agree. Corps provost unit was ten motor-cycles under establishment, and there was no hope of replacements. To create this pool for any military policeman to use was asking for trouble.

Staff officers who went out on to the road during this period wished to see a military police motor-cyclist every five hundred yards, forming a "White Line" between the two streams of traffic. Perhaps they were calling to mind a Corps Provost Company on British War Establishment with nine sections and a fleet of motor-cycles in a unit, in which every man could ride efficiently. Certainly they forgot that the police had other duties to perform, such as the encirclement of Imphal with a ring of traffic posts for security purpose, to enforce A.R.P. and anti-malaria measures, enforcing the joint military and civil curfew order and bathing and water point regulations; prevention of theft and pilfering, assaults and affrays; enforcing a rigid price control and traffic discipline.

Fortunately, there was no refugee problem. There was a certain movement of Manipuri from the hills into Imphal, but the movement was never so great as to cause dislocation to traffic or embarrassment to the civil authorities.

Relations between the military and civil population were amicable. There was a certain ill-feeling over profiteering and outbursts of assaults and affrays, but this was never serious enough to cause major incidents. The new location of troops in box areas entailed the evacuation of civilians from many local villages for security purposes. These civilians were moved into areas in Imphal which had been vacated by units. Military police assisted in the evacuation.

A cage to accommodate a maximum of thirty Japanese prisoners was erected at 4 Corps Provost H.Q. as Intelligence anticipated that it would never be necessary to hold in excess of this number. In fact, few prisoners were captured during the withdrawal of the divisions. 17th Division Provost erected a small wire cage at each staging camp. 20th Division Provost solved the problem by keeping prisoners in a deep trench roofed in with a sheet of corrugated iron with sandbags on top.

When the Divisional H.Q. took up more static locations, all provost units erected small barbed-wire cages. These cages were "holding depots" in which prisoners could be kept overnight before despatch to the Corps cage. Most prisoners were wounded, and a wired enclosure was built by Corps Provost to accommodate them. Ps.W. were flown out as soon as fit.

To assist in the control of traffic during the return of 20th Division, the A.P.M. got two radio sets from Divisional Signals. He mounted both in jeeps, one being left at Divisional H.Q.; the other was given to the second-in-command, who toured the network of roads and told the A.P.M. what was happening. The A.P.M., who was also in touch with the traffic posts on the road by telephone, then gave orders as to the volume of traffic which could be allowed into the main road. The Tamu road was not cut by the enemy for some time, but Japanese sprang up at various points from day to day. In this connection the police from traffic posts gave valuable information to the A.P.M. as to whether the road was open or not.

The Tiddim road was so narrow in most places that patrolling up and down the moving column was not possible. The police rendered most assistance by walking up and down the line, pushing completely broken-down vehicles over the side, and making towing

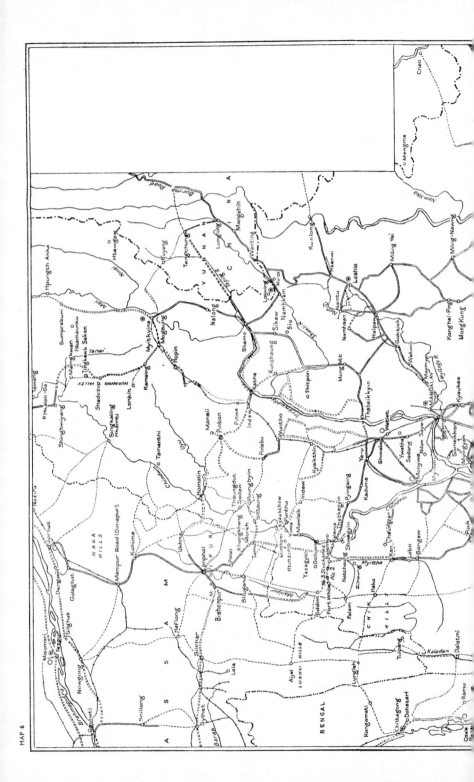

MAP 6

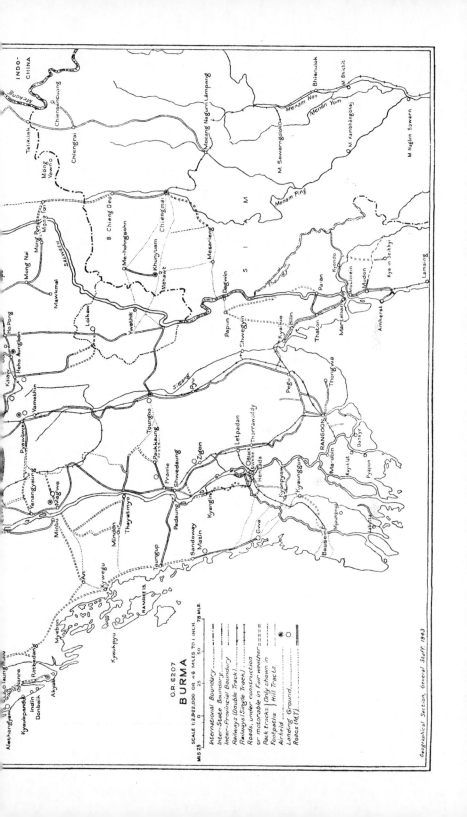

O.R. 6207

BURMA

SCALE 1:2,922,000 OR 46 MILES TO 1 INCH.

MLS 25 0   25   50   75 MLS

International Boundary	....
Inter-State Boundary	....
Inter-Provincial Boundary	....
Railways (Double Track)	———
Railways (Single Track)	———
Roads, under construction or motorable in fair weather	===
Pack tracks } Only shown in	....
Footpaths } Hill Tracts	....
Airfield	⊙ ○
Landing Ground	....
Roads (M.T.)	———

Geographical Section, General Staff. 1943

arrangements for others. In the harbour areas, police undertook duties at bathing, petrol, water, ammunition and supply points.

Stragglers' and information posts were also set up in each harbour. Much hard work was done by officers and men in scouting around the area in the early stages, in order that accurate information could be given.

When the battle settled down in the Imphal Plain, traffic control ceased to be the problem it had been during the preceding weeks. There were two reasons for this: (a) The four divisional axes were situated along four two-way roads; and (b) due to the supply situation, the running of all vehicles was restricted to a minimum.

A big problem was where to accommodate and how to deal with prisoners awaiting trial, dispatch to military prisons, promulgation of sentence, dispatch to civil prisons or undergoing field punishment or detention for periods from twenty-eight days to three months.

Staff and equipment of a prisoner-of-war unit had some months previously been loaned to the A.P.M. for this purpose, but proved unequal to the task. At one point this guard thought fit to pilfer kit from a nearby site from which a unit had just moved out, and the entire guard had to be interned in the cage they had just been guarding. In such conditions a system of strict and efficient punishment was difficult.

26th Divisional Provost Unit was to have gone in with the assault on Rangoon, but it was not finally involved in the operation. During the first two or three days of the assault, Rangoon was chaotic and much looting was done.

By June the greater part of Burma had been cleared of the enemy, who, however, still maintained themselves east of the Sittang river, blocking the way to Malaya, until the Japanese surrender in August.

CHAPTER IX

SECOND WORLD WAR: OTHER THEATRES AND STATIONS OVERSEAS

Norway

IN the early spring of 1940 Germany invaded Norway. As an essential strategic counterstroke a Norwegian Expeditionary Force was sent from Britain. This force included No. 6 L. of C. Provost Company, attached to the 49th (Yorkshire) Division, which sailed from Glasgow towards the end of March, 1940, and landed at Harstad, on the Isle of Hinnoy—just north of the Lofoten Isles. The force was mostly composed of young Territorial battalions with a stiffening provided by the Scots and Irish Guards, and reinforced by a detachment of the French Foreign Legion and the Chasseurs Alpines.

During the disembarkation the first air raid occurred and an advance party of provost was sent ashore. This party immediately took control, shepherding the young and inexperienced troops to shelter. One military policeman went to the assistance of an officer and succeeded in getting him under cover when he himself was killed—the first casualty. The remainder of the troops were eventually disembarked and dispersed, leaving the military police in solitary possession of the docks where they acted as stevedores, unloading the ship.

The company set up its billets in the house of the German consul, and from there carried out security duties at the docks, town patrols, and point duty on the approach roads to the base. Reconnaissances were then made on the mainland and the roads patrolled to Narvik throughout the twenty-four hours. Little help was given by the local inhabitants, whose surly and disinterested attitude was more of a hindrance than otherwise. Air raids were both numerous and intense, but throughout the police maintained communications and kept convoys on the move. Security patrols were also carried out and thorough searches made for cameras, binoculars and weapons, with surprising results.

One well-known business man was arrested by the military police. He had in his possession two Browning machine guns and ammunition belts, a Very pistol and cartridges, several cameras and films, twenty-four Browning automatics and thousands of rounds of ammunition, a large sum in cash and marked maps. Later enemy parachutists actually landed at each point marked on the map, and an aerodrome then in course of construction for the R.A.F. and clearly shown on the map, in addition to a destroyer whose anchorage was shown, were both bombed and destroyed. This man was lodged by the police in the city jail, but he escaped.

The military police did excellent work in the evacuation, organizing the embarking of wounded and troops and the destruction of equipment. A thorough search was then made of all billets and areas occupied by our troops and many abandoned weapons retrieved and security documents destroyed. When the evacuation was near its end it was decided that, in order to obviate any panic or rush for the boats, the local population should be kept in ignorance of it.

Accordingly, through a ruse in which a police corporal played the leading part, this was successfully achieved. Just outside the town it had been customary to have an M.P. pointsman; the local population looked upon this point as a symbol of British presence. At the time of the withdrawal a corporal was detailed for duty and, wearing white sleeves and red top, maintained this point. Just as enemy tanks appeared three miles down the road the signal was given on the destroyer's siren. The corporal calmly removed his traffic sleeves, neatly folded them and placed them on the roadside as though for his successor, mounted his motor-cycle, rode to the docks, and was the last man to leave Norwegian soil. The Company arrived back in Glasgow on the 2nd June, 1940. Later in the war plans were made for a second landing in Norway; the 52nd (Lowland) Division was selected for this role, and underwent a thorough training in snow and mountain warfare. The presence of this division in Scotland no doubt pinned down many German divisions in Norway. The Divisional Provost Company, then commanded by Captain S. Hallett, had very specialized commitments in these circumstances, particularly as all roads were considered to be "one-way only" and frequently the "roads" were "mountain tracks."

At the direction of the divisional commander, Major-General Neil Ritchie, the company was issued with No. 22 wireless sets, and a section was trained by Signals to become competent operators.

In addition to normal wheeled and tracked vehicles, complications invariably arose with animal pack companies, man-pack operations, and the dropping of supplies by air. Perhaps the most important feature of this rigorous form of training was that of man-management and the care of arms and equipment in sub-zero temperatures. Special mountain clothing was issued to each officer and man. It may be of interest to note that the most valued garment was the open knit string vest worn next to the skin and which, after a little preliminary uneasiness, proved to be the surest way of conserving body heat.

All the men were called upon from time to time to live for days in snow, their shelter being either a snow hole, which was found to be singularly comfortable, or in a flimsy eight-man tent. The latter was really small and was entered through a small fabric tunnel. One man or even two sleeping in a tent of this nature would, in theory, freeze to death because they could not generate sufficient heat.

Living in such circumstances, rations were cut to a minimum and carried in sealed tins. Pemmican, boiled sweets and sundry tablets to balance the vitamin rate were the chief features of this highly concentrated diet. In the case of provost, ski-ing was confined to officers, and instruction in this was undertaken largely by Norwegian officers attached to the division.

Despite the rigorous nature of this training, the wastage through sickness was low and the officers and N.C.Os. of the company built up a stamina and qualities of endurance which were to stand them in good stead in later battles. It is ironical that, despite this training, the division, after passing through further training in combined operations and as an airborne formation, was called upon to make its first contact with the enemy below sea-level on the islands of Beveland and Walcheren!

*   *   *   *   *

Faroe Islands

A SMALL detachment of military police was stationed in the Faroe Islands. While there is little to say about their duties, the cheerfulness with which they tackled a dreary and thankless task and overcame stagnation and boredom should be recorded.

*   *   *   *   *

Iceland

IN May, 1940, British troops landed in Iceland to forestall its seizure by the enemy; there they remained until the Americans took over later in the war.

The provost company with the Icelandic Force was one of the first units to arrive, and was billeted in an ice factory—a somewhat cold welcome. Contact was immediately made with the local police, who placed their station at the disposal of military police. Between provost and the Icelandic police there was close co-operation, and their relations were cordial once the original aloofness was broken down by tact and understanding. The Icelandic police came to adopt many of our methods, especially in administration, C.I.D. work, traffic control, and accident reports.

In Iceland there were no large-scale maps available, without which the movement of large bodies of troops, and the recognition of points of strategical importance in the defence scheme was impossible. It fell to provost to carry out a rough survey of the island and prepare the necessary maps, which served until Survey units arrived. With these maps they carried out movement of heavy coastal guns, which required many diversions to be made for civilian vehicles and convoys.

Reporting on road conditions was one of the vital tasks, the road surface being, in most cases, of lava dust, easily broken up by frost, snow and ice. In all weathers the dangerous and difficult job of maintaining motor-cycle road patrols was carried out, and it was only by their efforts that communications on the island were kept open. The general conditions can be gathered from the fact that over the period of occupation over three thousand accidents were reported and dealt with amicably.

The duty next in importance was in connection with shipping. Every boat was under military police supervision and a watch was kept in every hold discharging cargo—especially petrol tankers. All boats had to be searched for uncensored mail or photographs. All boats going round the island, carrying military stores to defence points, carried a military police guard. Criminal investigation and accident departments were set up in conjunction with the local police. The provost companies also took over the custody of prisoners of war landed from calling ships, and rounded up and interned certain Nazi sympathizers.

*　　*　　*　　*　　*

Gibraltar

A NECESSARY role was performed by the military police in Gibraltar. After the fall of France no one quite knew what was to be the fate of the Rock and its garrison, whose strength rose to a maximum of 15,480 in 1944. It prepared for siege from all sides, and although military police were issued with rifles in addition to their normal weapon, the pistol, they never had to use them.

Before the war and up to June, 1940, the Gibraltar provost detachment was 1 sergeant, 2 corporals and 12 lance-corporals —a proportion of one M.P. to every 256 soldiers. In 1943 there were 90 "Redcaps" on the Rock—about one to every 160 soldiers. There was a section of mounted military police with ten horses. Its creation was brought about by the formation of a pack-transport company and by the presence on the Rock of a number of privately owned horses which could not be evacuated. These were bought from their owners at a nominal sum and on being found unsuitable for pack work were handed over to provost. Although the value of the section was open to debate as its main use was only ceremonial, there is no doubt it was a credit to the Corps and added to the dignity of the ceremonial parades it frequently attended. The mounted section assisted to a minor degree in traffic control and patrols were carried out twice daily.

The military police had to undertake considerable quayside commitments, and one section was wholly engaged on anti-pilfering duties in the port area, a type of work which was heaviest at the time of the opening of the North African campaign. This section, which consisted of men of some experience in investigation work, later carried out S.I.B. duties. In December, 1944, three S.I.B. sergeants were posted, but by then the garrison was considerably reduced and scope for their particular role proportionately limited.

In May, 1944, a company composed of low category personnel from the R.A. arrived for duty at vulnerable points. The personnel were later transferred to the military police (Vulnerable Points Wing). Inter-service relations were good. A close liaison between military police, the standing naval patrol and R.A.F. police was maintained over a period of years, and at night a combined patrol under a military police sergeant and chief petty officer worked smoothly and effectively. The colony had its own civil police force, run on similar lines to the force at home. Here again co-operation was close, help being freely given on both sides.

The disciplinary side of provost work was normal, though, possibly due to the uncertainty of life in the garrison, drunkenness was prevalent for the first three years of the war, declining later. The tracing of stolen stores was extremely difficult, for throughout the war the colony was supplied with food consigned and marked N.A.A.F.I. Certain Ordnance stores including petrol and tyres were issued, and civilian firms carried on business in W.D. and naval transport driven by Spaniards with access to military stores.

*　　*　　*　　*　　*

Eritrea

IN January, 1941, two offensives, one from the north and one from the south, were launched to clear the Italians from Eritrea, Somaliland and Abyssinia.

For the northern offensive a striking force of British and Indian troops was formed, and, after the preliminary battle of Kassala, advanced through Tessenei, Barentu, Keren and so to Asmara, the capital of Eritrea. Although the enemy were entrenched on the heights of a steep hill, with an estimated numerical superiority of some eight to one, yet the force captured it in less than forty-eight hours' fighting. With these troops went both British and Indian military police.

When the fighting was finished and the Middle East Force

had joined up with the East African Force that came up from the south through Abyssinia, provost became more important. Until an Eritrean police force was set up under British military administration, military police were in complete control. Among the Italians, Fascists and anti-Fascists had to be separated and the former confined when necessary; the local civilian police had to be "screened," as the only solution of the usual lack of provost was to use the anti-Fascist elements for traffic and local civilian control. It was a strange sight to see Italian police in Asmara and Massawa, in Italian Fascist uniform and armed with automatics, calmly—or as calmly as an Italian can—directing civilian and military traffic.

In the Sudan, except in towns, there are no roads; there is a graded track from Khartoum to Kassala, thence to Tessenei, where a metalled road starts and runs right through to Asmara and Massawa; apart from that, all travel is by train or Nile river-boat. Check-posts and traffic control are unknown and the military policemen concentrated on discipline.

✷   ✷   ✷   ✷   ✷

Greece

IN October, 1940, Italy invaded Greece; and in March, 1941, a British force which included three sections of the 2nd Armoured Divisional Provost Company was sent to Greece from Egypt.

During the journey from the Greek port to the company's destination the whole of the route through the suburbs of Athens was lined with civilians who cheered, clapped and threw flowers on to the vehicles. At that time Greece was not at war with Germany and the German Ambassador was still in residence. Pamphlets were distributed amongst the military police. These pamphlets, which showed photographs of the German Ambassador, in civilian clothes and in uniform, wearing a monocle, bore the words "Beware of this man. He walks about your camp asking questions. Don't tell him anything."

Later, when it became clear that war between the two countries was imminent, military police were stationed at the front entrance of the German Embassy to prevent disturbances between British soldiers and the staff.

On 6th April Greece was invaded by Germany, and on 21st April was forced by the overwhelming strength of the enemy to capitulate.

During this very short campaign work was extremely heavy for the police in Athens. The town was overcrowded with services, amongst whom were thousands of Australians and New Zealanders, all of whom were in camp several miles outside Athens, and were without transport or means of getting back to camp at midnight after a night in town. Omonia Square was the control point at which everyone gathered in an endeavour to obtain some means of getting back. Any taxi or private car appearing in this square was immediately surrounded by hundreds of soldiers, and if the driver refused to go where he was requested, his vehicle was sometimes smashed up.

Fifth column work was extensive. Military police, by climbing from housetop to housetop, arrested a Greek civilian firing coloured Very lights from the top of a building during an air raid.

An N.C.O. of the Corps has given the following account of evacuation from Greece.

"About 16th April, when it was apparent that an evacuation was to take place, the remainder of the military police were formed into sections and detailed to prepare routes down to the Corinth Canal and onwards to the evacuation beaches. All office records had been destroyed and I had been assigned to one of the above sections.

"We went from Athens through Eleusis along the Coast Road to the Corinth Canal and inwards to Argos and Naphlion. N.C.Os. were left at various points *en route* and Franco signs were erected to assist convoys returning from the forward areas to the evacuation beaches. The whole route was being bombed and strafed by enemy planes continuously.

"At Naphlion we came upon a scene of great disorder. Abandoned and burnt-out trucks and equipment lined the roads, large numbers of Greek soldiers, British airmen and troops were wandering aimlessly around, and turning over the abandoned equipment in search of food. Lieut.-Colonel Wainman and the remainder of his small party of British military police set to work to establish some kind of order from the existing chaos. An R.A.S.C. unit was contacted and rations were brought up.

"Troops were organized into parties of fifty under a senior N.C.O. or officer and dispersed in the orchards on the hillside. All vehicles that could be moved were placed under cover or driven over the cliffs into the sea. Outlying points were established to guide incoming convoys into dispersal areas, and dispatch riders were organized to guide these convoys.

"The following day was spent in this manner, despite the attention of the Stukas. That evening was the first evacuation from the beach. An evacuation headquarters had been established, to which the officer or N.C.O. i/c party reported, and was detailed to one of these beaches. The party was marched from Headquarters to the cross-roads, where Colonel Wainman was doing duty, and from there they were directed to the beach to which they had been allotted, to be taken off by small boats to the waiting destroyers and troopers.

Military police lined the routes from the village to the beaches and maintained discipline. During this night approximately 4,000 troops were taken off without casualties. Evacuation ceased at about 6.0 a.m. when the Luftwaffe again started their hourly visits.

"The next few days were spent in the same duty, the N.C.Os. snatching what sleep they could, until 29th April, when we were informed that this would be the last night, and that we were to be taken off at 11.0 p.m. On this day the Germans landed glider troops at Argos, about three miles away. The number of troops to be evacuated that night was small and by 11.0 p.m. the area was deserted. The military police were formed up and marched down to one of the beaches, the only exceptions being Lieut.-Colonel Wainman, Lance-Corporals Kelso, Small and myself, who were doing duty at the cross-roads. The main body of police were taken off by naval launch. I have since learnt that this launch capsized and Lance-Corporal Rogers was drowned. At about 2.30 a.m. the remainder of the personnel and stragglers were rounded up and proceeded to the beach, where a tally was taken and it was found that there were 63 in the party, including one naval officer. A fishing boat named the *St. George* was requisitioned and the whole party was embarked.

"After a three days' trip in this vessel, during which we were constantly machine-gunned, we reached Suda Bay, where we were transferred to H.M. Destroyer *Kingston* and joined a convoy bound for Alexandria."

✻ ✻ ✻ ✻ ✻

Paiforce

HARD on the fall of Greece came that of Crete, captured by the Germans on 1st June after an airborne invasion of unparalleled intensity. Meanwhile the enemy had also got control of the Ægean islands; and our strategic position in the Middle East was now seriously threatened.

Local troubles on a big scale, fomented by the Axis, broke out in Iraq early in April and in Persia in August, and we were forced to enter both countries to protect vital oil supplies, to safeguard Imperial communications, and to keep open Russia's indispensable supply-line through the Caucasus and the Caspian ports.

When Tenth Army arrived in Persia and Iraq during the troubles in 1941, some Indian provost arrived with it. Major Hodder, 1st Gurkhas, was the senior provost officer and A.P.M. It was not until October, 1942, that a Provost Marshal was appointed—Colonel Forbes, K.O.Y.L.I., being sent from Middle East. About this time drafts of military police began to arrive, and some of the Indian provost (British) were sent to the depot, Almaza, on courses. An Indian C.M.P. School was formed in Baghdad.

There was no S.I.B. in Paiforce until June, 1942, but before this Lieutenant Beck had been posted from India to deal with bribery and corruption and, curiously, was placed under control of the General Staff (Intelligence). He had the assistance of eight inexperienced ex-Indian civil policemen. He successfully closed two bribery cases involving together £220,000.

In June, 1942, a detachment of S.I.B. arrived from Middle East, and the Indian section was disbanded on orders from Middle East. Up to the time of Colonel Forbes's arrival and appointment as Provost Marshal there was no control of "Aid to Russia" traffic on roads, and no anti-pilferage organization at Margil Docks. Pilfering of all goods was prevalent.

Traffic control posts were established on the route Khanaqin to Kazvin. From November, 1942, onwards, traffic on this route increased rapidly and, in addition, assembled vehicles started using the South Persian route from Khorramshahr through Andimeshk to Malayer, Hamadan, where it joined the Khanaqin route to Kazvin. Many difficulties were encountered and overcome; the control of civilian drivers on contract vehicles proved troublesome, addicted as these drivers were to taking hashish. Ten-ton lorries would at times do 50 m.p.h. on favourable, and sometimes unfavourable stretches of road. At other times they broke down at most inconvenient places. This required an M.P. on duty for twenty-four hours and longer, to pass traffic by safely. There were many accidents, and not a few deaths among civilians.

By June, 1943, there were as many as two thousand vehicles a day using the Hamadan–Kazvin road in both directions. At the same time the Americans took over traffic control on the South Persia route right through to Kazvin, and military police posts were confined to the Khanaqin–Hamadan section, with outposts for disciplinary purposes at Takistan and Tabriz.

Meanwhile fresh drafts of military police had been arriving in the Command, and the small original band of Indian provost had grown to about sixteen sections British C.M.P. and eight sections Indian C.M.P.

★   ★   ★   ★   ★

Syria and Lebanon

UP to the middle of 1941 Syria and Lebanon were under the control of the Vichy Government, who were pressed by the Germans, after the fall of Greece and Crete, for the use of the Syrian airfields. Vichy agreed; the British Government accordingly decided to strike without delay.

Tenth Corps was sent out from the United Kingdom on 1st June, 1941, to handle the invasion; but the intrigues of the Vichy French in collaboration with the Germans and Italians, had made it imperative that action should be taken before the arrival of Corps H.Q., if the Allies' vital life-line down through Turkey to Palestine and the Suez Canal was to be safeguarded. 6th Australian Division was withdrawn from the Western Desert, advanced bases in Northern Palestine were quickly established and other troops were dispatched. On 8th June British, Imperial, and Free French Forces crossed the frontier.

The Vichy French put up a reasonable show of resistance, but their hearts were not in the business, and it has been stated since in Syria and Lebanon that they would not have offered any resistance at all had not Free French Forces been included in the invasion. Be that as it may, the campaign was of short duration, and Damascus and Beirut were entered less than forty days after the frontier had been crossed—to be exact, Beirut on 16th July, 1941, and Damascus a few days later. Throughout the campaign, British military police were attached to 6th Australian Division.

The armistice was signed in the ancient city of Tyre, on the sea-front. During the preliminaries an amusing incident occurred. In the house used for the signing of the armistice, the lights failed, so an Australian policeman was instructed to place his motor-cycle on the front steps of the house and turn on his headlamp. Unfortunately, his battery was out of order; he had to run his engine. Thus the historic document recording the handing over to the Allies of the only Vichy French stronghold in the Eastern Mediterranean was signed to the accompaniment of the exhaust noises of a police motor-cycle.

As can well be imagined, the local population were in a highly-strung condition. Beirut and Damascus had been bombed by British planes, although it was afterwards discovered that at least three of the raids had been made by the Germans, who had taken advantage of the general confusion prevailing at the time to carry out these raids in the hope that the Lebanese would think that the British were guilty of indiscriminate bombing. However, after the first three or four days, the populace came to recognize that they had real upholders of law and order in the persons of the military police, and the latter were treated with great respect and affection.

For the first four months, all the military policing of Syria and the Lebanon was carried out by 1 officer, 1 sergeant, 2 corporals and 13 lance-corporals at Damascus and the same at Beirut. The Australian provost provided one section in each of the towns, but they looked after their own men only, a colossal task that proved

M

beyond their powers. Mixed patrols of British and Australian police were instituted, which were somewhat more successful but by no means ideal. The D.A.P.M. had to deal with British, Australian and Free French troops, Vichy-French civilians and disarmed troops and civilians of almost every nationality in the world, all exhilarated by the recently finished "pocket-war." However, after the first excitement things quietened down, and when the Vichy French returned to France life returned more or less to normal.

Beirut, with its sea-bathing, good hotels and varied attractions in the summer, and its proximity to the mountains of the Lebanon range for winter sports, became the most popular leave resort in the Middle East. H.Q. Paiforce began to run large leave parties, and during that summer the floating leave population of Beirut ran into many thousands daily. A detachment of military police, never more than fifty strong, had to control these men, some of whom had not been in a civilized town for months.

*   *   *   *   *

Madagascar

THE penetration of Japanese warships into the Indian Ocean, after the reduction of Malaya and Burma in the early months of 1942, underlined the menace which their seizure of Madagascar would be to our sea-routes round the Cape to the Middle East, and Australasia.

To forestall any such disaster it was decided that we must ourselves occupy the island, and for this purpose 121 Force was assembled in Scotland and left the Clyde on 22nd March. The basis of the force was 29th Independent Brigade, No. 5 Commando, Artillery, armour and service detachments, all trained in combined operations. The provost element consisted of a D.A.P.M. and two sections of 200 Provost Company, which had done extensive combined operational training in Western Scotland.

The initial landings were made at Courier Bay on the West coast of Madagascar just before first light on 5th May, 1942. This was the first occasion on which provost had taken part in beach-landing operations, which were destined to play so big a part in later campaigns. The immediate problems were those of organizing the beach areas for personnel and vehicles, maintaining contact with the advancing troops and the disposal of Ps.W. As the action developed it was necessary for the Commander to call in 13th and 17th Brigades of the 5th Division who were lying out at sea, and on their arrival the provost strength was increased by the addition of one subaltern and two sections.

When fighting stopped, the D.A.P.M. therefore found himself with a provost company consisting of one officer and four sections with which to set about organizing the town and harbour of Diego Suarez, together with the occupied hinterland to the south. The duties consisted of normal traffic control, maintenance of discipline and anti-malarial precautions amongst military and naval personnel, assisting fighting services personnel in security duties, and supervision of ships unloading in the harbour. In addition, there were such duties as settling private strife amongst the natives, and surveillance of prostitutes. It was interesting to see, however, the unlimited faith the natives had in the British policeman, and there was always a trail of callers seeking help and guidance, often on the most embarrassing points.

In addition to normal provost duties, the D.A.P.M. was involved in continuous liaison, particularly with political officers, supervision of civil police, and the prosecution of native delinquents before the military court. On one particular occasion the D.A.P.M. was called upon to put to sea to settle a minor mutiny on board a vessel which had come under the orders of the Naval Officer in Charge. The settlement of the row was a mild affair compared to the ascent and descent of a Jacob's ladder in rough weather.

The two sections of 5th Divisional Provost Company subsequently rejoined their division, and the occupation force was reinforced by the introduction of a South African Brigade which included a section of South African provost. In September, 1942, it was necessary to make further attacks in the centre of the island, and landings were made at Majunga and Tamatave. An East African Brigade was introduced as follow-up troops, and East African provost (Askaris), under one European officer and two European N.C.Os., were included.

The fighting really ended with the capture of Tananarive, the capital city of Madagascar. The provost available under the D.A.P.M. for the maintenance of some sort of order in the city was composed of Europeans, South Africans and East Africans— a cosmopolitan but efficient force. The D.A.P.M.'s chief worry was languages—a worry which was not lightened by the fact that every dialect from John o' Groats to Lambeth Road was spoken amongst what remained of the original members of 200 Provost Company. The control of Madagascar as a whole was handed over to East Africa Command in October, 1942.

✳   ✳   ✳   ✳   ✳

Malta

ONLY those who were marooned on the beleaguered island of Malta during its black months of siege can accurately assess just how much was contributed by the small C.M.P. detachment there towards the award to the island of the George Cross.

Malta's provost establishment, which began on 3rd September, 1939, with a section of 1 sergeant, 2 corporals and 8 lance-corporals with 6 men attached from infantry units stationed on the island, never rose to large proportions, for though an adequate establishment was approved in step with the influx of troops, reinforcement difficulties during the siege prevented its early fulfilment. It was not until November, 1943, that it was found possible to bring the detachment up to its authorized total strength of 2 warrant officers and 63 N.C.Os., and several months more were to elapse before S.I.B. personnel were posted in sufficient numbers.

In the early days the C.M.P. detachment was a part of the establishment of H.Q., Malta Command, and was administered by the garrison adjutant. It came under the Naval Provost Marshal for discipline and reports, a state of affairs which existed until 8th March, 1943, when a D.P.M. was appointed.

At the outbreak of war the strength of troops in Malta was 7,200, rising to a maximum of 75,000 in the summer of 1943. The strength of provost increased in rough proportion, though there was always a time lag in posting authorized reinforcements. One of the chief difficulties lay in finding trained personnel. In March, 1943, practically every man in 226 Provost Company had been enlisted direct from local units and had had no military police training, as it was impossible to run a police course in addition to normal duties.

With the declaration of war by Italy came a wave of drunkenness and absence, but by the end of 1941 the former charge had become non-existent. Provost claim no credit, however, as by then liquor stocks on the island were just as scarce as policemen.

But Provost's chief task lay in the quick turn-round of those vital convoys and in ensuring safe conduct of the stores once they were off-loaded. The story is told of one convoy which arrived hoping to make a quick get-away, only to find the native dockers forced underground by an air raid. The provost company heard of the captain's dilemma and, turning out voluntarily, aided by the ship's company, set up an unloading record during one of the worst air attacks the harbour had ever experienced.

In 1942 it became evident that considerable quantities of Government property were going astray, and in an attempt to prevent this, a warrant officer and three N.C.Os., none of whom had any training in S.I.B. work, were earmarked for counter-theft duty. Representations were made to H.Q., Malta Command, for an S.I.B. section to be posted, but it was not until 1944 that they arrived. Meantime specially selected N.C.Os. from within the company attained a fair measure of success. Pilferage of food and clothing, both scarce on the island, continued. The thefts lessened when a system of dock-to-dump escorts was introduced.

Within six months of this S.I.B.'s arrival in 1944, thefts were down to a satisfactory level. Recovery of stolen property proved to be extremely difficult as at some time or other general issues of food, clothes, petrol, tyres and batteries were made to the civil population. Pleas that suspected stores were issued "two or three years ago" were frequently accepted by the courts. Nevertheless property worth £4,640 was recovered by August, 1945, and 800 cases investigated. The S.I.B. maintained a close liaison with the Malta C.I.D., whose co-operation was at all times freely given.

There was for a time on the island a dog section. Introduced in May, 1943, for the Middle East, the section contained 10 dogs and 11 handlers.

The island's role in connection with the build-up of forces to participate in the invasion of Sicily should not remain unmentioned. During this period provost were heavily committed in connection with convoys and handling troops and stores, and routine duties went by the board.

Malta's provost company did not survive the repeated bombings unscathed. In March, 1941, their barracks were destroyed by an enemy mine. One N.C.O. was killed and several wounded. Further billets were occupied adjacent to the Royal Naval picquet-house, but subsequent enemy action caused a second move. Later in the year another N.C.O. died following enemy action, and about the same time the company's billets were damaged and partially demolished, fortunately without casualties.

*   *   *   *   *

South Africa

"I WISH to state emphatically that never in the history of the Provost Service can such a small number of military police have had to handle such colossal numbers of troops or to operate in such a vast area in a country in which, owing to the political situation, the duties of British military police were so difficult."

This claim, taken from a report in 1943, appears after a study of the facts to be justified, for provost in South Africa had a difficult task.

Owing to more urgent demands from operational commands, South Africa had to cope with huge numbers of East-bound troops in transit with but a handful of policemen. In December, 1940, one officer and his detachment of ten M.Ps. disembarked at Durban to face the duty of policing South Africa! They were stationed at Natal Command H.Q. in Durban and remained there throughout the war.

The difficulties experienced by the detachment are easy to imagine when it is realized that they had to handle convoys of anything up to 40,000 strong. Beginning early in 1941 as a trickle and growing into a steady flow in 1942, troops from the United Kingdom bound for India and the Far East frequently hit Durban in their thousands and really let themselves go.

The transformation from blitzed, blacked-out Britain to care-free Durban, with its night lights and freedom from licensing restrictions, not unnaturally proved too much for many of the troops, whose behaviour was frequently exuberant and riotous at slight provocation. After being cooped up on overcrowded troopships for five or six weeks there is little wonder that Durban and its military police braced themselves for each successive "assault landing" and heaved a sigh of relief when the convoys sailed again!

There was also in existence in Durban a South African provost company with which the small C.M.P. detachment worked in close contact, but they would prefer no charge against Imperial soldiers. Thus it became necessary to call in the assistance of personnel from visiting convoys to help with the picqueting of Durban.

Thirsty troops landed to find bars open continuously from 10 a.m. to 11.30 p.m. Drinks of all kinds were to be had, and if thirsts were not slaked by 11.30 p.m. there were dozens of night clubs which would oblige at fancy prices. Shore leave would be granted from noon until midnight, and the first calls to attend drunks would begin at about 2 p.m. and continue without interruption often until 3 or 4 a.m. All provost could do was to remove offenders as quickly and quietly as possible from the eye of an openly-critical population. One evening no less than 63 incapable drunks were detained at one police station awaiting transport to their ships. During each convoy's stay of approximately five days the party of ten military policemen snatched sleep as and when they could. Nor were they able to relax as the ships sailed, for then began the round-up of absentees and deserters who had intentionally or otherwise missed their ships. To add to the difficulties military police were misused by being ordered away as escorts to absentees apprehended by the civil authorities as far apart as the border of Portuguese East Africa and the western extremes of the Cape Province. The arrival of a new convoy often found the Durban detachment thus depleted.

Another flagrant waste of men trained to a specialist duty occurred when a detention "section" for absentees and deserters was opened in February, 1941, and handed over to provost to guard.

Following repeated pleas for reinforcements, ten further military police arrived in January, 1942, with instructions to establish a detachment at Cape Town. An officer and eight men went to the Cape, the remaining two reinforcing the Durban contingent. In July of the same year 42 more N.C.Os. arrived, 14 of whom were posted to Cape Town. By 1942 Provost were being assisted in another way. Durban was no longer the gay town of 1941. Its lights were blacked-out and licensed hours restricted, a welcome though belated respite. Moreover, convoys were decidedly smaller and visits shorter.

An ever-present problem was the colour bar—very strong in South Africa and little understood by visiting Europeans. A constant look-out for infringements, mostly in the form of fraternization or intimate relations with native women, had to be maintained, for political repercussions were often considerable. Patrols amongst the unlicensed brothel areas where shady and dangerous gambling dens abounded were another responsibility.

Pietermaritzburg, fifty-five miles from Durban, had usually from 4,000 to 5,000 hospital and convalescent troops, and parties of provost were sent there when possible.

*   *   *   *   *

West Africa

WHEN, as a result of the virtual closure to our shipping of the Mediterranean, the West Coast of Africa became a halting point for the Middle East, dock and disciplinary duties called for adequate military police personnel. Thus, on 16th January, 1942, there came into being the Corps of West African Military Police.

At first sections were established in Nigeria, Gold Coast and Sierra Leone, but later Gambia received a section, and five railway sections were formed. In addition, Sierra Leone had a section of military police and two sections were sent to Burma with 81st and 82nd West African Divisions.

It was found, however, that the West African could be developed into a useful policeman provided the material was carefully chosen from trained soldiers, that care and patience were exercised over a training period of at least four months, and that he was well led both during this training period and on being posted. Finally, if best results were to be obtained, good, well-seasoned European N.C.Os. were essential both as instructors and as section sergeants. Apart from the two divisional companies mentioned earlier, the role of West African Provost was static, main duties being general discipline, patrols and supervising docks. The European population was a floating one, for large transit camps were constantly being filled and emptied.

Crime amongst European troops was comparatively infrequent, but amongst African troops it was fairly high and covered a wide field. Thefts involving literate Africans were quite well organized, suggesting European co-operation. A high proportion of crimes against W.D. property involved a civilian element. Most of the receivers were Syrians or African civilians, who were found to be responsible for many of the burglaries in Army messes and living quarters. Many cases of assault on European soldiers occurred after dark, particularly in the Sierra Leone area, where pimps and pick-pockets abounded.

To combat the wave of theft in Service lines, units were encouraged to send selected Africans to C.M.P. H.Q. for a basic police training course.

Organized thefts in dock areas led to the appointment of a D.A.P.M. (Docks), responsible for Sierra Leone, to the attachment of S.I.B. personnel and to joint action by civil and military police. Motor-boat patrols protected ships and lighters from water-borne thieves and military police were detailed for duty aboard ships during discharging and loading. Within twelve months organized theft was thus reduced to petty pilferage.

Civil and military police always worked in close accord, a liaison which was materially assisted by the fact that many African units served with the colonial police before the war. In Sierra Leone all C.M.P. personnel were sworn in as special constables.

It was not until 1945 that S.I.B. became established in West Africa, but there was still plenty of work to occupy a larger section than that provided.

CHAPTER X

THE SPECIAL INVESTIGATION BRANCH

THE advance units of the British Expeditionary Force landed in France on 9th September, 1939, and from that day stores of every description began to pour into France.

To deal with the off-loading of these stores at ports, their formation into dumps and depots and their subsequent distribution, an ever-growing number of men were needed.

The presence of so many attractive stores in often inadequately guarded docks, dumps and depots was accepted by some dishonest soldiers as an invitation to help themselves.

The professional thieves soon established contacts with local receivers, and the French police, already overburdened with work caused by the war, had little time to spare for the affairs of their allies. Then there were many cases of younger soldiers, finding the French drinks attractive and cheap, who over-indulged with the result that there were many reports of assaults, wounding and sexual crimes.

In Rennes, with a civilian population of 125,000, there were approximately 6,000 troops. Yet the crimes recorded between 11th and 28th October, 1939, included a smash and grab raid on a jeweller's shop with watches and jewellery valued at 80,000 francs stolen; four cases of driving away civilian cars (one being the official car of the local French police); one case of housebreaking; two cases of robbery with violence; six cases of larceny; and fifteen other serious cases of assaults, damage and fraud.

In Nantes, where there were 13,000 soldiers (mostly labour companies), the following crimes, alleged to have been committed by our troops, were reported between 30th November, 1939, and 16th December, 1939: one suspicious death of a soldier, three cases of breaking and entering, twenty cases of theft, five cases of car stealing and eight cases of assault. From these statistics recorded in only two cities it will be appreciated how serious the situation was becoming. Nantes, Brest and St. Nazaire were suffering particularly badly from shipping thefts, and property which successfully survived the depredations there was being looted while in transit to its destination. Vehicles were arriving in the forward areas stripped of batteries, tool-kits and essential spares, and it appeared that they had been looted by the convoy guards or by the local population when in transit by rail. N.A.A.F.I. stores suffered very badly.

The French Gendarmerie, harassed by overwork were unable to give much assistance and turned to unit commanders for help, who, with the best will in the world, were unable to do much; and the French police, discouraged at finding no one with whom they could collaborate, took little or no action to solve the crimes. The few cases that were successfully concluded from an investigation point of view were handed to officers for disciplinary proceedings, but, because of the inexperience and lack of knowledge of military law of many of them, many cases were so hopelessly prepared that the Judge Advocate General's department had no alternative but to recommend that proceedings be dropped.

This, then, was the position when, in late November, 1939, the War Office asked for the help of the Metropolitan Police. The then Commissioner of Police of the Metropolis, Sir Philip Game, directed Chief Inspector Hatherill to go to France and make an appreciation of the situation. Accompanied by Colonel Kennedy, Provost Marshal B.E.F., and Detective Constable Nicholls, Chief Inspector Hatherill made a comprehensive tour of France which involved visits to docks, depots and the L. of C. and forward areas. Notes were made of specific cases of crime, together with the steps taken by the French police to combat them; and, on his return to London, Mr. Hatherill submitted his report recommending the formation of an army C.I.D. to work in conjunction with the French police.

This was a somewhat radical suggestion; but it was seen that it was necessary, and that, if such a unit was raised, it must come under the control of the Provost Marshal as the officer responsible for the maintenance of discipline in the field. It was, therefore, natural that such a unit should be a part of the Corps of Military Police, working with and receiving much of its information from them, exactly as in any modern civil police force.

A War Establishment was drawn up and entitled "An Investigation Section of the Corps of Military Police," which allowed for 1 major (A.P.M.), 1 staff lieutenant, 6 lieutenants (investigating officers), 6 W.Os.II (investigators) and 45 sergeants (investigators). In January, 1940, the Commissioner of Police of the Metropolis was asked to release the requisite personnel. It was in no way because of lack of co-operation, but because of the many new duties which the war thrust upon the civil police, that at first he could only release 19 detectives of various ranks, all of whom had volunteered on learning of the proposed formation of the section. Of these, 7 were granted immediate emergency commissions and the remaining 12, after attestation, received immediate promotion—6 to the rank of W.O.II and 6 to sergeant.

On 12th February, 1940, the party under command of their A.P.M.—Major C. E. Campion, who had been the detective superintendent in charge of the Criminal Record Office at New Scotland Yard—left for the C.M.P. Depot and Training Establishment, at Mytchett, Aldershot, to undergo a short course before embarking for overseas. Fortunately for them, certain sections of the Army Act form part of the training of civil police C.I.D. and, so far as law and its application were concerned, it was only necessary for them to "get down" to King's Regulations, Rules of Procedure and Court-Martial procedure. Structure of the Army, chain of command, channels of communication, foot-drill, small-arms instruction and the army systems of indent, issue and accounting were all duly absorbed in so far as the limited time available allowed, and on 28th February, 1940, the section, with its stores, embarked at Southampton, to disembark at Le Havre on 29th February, 1940.

On their arrival in France, their small number was increased by one officer, Captain Attfield, also a member of Scotland Yard, who assumed duty as administrative officer to A.P.M. at G.H.Q. At Le Mans the section divided itself, one officer, one W.O. and one sergeant going to each of certain prearranged towns. Lieutenant Dibbens took his two O.Rs. to Brest, Lieutenant Ellis to Nantes, Lieutenant Elliott to Rennes, Lieutenant Hooper to Le Mans, Lieutenant James to Dieppe and Lieutenant West to 1 Corps. Here they were welcomed by the respective A.P.Ms. of these towns and were given every help and facility to begin their work.

In the provost companies already in France were a number of civil police reservists, recalled to the Colours, and some of these were selected for attachment to the detachments of the Investigation Section. These detachments of S.I.B. were received with mixed feelings among the various units of the army. Some C.Os. saw a possible source of interference with their maintenance of discipline within their units, others saw in the Branch the possible precursor of an army Gestapo, but by most they were welcomed. As soon as they started their work it was found an easy matter to dispose of mistrust about their aims, and the majority of their successfully completed cases owed much to the co-operation of C.Os.

Every type of crime was dealt with, from murder downwards, and they soon found that they had not much spare time. Lieutenant Ellis quickly found himself involved in stamping out a large-scale racket in connection with N.A.A.F.I. stores, Lieutenant Dibbens found so much work in the docks at Brest that he never seemed away from them, and Lieutenant Elliott and the others were equally fully occupied in their respective districts.

Then came the invasion by the enemy of the Low Countries and, with the consequent re-grouping of the corps and divisions and their advance, it became impossible to carry out investigations. The enemy's success grew, and finally all S.I.B. personnel found themselves absorbed into provost companies for traffic and refugee control duties.

On the evening of 19th May, 1940, during an enemy air raid on Rear H.Q., which was then at Boulogne, Major Campion was wounded in the head by bullets from a low-flying aircraft and died the following day from his injuries. As the enemy's advance increased, all S.I.B. finally withdrew to embarkation points and returned safely to United Kingdom.

After the evacuation of France the S.I.B. personnel were not employed on investigation duties and there was much discussion as to whether they would be released from the Army to return to their respective police forces. It seemed that the United Kingdom was the one place in the world where S.I.B. were unnecessary in view of the fact that the country was adequately covered by efficient civil police forces. After further discussion, however, it was decided to post the remaining 18 of the 19 members who had crossed to France, in their original groups of 3 (1 lieutenant, 1 W.O. and 1 sergeant) to the six Commands.

At first their help was sought only in cases where continuation of inquiries from a military point of view was required, but gradually, as confidence in the S.I.B. was established and war-time legislation was introduced and laid specific duties and authority on members of the Forces on duty in uniform, more and more inquiries were handed over in their entirety to S.I.B.

In December, 1940, Lieutenant Elliott left Southern Command and United Kingdom to take a few men to the Middle East to assist in the formation of S.I.B. there, and his place was taken by 2/Lieutenant Good. It was about this time that inquiries were started in Northern Ireland and Scottish Command into what proved to be the biggest fraud investigated by the branch up to that date.

Interception of a peculiarly worded signal to Belfast from Scotland led to inquiries into a set of circumstances which revealed large-scale corruption and fraud in connection with conservancy contracts. Ellis and his men in Belfast spent long months carefully building up their case, all the time maintaining close liaison with James in Scotland. The inquiries were finally completed and, in conjunction with the Royal Ulster Constabulary and the Scottish police, S.I.B. in both countries arrested some soldiers and civilians. Some civilians, two or three officers and several O.Rs. received heavy sentences before the respective civil and military courts, upwards of £3,000 in cash was recovered and credited to the public, and an annual fraud of over £30,000 against the Government was prevented.

Eire's neutrality created a further problem and it was ultimately found necessary to form a special detachment of the military police, composed of "Redcaps" and S.I.B. detectives, to patrol the frontier and deal with crimes committed in that region. Excellent liaison existed with the Garda Siochana and, within the limits possible between a belligerent and a neutral country, every help was given.

Food and petrol rationing regulations were beginning at this time to become more stringent and there was a large increase in cases of theft of rationed commodities. In spite of the addition of a substance which changed the colour of the petrol, there were plenty of people prepared to steal it and plenty of motorists prepared to buy and use it. Many were the subterfuges used to avoid detection. One motor-cyclist, long suspected of improper use of W.D. petrol, was finally thoroughly searched by S.I.B., who found that though the petrol tank of the machine was filled with ordinary petrol, two flat cans of W.D. petrol were concealed in an anti-gas respirator carried in the "alert" position and a pipe led therefrom to the carburettor of the machine. Other motorists cut out the petrol pump on their cars and fed the carburettor by gravity from cans of W.D. petrol concealed under the bonnet of the cars.

In the summer of 1941, after the formation of South-Eastern Command, Lieutenant West—who had recently been transferred there—and his men cleaned up a very large-scale conspiracy involving the forgery of indents for civilian transport and conspiracy between certain R.A.S.C. personnel and civilians. After protracted inquiries a suitable crop of courts-martial and civil police court proceedings followed and some heavy sentences were awarded to the offenders. A final assessment of the amount involved in these dishonest practices was around £40,000.

It was in May, 1941, that the first big draft of reinforcements assembled at the C.M.P. Depot at Mytchett to go to M.E.F. After some two months at the Depot, they sailed towards the end of July for Suez. Included among them were many who were to achieve field rank, and their journeyings and subsequent story is told in the portion of this history devoted to S.I.B. in the M.E.L.F. Thereafter, up to the end of the war there was a constant intake into the Branch to meet reinforcement demands from overseas theatres and commands.

The establishment of an S.I.B. section in the early summer of 1941 was 1 lieutenant, 1 C.S.M., 8 sergeants and 2 corporals, and it so remained until March, 1942, when it was increased by 1 C.S.M. and 4 sergeants and reduced by 2 corporals. In August, 1942, a further increase of the War Establishment was authorized, allowing an additional officer, a captain, but increasing commitments called for a further review of the War Establishment, and in January, 1943, it was again increased (for sections in the U.K.) to the strength per section at which it remained to the end of the war, *i.e.*, 1 captain, 2 lieutenants, 1 R.S.M., 2 C.S.Ms., 20 sergeants and 2 corporals.

To deal with the training of recruits to the Branch, in March, 1942, Captain Ellis was transferred from Belfast to the C.M.P. Depot, where he formed an S.I.B. Training Wing. At first, this catered for an extremely short course of instruction, which was really designed to test a recruit's claim to have knowledge of C.I.D. duties. These courses were later extended in time and scope and continue to the present day. "Refresher" and "Advanced" courses were also begun and Captain Ellis and R.S.M. Wilsdon remained as instructors until their departure for North Africa.

In 1945 alone, the S.I.B. in the U.K. were responsible in all commands for 6,727 investigations, 4,277 arrests and the recovery of W.D. property to the value of £68,695. These figures take no account of potential loss prevented by the breaking up of conspiracies, frauds and cases of corruption.

The names of the hundreds of investigators who worked with S.I.B. in United Kingdom during the war years obviously cannot be mentioned individually, but, wherever they may now be, they can look back on the knowledge of a good job well done and the fact that they were among the "founder-members" of what the Army Council has now approved as a permanent branch of the military police—the Special Investigation Branch.

An S.I.B. section landed in Algiers in November, 1942, under the command of Captain W. Heddon. The demands on S.I.B. services were heavy and the need for early expansion soon became evident.

By March, 1943, five sections were operating in North Africa and H.Q. S.I.B. was formed, consisting of 1 D.A.P.M. (Captain Heddon) and 5 N.C.Os. or Warrant Officers.

By June, 1944, Captain Heddon had become the D.P.M. S.I.B., and the number of sections had grown from five to thirteen and was operating throughout North Africa, Sicily and Italy, and an average of 2,000 arrests were being made each month. An additional section was formed early in 1945 and used solely to counter the high incidence of theft of W.D. stores on railways.

The war against theft of W.D. arms, equipment and stores in Italy involved operations against armed bands of Italians and deserters from the Allied Armies.

In the different countries in which S.I.B. were employed they had to learn something of the complicated local police systems, and, since the occupation of Italy and Sicily, Allied Military Government proclamations, courts, law and procedure. The armies of the Central Mediterranean theatre contained a greater variety of races and creeds than any other major theatre in the world. In dealing also with the Allied, Dominion and Colonial troops with their different morals, customs and languages, many new problems called for solution by the police.

Available records show that the total number of cases investigated by the S.I.B. during the campaign was 22,809 resulting in the arrest of 38,257 soldiers and civilians. The value of W.D. property recovered was enormous.

Lieut.-Colonel W. Heddon directed S.I.B. affairs with marked success from the beginning to the end of the campaign.

Captain H. P. Clarke and Captain W. H. Cooper, who led operations against Italian gangsters in Southern Italy, and Captain Archer was responsible for dealing with serious crime in the Rome area, a formidable task which he carried out with success.

In addition to the prevention, detection and investigation of serious crime of all kinds, the S.I.B. were called in at the latter end of 1944 to investigate alleged war crimes, and two special sections were raised for this purpose.

The scope of these investigations widened rapidly and the operations of these sections covered 1,100 miles of territory. This sphere of investigation had been allotted to the S.I.B. as there was no other organization capable of undertaking the work. There is no doubt, however, that the assumption of these extra and very heavy responsibilities by the already strained S.I.B. machine seriously affected the efficiency of the work of dealing with serious crime.

★　　★　　★　　★　　★

THE work of S.I.B. in North-West Europe was so vast that it is not possible to do more than give a brief outline of its activities and some statistics.

The first section to land was under command of Lieutenant Fawcett, formerly of the Isle of Wight Constabulary. This section landed on the Normandy beaches on D+2.

It would be dishonest to exclude from this history the fact that almost the first case investigated by Lieutenant Fawcett's section involved military policemen. A member of a provost company was found to have stolen 18,000 francs from a German prisoner committed to his charge for escort. He was tried by court-martial and sentenced to 18 months' imprisonment. Almost immediately afterwards S.I.B. discovered that larceny from prisoners of war was taking place at one of the P.W. camps. A search disclosed that nearly every member of the vulnerable point police guard was in possession of articles of property taken from prisoners. The N.C.Os. were court-martialled and the private soldiers warned. The case, which received widespread publicity throughout the theatre, had a salutary effect and there were no further cases of that nature.

With Second Army headquarters was Captain Frank Pollard

and his section. This officer gave service of the highest order throughout the campaign and later became Assistant Provost Marshal S.I.B. at H.Q., 21 Army Group.

As the theatre of operations and the area of liberated country increased, a ready black market offering attractive prices for goods was soon in full swing, but its prosperity was often short-lived through the attentions of the S.I.B.

To counteract this threat a total of 15 sections, each section consisting of 1 captain, 1 lieutenant, 2 warrant officers and 12 other ranks per section, were in operation and hundreds of thousands of pounds' worth of Army stores were recovered.

Towards the end of the war the number of crimes involving the sale of military property in the French and Belgian black markets became so great that additional S.I.B. sections had to be sent out from England. Even with these reinforcements it was never possible to catch up with the arrears of work. S.I.B. officers and N.C.Os. worked to the limit of their endurance, but there would have been ample employment for ten times their number.

The following figures compiled for the campaign up to 31st March, 1945, of the North-West Europe theatre of war indicate what they achieved:

Arrests			Property recovered (value)		
Military ...	...	... 2,335	War Dept. ...	...	£134,827
Merchant Navy ...		... 123	Allied ...	...	£18,150
Allied Forces	...	... 129	Enemy ...	...	£194,834
Civilians ...	...	... 5,288	Civilians ...	...	£36,753
	TOTAL	7,875 persons		TOTAL	£384,564

The following figures show the total cases reported to and completed by the S.I.B. up to the same date. These figures include both military and civilian offenders; but as in many cases both were involved, it is not practicable to separate civil from military crimes in these statistics.

	Cases reported	Cases completed
Larceny, fraud, etc.	1,531	1,222
Looting	152	122
Receiving, etc.	3,431	3,395
Breaking offences	110	64
Murder, assault, robbery with violence, etc.	141	113
Rape, indecency, etc.	112	91
Miscellaneous	927	873
	6,404	5,880

In addition to their ordinary duties of the detection of crime, S.I.B. personnel were often called upon to undertake extraordinary tasks. Much of the credit for the successful trial and conviction of Kramer, "The Beast of Belsen," and his subordinates should go to

Major Pollard, Captain A. J. Fox and C.S.M. Liddle of the S.I.B., who were sent to the concentration camp to select witnesses and take statements of evidence concerning atrocities.

★   ★   ★   ★   ★

WITH the increase of number of troops in Egypt and Palestine, following the entry of Italy into the war, crime increased proportionately. Conscription had brought into the army a percentage of soldiers with criminal antecedents or tendencies. Many of these were drafted to the Middle East.

By September, 1940, there was no S.I.B. and, indeed, pitifully few provost in the theatre, but there was an ever-growing incidence of crime which was causing some concern to the staffs of all three Services. S.I.B. help was requested and Lieutenant F. Elliott was directed to join a draft for Middle East, taking with him a C.S.M. and four sergeants of the Branch.

On arrival in Egypt they found that a number of soldiers had decided that the delights of Cairo and Alexandria were infinitely preferable to the monotony, discomforts and dangers of the Western Desert and East African campaigns. These deserters combined to form troublesome and dangerous gangs which were to become very familiar to the Branch under the names of "The Free British Corps" and "The Dead End Kids."

Before the arrival of this section, however, the Provost Marshal, Colonel F. Bryant, selected Captain Harper to organize a local S.I.B. force. Captain Harper formed his headquarters at Bab-el-Hadid Barracks in Cairo and, at first, concentrated his efforts in that city and on the Suez Canal. But with the arrival of the sections from England new detachments were opened.

Not a day passed without many arrests being made. Most of them were for larceny and many were items of only a few shillings in value. In the docks and on the railways incalculable harm was being done to the war effort by the wholesale thieving by the natives. Railway employees marked wagons loaded with attractive stores and failed to seal them properly and thus ensured that the heavily overloaded trains, travelling at little more than walking pace, were looted before arrival at their destination.

In July, 1941, the detachment in Canal North recovered two aeroplane engines which had been stolen from the train by being pushed off flat cars, levered into position near some sand dunes and then covered in sand.

In spite of a small, steady flow of recruits to the Branch, its numbers remained woefully inadequate. However, further reinforcements were *en route* from England, and on 20th September, 1941, everyone was relieved to see the arrival at Suez of Lieutenant Dib-

N

bens with half a dozen subalterns—Lieutenants Thrift, Crocker and Nicholls among them.

At the close of 1941 there was one section working in Cairo; one in Alexandria, which performed anything required of them in the Western Desert; one in Canal Area working from Port Said in the north to Safarga on the Red Sea southwards and to Zagazig and Damanhour in the Delta; one in Palestine with its commitments in the Levant; and small detachments in Cyprus, Sudan, and Eritrea.

One of the biggest worries of the S.I.B. remained with them until the last day of the war, in spite of hundreds of arrests and convictions. Most Arabs regard the possession of a firearm as the sign of manhood. The Jews in Palestine were anxious to obtain all the firearms possible and so were numerous other parties, some subversive, some patriotic, in the Middle East. Gangs of rifle thieves operated on the troop trains, others entered camps at night. Some gangs concentrated on raiding dumps for arms and ammunition, others relied on the carelessness of soldiers and waited for the rifle to be leaned against a wall and the soldier to turn his back for a moment. The number of thefts of arms of all types and ammunition was appalling, and "The Dead End Kids" were responsible for many of them. These deserters lived by becoming friendly with soldiers they met, getting themselves invited to a canteen or some place in a unit lines, and then taking advantage of opportunity to steal whatever they could lay their hands upon.

Tel-el-Kebir, where there was one of the largest Ordnance depots of the Middle East, remained a problem all through the war. Fullest advantage was taken of the decree of the Egyptian Government permitting the use of firearms in the protection of W.D. property, and a large number of would-be thieves were shot and killed by S.I.B., as well as by unit guards.

Drug-running was another crime which was beginning to reach alarming proportions. Hashish and opium were the main drugs. These have always been the curse of Egypt, but the Lebanese authorities have always tolerated the growing of the hemp plant and were loath to destroy crops. The Egyptian Government retaliated by training a first-class anti-narcotics organization, which co-operated closely with the Palestine Police. By this means the trade had been cut down considerably by the outbreak of war.

The answer of the drug-runners was to use W.D. vehicles and drivers who were immune from search by the Egyptian Police at the frontiers. Profits from the sale of the drugs were high and the smugglers were able to offer high rewards to any soldier who was prepared to risk being caught. Numberless cases were successfully dealt with by the S.I.B., but right up to the end of the war the smugglers always found some soldier who could be corrupted by promise of large rewards for consignments successfully delivered.

With the victory at Alamein and the advance into the desert it became necessary to extend the Alexandria and Western Desert section. By mid-November detachments had been placed at Daba, Mersa Matruh, Sollum and Tobruk. It also became necessary to open detachments in the Delta to intercept the loads of captured enemy stores which were being stolen and brought by camel into the Delta. Ultimately, the Alexandria section withdrew to the frontier at Sollum and a new section was formed under Major Crocker to perform duties in Libya.

Lieutenant Good—one of the officers who had arrived in September, 1941—had opened a small detachment in Baghdad. His health suffered and he was transferred to Cyprus, his place being taken by Lieutenant K. Thrift, who was to remain there in charge of the destinies of S.I.B. in Persia and Iraq, both during the time that these two countries were included in Middle East Command and when they came under Paiforce.

Thefts continued wholesale on an alarming scale. At the various ports and wharves everything capable of being stolen was fair game for the natives. Much of the unloading of vessels was done by lighters, and cases of foodstuffs and other marketable commodities were pushed into the water, later to be retrieved by gangs of thieves who had gone into partnership with "bum-boatmen." So high became the incidence of thefts carried out by these water-borne rascals that S.I.B. in port areas were allocated launches, and these were operated with a marked degree of success until the end of the war at Suez, Ataka, Port Said and Alexandria.

Many contracts were entered into between the Army and local contractors for the supply of items which could be produced locally, thereby saving valuable shipping space. There were many abuses and convictions were obtained against soldiers who had succumbed to the temptation to accept a sum of money for merely turning a blind eye to the contractors' deficiency in quantity, quality or both.

A new section had also been formed in the Levant States— Syria and Lebanon—and was very fully occupied. These countries are very poor and the native thieves found a market for all types of W.D. stores, especially motor vehicles and tyres. H.Q., Ninth Army had a large number of troops under command to resist any attempt by the enemy to breach the neutrality of Turkey. Air strips and roads were being built or improved, largely by local contractors under R.E. supervision, and many abuses of specifications and quality of materials were uncovered.

One bad case concerned the building of a road which, had the Germans attacked through Turkey, would have been of great importance. The R.E. officer who was supervising the local contractor received gifts of money and valuable jewellery to pass inferior work on the road. When the offence was brought to light it was found that instead of being a good, hard-core built road it was little more than a strip of tar sprayed on the desert and would scarcely have supported a motor-car, much less tanks and their transporters.

In Alexandria, a gang of deserters were making a lucrative business of stealing motor lorries, driving them to Alexandria Docks and, by means of forged gate passes, work tickets and movement orders, loading up with attractive stores and taking them to the Lebanon. Here the goods were sold with the connivance of a member of the Lebanese Chamber of Deputies and the proceeds invested in hashish, which was loaded into four-gallon petrol tins and sealed and transported to Egypt, where it was sold at an enormous profit. When the ringleaders were finally arrested they were occupying a magnificent villa at Sidi Bishr, possessed a houseful of expensive furniture and two or three cars. Tins of hashish were found buried in the garden and currency notes to the value of several thousand pounds were hidden throughout the villa.

Shortly after the arrests a civilian lorry was seen by S.I.B. carrying mild steel bars of the type used in reinforcing concrete and which were unobtainable on the civilian market. It was followed and inquiries showed that large quantities of such steel had been stolen from various R.E. dumps and sold to various civilian contractors for constructing houses. The case became more and more complicated and almost caused an Egyptian Government crisis, due to the high social positions of some of the people involved. During the inquiries a large quantity of naval stores were recovered and the total "bag" of prisoners amounted to over fifty.

During the Cairo Conference of Mr. Churchill and Mr. Roosevelt, held at Mena House Hotel, S.I.B. were selected to arrange for the security of the perimeter of the building and to escort the principals. Although slightly outside the normal scope of S.I.B. duties, everything went off so well as to earn commendations from Army and diplomatic authorities.

★   ★   ★   ★   ★

THE suggestion that an S.I.B. should be formed for India received the approval of the War Office in the early autumn of 1943, and by 20th November, 1943, two sections of S.I.B. of the C.M.P. (India) had been formed and were allotted to Eastern Command and Southern Army. Early in 1944 Major Ellis transferred from Italy and became the first D.P.M., S.I.B., India, under Brigadier F. Forbes. A few members of the Branch were transferred to India from the Middle East and, with these and the two sections already raised in India, S.I.B. began to expand until there was a section or detachment in all principal towns and districts.

Records show that during 1944 2,557 cases were investigated, 3,112 arrests were made and property to the value of £786,500 was recovered.

The S.I.B. were highly and efficiently organized. A *Police Gazette* parallel in every way to that of New Scotland Yard, was circulated to all Indian Civil Police Forces, heads of various services and Provost and Intelligence sections, British, Indian, and Allied, throughout the theatre. The S.I.B. Training Establishment, which was situated within the C.M.P. (1) Training Centre and Depot at Secunderabad, was well established, and the chief instructor, in order to facilitate the instruction of S.I.B. personnel in Indian law and police methods, attended and successfully passed the examination of the Police Training College in the United Provinces.

Almost one of the first cases dealt with by S.I.B. India was that of the discovery of a fraud which involved civilian contractors and a major of the Indian Engineers. Bogus claims for payment (some of which were paid by the Burma Government) were submitted by the civilian contractors and passed by the major who was acting as D.C.R.E. Protracted inquiries by Lieut.-Colonel Ellis, Major Beck and R.S.M. Flynn, in conjunction with the civil C.I.D., resulted in sufficient evidence being obtained to warrant the arrest of the officer and certain civilians. The officer was traced to Imphal, which at that time was besieged by the Japanese and unapproachable except by air. A special plane therefore was chartered and an officer of the S.I.B. flew over Japanese-held territory into Imphal; the officer was arrested and brought back to India by the same means. The civil police arrested 25 contractors, and £300,000 was recovered for the Government of Burma. Another *cause célèbre* about this time was that of the arrest of an assistant military secretary in G.H.Q. India who, being responsible for postings of all officers of the R.I.A.S.C., was accepting bribes from officers anxious to avoid overseas service. They received improper postings, and the result of this case was that five officers were cashiered and several others received lesser punishments.

After the Bombay explosion, when considerable gold bullion was blown up and lost, S.I.B. patiently followed up many rumours and anonymous letters and succeeded after four months in recovering seven bars of gold, to the value of Rs.670,000, and these were safely returned to the reserve, Bank of India.

India, throughout its turbulent history, has had the reputation of being a country where fraud and corruption are rife, and the war seemed to worsen the country's reputation. A conspiracy at Dum Dum airport lead to the arrest of two officers and nineteen others for conspiracies to defraud the Government in connection with forged and fictitious muster rolls for coolie labour. More than six months' investigation revealed a large conversion of Government money. At the same time that this inquiry was proceeding the section was also engaged with the civil police in inquiries into the black marketing of medical supplies and drugs. Ultimately forty persons were arrested and German and Italian drugs, then practically unobtainable, to the value of Rs.229,000 were recovered.

Cases of dacoity were an ever-present menace to lonely British troops, and after a large number of reports of such cases, a group of S.I.B. N.C.Os. were struck off other duties specially to deal with this menace. After weeks of patient observation the time was considered ripe to act, and C.S.M. Allen of 117 Section bravely volunteered to act as a decoy. The trap was successful and four dacoits were arrested and later found to have been responsible for twenty-three such cases. Sergeant Clarke of 116 Section was similarly engaged about this time, and with some of his comrades finally rounded up nine native armed robbers who had for some time been operating in and around Ranchi.

★   ★   ★   ★   ★

The value of investigation cannot be measured by the value of the goods recovered. Many crimes are not committed because of the deterrent effect of the known presence of detectives in the Army. Many serious crimes adversely affecting discipline and morale, such as rape, murder, arson, in which there is no monetary object, are investigated.

★   ★   ★   ★   ★

THROUGHOUT the war, both in the United Kingdom and Overseas, criminals, black-marketeers and receivers developed remarkable skill in getting their spoils through the network of checks and guards, and in disposing of them.

Commanders everywhere recognized that only the ability of the S.I.B. prevented this type of crime getting out of hand.

Several crimes were exposed simply because a member of the S.I.B. spotted a small incongruity which would have escaped the notice of a less highly trained observer.

The S.I.B. were about the hardest-worked people in the Army; often nothing but their enthusiasm kept them going, and nothing short of great efficiency could have produced such good results.

Their duties, not infrequently, included the interrogation of senior officers, sometimes as potential offenders. That the S.I.B. did this with tact and persistence and without fear or favour is a high tribute to the value and integrity of these fine investigators.

CHAPTER XI

THE DEPOTS : PORTS POLICE : A.T.S. PROVOST

THE DEPOTS

TO understand the importance of the Depot at Mytchett and the subsidiary Depots during the Second World War it is necessary to appreciate three things:

Firstly, that the provost service should be able to rely upon a high and steady standard of basic training in reinforcements, who, on joining military police units, were at once fully employed under active service conditions in the U.K. and overseas.

Secondly, that this standard must satisfy, not only the Corps, but also the rest of the army, who for many years had looked to the military police to set an example in dress and conduct.

And thirdly, the unique responsibility of lower ranks in the Corps; the lance-corporal in the "Redcaps," the private in the traffic control and vulnerable point companies. In turn-out and discipline these men had to set an example to all; on duty they had to act, often single-handed, with cool judgment when harassed on the traffic routes, with discretion and determination when enforcing orders or discipline. In all this they had to deal tactfully and incorruptibly with officers and N.C.Os. of every rank. No other arm or service in the army, save perhaps the Commandos, thrust a comparable responsibility upon single soldiers of the lowest ranks.

During the courses, shortened to three months by the exigencies of war, and without the means of extensive field training, the Depot was not expected to turn out the finished article; that was the subsequent job of units. The Depot's task was similar to that of a steelworks, which takes in selected and graded raw material, works upon it to eliminate faults and impurities, and supplies the manufacturer with well-tempered and high-grade metal from which the finished article may be produced.

The business of the Depot, therefore, was to ensure an exemplary level of drill, turn-out, and deportment; a solid knowledge of police powers and duties, report-making and the rules of evidence, etc.; first-class motor-cycle riding; the all-important role of helpfulness; and, finally, that all reinforcements should leave the Depot with that high morale which comes from self-confidence and self-respect.

To produce these results a Depot of an unusual character was needed. Alongside good organization and sound instruction it was essential to create an "atmosphere." The tone and character of any institution is invariably set from the top. The Corps owes a special debt to the leadership of Lieut.-Colonel Sykes, Commandant at Mytchett from January, 1941, to July, 1942, and to the no less solid and vigorous qualities of his successor, Lieut.-Colonel F. Wright.

But although the chief credit for the work of the Depot must go to these two officers, the support they received from a first-class staff must not pass unrecorded. It is perhaps invidious to single out names from so many fine officers and N.C.Os.; but space should at least be found to mention Major Norman, Major Reynard, Major Chiesman and R.S.M. Curtis (later to become D.A.P.M., 12 Corps, 21 Army Group).

Tribute should also be paid to the work of the Command Depots, who, as will be seen later, acting in relief of Mytchett, successfully copied the example of the mother-Depot.

At the outbreak of war the Provost Marshal was faced with two problems: Recruiting and training. Provision for expansion of the army had already been made, but not for the highly qualified and highly trained men to police it. Immediate steps had therefore to be taken to find the right men and to train them.

To meet the first requirement an officer (Captain Reah) with the appointment of D.A.P.M. was appointed and instructed to obtain recruits on a volunteer basis; a task which he discharged throughout the war with conspicuous success. His duty was to fill the new training establishments with a steady flow of volunteers; his equipment was an office, a clerk and a motor-car. He had authority to interview every recruiting officer in the country and to employ whatever publicity, in the way of poster and newspaper advertising, that the Public Relations branch of the War Office thought proper.

It was soon clear that potential military policemen could be found all over the country. Volunteers poured in, but where were they to be trained? Mytchett Hutments, Ash Vale, the peace-time Depot and Training Establishment, was inadequate from the point of view of training large numbers—geographically it was badly placed. With busy recruiting centres such as Manchester, Liverpool and Leeds, to say nothing of the equally busy and lively centres of Glasgow, Edinburgh and the prolific towns across the Border, it became apparent that two Training Establishments must be set to work.

Mytchett, although now inadequate for the large numbers of recruits, had for many years been the training centre for the military police. A visitor would have seen, amongst a collection of wooden huts, a large and imposing modern barrack building. This, however, had nothing to do with the police, but was the Army School of Hygiene which has been built right in the middle of the Military Police Depot.

There was no lecture hall and the probationers had their lectures in their own barrack huts. There was no gym and no swimming pool, but there was a N.A.A.F.I., a fine new building and about the only erection at Mytchett which could accommodate all the probationers at one time. Life for the probationer was strenuous, for if the Depot was small, it had a proud tradition to keep up. Most of the instructors, in the early days, were ex-Guardsmen who had joined the civil police. Discipline was up to Brigade of Guards standard.

Mytchett received the civilian volunteers who fulfilled the peace-time standards of height, weight and conduct. Many of them were soon commissioned and achieved distinction as officers of the Provost Service. A corporal instructor at Mytchett in 1940 was called before the A.P.M. of his formation in France in 1944 on a disciplinary matter. To his astonishment he found that this angry field officer was none other than a probationer who had been in his squad at Mytchett.

But another depot had to be found, preferably in the north. It was eventually discovered that at Northallerton, a country town within easy distance of Leeds, York and Newcastle, there was a civilian prison unused since 1922.

Forbidding as the building was, with its high walls, its cells and enclosed yards, it possessed all the requirements for an up-to-date, lively training establishment; and so it became. Major Sykes was appointed Commandant of this establishment which was provided with instructors who were all civil policemen who had served their time with the Brigade of Guards. There was a regular intake and output of 50 men per week.

The north-country men volunteering during these months for the Corps played their part in the "build-up" of the Corps—for example, the clerk who compiled the documents was, towards the end of the war, met by his former Commandant, when this ex-corporal had become D.P.M., Ceylon. Many other inmates of the "prison" at that time gained promotion to high rank.

During the period up to January, 1941, the establishment trained between 500 and 530 men.

In January, 1941, a reorganization of Mytchett took place. Major Sykes was appointed Commandant with the rank of Lieutenant-Colonel, relieving Major Kitwood and was himself succeeded at Northallerton by Major Dunkerly. To Mytchett with Lieut.-Colonel Sykes went half a dozen key members of the staff, including R.S.M. Baker, afterwards becoming Chief Instructor, at the new post-war Depot at Inkerman Barracks.

Towards the end of April, 1941, it became apparent that the intake allowed by the personnel Branch would not be sufficient to justify two depots. It was therefore decided to amalgamate them, and the depot at Northallerton became a military prison.

The number of trainees at Mytchett during July, 1941, rose to the record of 1,400. About this time the late Duke of Connaught made what must have been the last of his many inspections—as he had always taken a great interest in the Corps. During the next three years many distinguished visitors were shown around the Depot, which the Provost Marshal considered had now become one of the finest training establishments in the country.

In July, 1942, Lieut.-Colonel Sykes became D.P.M., First Army, later to take part in the Allied invasion of North Africa. His successor was Lieut.-Colonel Wright, then Chief Instructor at the Depot.

Earlier in the same year, as no more C.I.D. men could be spared for the army, a wing for training selected military policemen in S.I.B. duties was started at the Depot. Major Jack Ellis, one of the C.I.D. officers in the original S.I.B. detachment with the B.E.F., France, was the first chief instructor, and organized a first-class school which turned out some excellent material. Ellis later became Lieutenant-Colonel and D.P.M. in India and later Inspector at the Metropolitan Police Detective School, Hendon.

Lieut.-Colonel Wright remained Commandant until well after the end of the war; to trainees who had passed out he used to give this slogan, which aptly reflects the spirit of helpfulness taught at the Depot: "Guide the responsible, check the irresponsible, incarcerate the incorrigible!"

Early in 1941 small Depots were formed in each Command to train men for the new Vulnerable Point Wing. These Command Depots soon expanded, first to include Traffic Control recruits, later to train, in "Redcap" duties, selected men transferring from the T.C. and V.P. Wings into provost, and to run refresher courses for all three wings. They swiftly entered into a healthy rivalry with Mytchett and proved an indispensable addition to the limited resources of the mother-Depot.

During the Second World War many thousand officers and other ranks were trained at Mytchett alone. The reputation and achievements of the Corps, which are now history, are their own witness to the high standard, both of trainees and training, maintained at Mytchett and the other Depots.

★   ★   ★   ★   ★

PORTS POLICE

THE supervision of embarkation and disembarkation has always been an important military police function. In peace time a detachment of military police was stationed either at

Southampton or at the garrison town of Portsmouth. The mobilization scheme in 1939 provided two provost officers and seventy military police for duty in ports. Of these, one A.P.M. and thirty other ranks were allocated to Southampton and the remainder to other ports.

But the pilfering problems at ports and in transit soon became acute, and it was decided to form special Ports Police Companies with considerably extended duties and powers. The first of these were formed in 1941; and as sufficient provost sections were not available authority was given to supplement the deficiency with twenty-five Vulnerable Point Sections. These men were raised gradually and brought the total strength up to 16 Provost and 25 Vulnerable Point Sections—368 all ranks by February, 1942. An A.P.M. (Ports), Major T. G. Ruttledge, was appointed.

A Special Investigation Section for Ports was formed under Captain J. W. Rignell, with H.Q. at Liverpool, in January, 1942. A further section was added on 15th November, 1943, and the total strength amounted to 5 officers and 40 other ranks. Owing to the growth of shipping on the North-East Coast, a Ports Provost Company was authorized for service at those ports on 22nd January, 1942.

In March, 1942, numbers were allotted to Command and Ports Provost Companies. This affected the latter as follows:—

North-East Ports Provost Company became 174 (Ports) Provost Company.

Bristol Channel Ports Company became 175 (Ports) Provost Company.

North-West Ports Provost Company became 176 (Ports) Provost Company.

Scottish Ports became 177 (Ports) Provost Company.

The preparation of the North African expedition in the early autumn of 1942 and the gradual resumption of activity at Southampton led to the formation at that port of 178 and 179 (Ports) Provost Companies. The latter was allotted to the North African Force and the former remained at Southampton for duty at South Coast ports. As preparation for the invasion of the Continent grew and the importance of the Port of London was recognized, 193 (Ports) Provost Company was formed and allotted to the South-East Coast ports. 181 (Ports) Provost Company was raised late in 1942 for duty in Northern Ireland, but was withdrawn in April, 1943, mobilized and sent to Italy.

The War Establishment of the Ports Provost Companies on VE Day was 28 officers, 1,371 other ranks.

The success of the ports police owed much to the wide experience and ability of Lieut.-Colonel Ruttledge, who had served with the provost service with distinction in the Great War, and in Northern Ireland between 1919 and 1922.

Eleven Ports Provost Companies were raised for service overseas. All but two of these were formed from men belonging to existing home ports provost companies. Two companies were formed from surplus sergeants of other units, largely from the Royal Artillery: this was an experiment which proved very successful, the two units in question going to the British Liberation Army at the end of 1944. The distribution of these eleven companies was as follows:

2 North Africa (subsequently Italy).

3 Italy.

5 British Liberation Army.

1 Singapore.

Throughout the war military convicts and prisoners were sent home and handed over to the ports provost companies for disposal. The numbers were usually small, only once rising to over 100 in any quarter up to the end of 1944. The following year, however, 1,120 came home. Thanks to good discipline, embarkation duties produced few troubles. Many millions of men were handled at the various ports, mainly without incident. The major task performed by the ports provost companies was now the prevention and detection of pilferage of stores in course of shipment overseas. This crime, prevalent as it has always been in peace time, grew to alarming proportions during the war.

The Ministry of War Transport set up pilferage committees at many ports and the ports provost officers attended their meetings. At Glasgow for over a year the A.P.M. sat as chairman of the port pilferage committee. The number of arrests by military police for pilferage at home ports was as follows: 1942, 796; 1943, 671; 1944, 1,210; 1945, 771. Of these 40 per cent. were Merchant Navy personnel, 30 per cent. belonging to the Armed Forces and a similar percentage were stevedores. About 32 million tons of military stores were shipped or discharged through home ports and were given military police protection.

It will be seen that the duties of the ports police expanded greatly during the Second World War; upon them fell responsibilities for security (not the normal function of the military police), and for an unrelenting vigilance against sabotage and pilfering of essential war supplies—which, unchecked, would have seriously crippled our war efforts. Overseas particularly their duties covered not only the fighting men but all civilians, civilian vehicles and shipping within the port areas; they undertook the duties of harbour and river police and, together with the S.I.B., had to search ships, crews, and crews' quarters. They had to learn their powers, the meaning of the various markings on packages and crates, the tricks to which dishonest stevedores might resort to avoid detection, and something, at least, of the construction of a ship.

These exacting tasks the ports police performed with a devotion and ability which matched that of the other wings of the Provost Service. That their efforts were successful in preventing a very great deal of pilferage is evident from the numerous complaints, voiced by commercial undertakings, of the alarming extent of this evil and the enormous losses sustained. No such great losses fell upon the War Department or the Air Ministry.

A.T.S. Provost

IN 1941 the Auxiliary Territorial Service was placed under partial Military Law, making auxiliaries liable to Sections 40 and 41 of the Army Act. As a result it was decided in the same year to form a Provost Wing composed of A.T.S. auxiliaries. A call for volunteers met with a good response and courses of instruction in provost duties for selected officers and other ranks began at the C.M.P. Depot at Mytchett in December, 1941.

The first allocation of A.T.S. Provost was made to Home Commands in February, 1942, when fifteen N.C.Os. began duty in London and twelve in Edinburgh. A.T.S. Provost Officers were appointed to the Staff as D.A.P.Ms. and Staff Lieutenants.

The immediate effect of the introduction of the A.T.S. Provost Wing was a striking improvement in the discipline and dress of the members of the A.T.S. when out of barracks. The appearance of A.T.S. "Redcaps" in the streets did not pass without some comment by the general public, but the concensus of opinion was one of admiration for their smart appearance and fine example.

At railway stations the A.T.S. Provost made full use of their opportunities and ability to help and advise service men and women. At a London terminus late one November night three infantry sergeants with full kit and evidently just returned from the Far East approached an A.T.S. patrol for advice about accommodation at the Union Jack Hostel, explaining that they were going to a demobilization centre for release. When told what the accommodation would cost it transpired that their funds were insufficient and a hurried and whispered conference by the patrol resulted in a loan being advanced to the sergeants to enable them to stay at the hostel for the night. After a lapse of several weeks, when the incident was almost forgotten, the senior member of the patrol received by letter repayment of the loan, together with profuse thanks.

A.T.S. Provost Wing in the United Kingdom has experienced a wide variety of duties outside its normal routine. Amongst them escorting German women prisoners of war captured in France, from South Coast ports to their camps, participation in a combined civil police and military raid on the Polish Army Camp in Norfolk from where it was suspected that the notorious Polish gaol breaker, Zobrowski, was receiving assistance. The A.T.S. Provost, whose task it was to search the women's quarters, were commended for the part they played in this raid, which resulted in the arrest and subsequent deportation of 56 Polish soldiers.

By the end of 1942 the strength of the A.T.S. in Middle East had reached such proportions that it was decided to form a Provost Wing there. Accordingly, in December of that year, the first party of A.T.S. Provost, consisting of Junior Commander MacDermott, Subaltern Wigmore and Sergeants Franklin, Lewis, Maynard and Dickinson, sailed from the United Kingdom to the Middle East. The first duty of this party on arrival was to recruit and train auxiliaries selected from those already serving there; these were mostly Palestinian, and training was carried out at the C.M.P. Depot at Almaza.

In addition to routine street patrols, there was the continual search for native A.T.S. absentees. Of the many duties the A.T.S. Provost Wing in Middle East was called upon to perform, those of the anti-smuggling patrols were, perhaps, the most interesting. Large numbers of troops and A.T.S. indulged in smuggling arms, jewellery, cosmetics, wines and spirits and miscellaneous army property from Egypt into Palestine.

On one occasion a member of the A.T.S. Provost Wing in Egypt arrested an A.T.S. sergeant suspected of being a member of the Stern gang and successfully escorted her to Jerusalem.

In the wake of the Army of Liberation in North-West Europe there came the first part of the A.T.S. Provost Wing of 21st Army Group. This party, under the command of Junior Commander Buckle—later to become A.P.M. A.T.S. at H.Q., B.A.O.R., consisted of Company Sergeant-Major Bodel, Sergeants Lewin, Woodhall and Bowles, three corporals and fifteen lance-corporals. They disembarked in France on 11th August, 1944. After a short period of duty at the A.T.S. Port Staging Camp at Vaucelles, the detachment moved to Brussels and sections were established at Antwerp, Ostend and Calais, with a further section staffing a civilian internment camp at Vilvoorde.

Policewomen of the A.T.S. guarded Mrs. Joyce, wife of "Lord Haw-Haw." In September, 1945, a section was specially formed to provide guards, court ushers and escorts for women prisoners during the Belsen trials.

A.T.S. Provost on the Continent found themselves saddled with many extraneous duties in addition to their normal routine.

Principal among these was the provision of escorts for German women prisoners attending war crime trials from various parts of Europe, guarding prisoners throughout the trials and escorting them to places of execution or internment, searching German women employed at military establishments, participation in brothel raids in conjunction with military police and raids on displaced persons camps in an effort to suppress the black market activities of the inmates.

The formation of the A.T.S. Provost was an experiment, but one which amply justified itself, and the Corps has become justly proud of the "Sister" Wing. They had indeed no easy task, but from the outset they performed much-needed and often troublesome duties exceedingly well.

CHAPTER XII

CORPS ASSOCIATIONS

"Broken Circle" Prisoners-of-War Fund

THE history of the "Broken Circle" Prisoners-of-War Fund is a story of an effort by a few developing into an organization which was to become an institution of great importance to prisoners of war.

4th Divisional Provost Company, on the initiative of their O.C., Captain Adrian Stokes, began in 1940 to send parcels of comforts and food to men of the unit who had been made prisoners of war that year.

In the same year the Provost Marshal, Sir Percy Laurie, sent a contribution of £150 to the funds of the Red Cross Society to send food parcels to C.M.P. prisoners of war.

The scheme inaugurated by 4th Divisional Provost Company had been such a success that it was decided to extend its scope, and Captain Stokes, as organizing secretary, then formed the C.M.P. Prisoners-of-War Society at Mytchett; in July, 1941, the balance of the fund raised by Sir Percy Laurie, a sum of £225, was handed over to this new organization. By August, 1941, over 200 members of the Corps had been posted as missing and, of these, some 120 had been definitely reported as prisoners of war.

The Society adopted the title and sign of the "Broken Circle," the sign of the 4th Division, to symbolize the plight of the few broken away from the main body.

The aim of the "Broken Circle" was to send in rotation a parcel of comforts one month, followed by a parcel of cigarettes and, in the third month, books and games. The parcel containing comforts was to be sent as from the prisoner's next-of-kin in order to help those relatives who would wish to send really good parcels and who, because of their circumstances, could not afford to do so.

In May, 1942, the "Broken Circle" was sending out something like 300 parcels of clothing and comforts quarterly besides arranging for parcels of cigarettes and books in the intervening months.

The fighting in the Western Desert, followed by the withdrawal to El Alamein, led to a large increase in the numbers of prisoners of war. Parcels destined for Italian camps caused much difficulty throughout. Many never reached their destinations at all and those that were delivered took many months to arrive.

The "Broken Circle" was never able to do anything for the

large number of men in Far East camps. News of about a hundred of these prisoners came through their next-of-kin, but no arrangements for the dispatch of parcels to individuals could be made. Even the Red Cross could only send limited and irregular supplies. The W.V.S. working parties provided a seemingly inexhaustible stock of knitted comforts of all kinds and sizes.

After the war one section of the correspondence remained in the hands of the Organizing Secretary—the letters of thanks and appreciation written by the released prisoners and their next-of-kin, and these letters, bound in a volume together, are now a much prized memento.

Captain Stokes was ably assisted by a willing band of helpers, not the least of whom was Mrs. Samuel, of Crowborough, the Assistant Honorary Secretary, upon whom fell most of the work involved.

The Council formed to conduct the affairs of the "Broken Circle" was composed:

President: Lieut.-General Sir Ronald Adam.

Chairman: Brigadier Sir Percy Laurie.

Honorary Treasurer: S. T. Dade, Esq.

Honorary Organizing Secretary: Mrs. Ernest Kleinwort.

Honorary Assistant Secretary: Mrs. Edward Samuel.

Council: Lieut.-Colonel J. N. Cheney, Lieut.-Colonel W. H. Diggle, Lieut.-Colonel W. D'A. Hall, Lieut.-Colonel C. T. O'Callaghan, Lieut.-Colonel P. J. T. Pickthall, Major L. R. Isherwood, Major W. R. Norman, Captain A. E. Stokes, Lady Laurie, Mrs. W. H. Diggle, Mrs. W. D'A. Hall, The Hon. Mrs. W. R. Norman, Mrs. C. T. O'Callaghan, Mrs. N. C. M. Sykes.

The sum of £16,752 15s. od. (after deduction of law costs) remained to the credit of the Fund at the end of the war and, following an order for disposal of that sum given by the High Court (Chancery Division) was shared among 217 ex-P.W. claimants.

★   ★   ★   ★   ★

THE CORPS OF MILITARY POLICE OLD COMRADES ASSOCIATION

THE Old Comrades Association for the Corps came into being in 1927. On the outbreak of war in 1939 the assets of this Association were frozen and all activities suspended, but in March, 1941, Lieut.-Colonel Mark Sykes, Commandant of the Depot, inaugurated the "Old Comrades (War) Association." The objects of the Association were to:

(i) Help members to find civil employment by setting up an office, when funds permitted, to keep in touch with employers of all types of labour.

O

(ii) Help members and their families financially by means of loan or grant.

(iii) To promote a lasting bond of friendship between past and present members of the Corps.

The subscription for life membership—there was no provision for annual subscriptions—was fixed at ten shillings, and the administration of the Association was conducted from the Depot.

At the end of the war the membership totalled 6,472 and the general fund stood at £5,183 19s. 5d.

Membership of this Association numbered 13,247 at 30th June, 1950, and total funds amounted to £4,101.

To overcome legal difficulties, a new association, known as the Royal Military Police Association, was formed on 15th June, 1946. This third and new association, which was designed to cater for the post-war entrants to the Corps and the members of both the "War" and "1927" Associations was formally inaugurated in March, 1947.

Branches have been established in London, Glasgow, Salisbury, Birmingham, Leeds, Bradford, Hull, Manchester, Cardiff, Aldershot, Durham, Lincoln, Northern Ireland and the Home Counties. These branches, formed under the general supervision of the D.P.Ms. of Commands, are administered by civilian committees (who are represented on the Central Benevolent Fund Management Trustees Committee by area representatives) and were originally financed with a grant of £25 each by the Central Committee; this was later increased to £50 from General Funds.

The branches have done splendid work; many pleasant reunions and social functions have been held. They have been instrumental in securing employment for ex-members of the Corps and, among their other activities, appeals for financial assistance have been treated with sympathy and understanding.

★   ★   ★   ★   ★

R.M.P. Central Benevolent Fund

THE first meeting of the Corps of Royal Military Police Central Benevolent Fund was held at the R.M.P. Depot, Mytchett, on 1st February, 1944, with Major-General J. Seymour Mellor, the Provost Marshal and founder of the scheme, in the chair. Also present were Lieut.-Colonel B. D. Armstrong, D.P.M. to the Provost Marshal, Lieut.-Colonel E. F. L. Wright, Commandant of the Depot, and the following officers and Warrant Officers of the Depot Staff: Major R. K. Chiesman, Second-in-Command; Captain G. Bice, Administrative Officer; Captain (Qrmr) W. Taylor, Quartermaster; R.S.M. W. H. Lobley, and

C.S.M. A. Naish. General Mellor became first President for the term of his office as Provost Marshal.

Mrs. Samuel, Secretary of the "Broken Circle" Prisoners-of-War Fund, was, at the first meeting, invited to become an additional member, and her extensive experience in this kind of work was to prove invaluable as the scheme developed. Mrs. Samuel did a tremendous amount of work behind the scenes, and it was with great regret that the Committee received a letter of resignation from her in June, 1946.

During the first six months of the Fund's existence, £9,370 12s. 9d. was subscribed, and by the end of the first year £15,619 8s. 8d. For the second year the figure had, by the end of December, 1945, risen to £24,634 16s. 11d., a very creditable effort on the part of units still labouring under the stress of war, and at the end of the year 1946 the Fund had reached the magnificent total of £32,303 9s. 11d.

From the inception of the Fund in 1944 the position of Secretary and Treasurer had been held by Major G. Bice, the Administrative Officer of the Depot. Owing to the many official duties occupying this officer's attention, it was decided, in February, 1946, to appoint Mr. R. A. L. Belben as a full time paid Secretary, while Major Bice, in his *ex officio* capacity, continued as Treasurer.

On relinquishing his appointment as Provost Marshal, General Mellor was succeeded as President of the Fund in July, 1945, by Major-General I. D. Erskine.

PROVOST MARSHALS OF THE UNITED KINGDOM AND OVERSEAS THEATRES FROM THE 16th CENTURY TO 1948

THE UNITED KINGDOM

1511	Henry Guylford.
1540	Osborne Itchingham.
1544	Thomas Audley.
1547	Sir James Wylford.
1549	Sir Anthony Kingston.
1557	Sir Gyles Poole.
1569	Sir George Bowes.
1582	Barnaby Googe.
1588	Peter Crisp.
1589	G. Acres.
1589	Humphrey Coningesby.
1590	Thomas Nevinson.
1595	Sir Thomas Wylford.
1597	William Bredyman.
1598	Captain John Owen Tudor.
1600	George Newcomen (or Newgent).
1643	William Smith.
1663	Richard Thompson.
1719	John Martyn.
1723	Joseph Garton.
1726	James Howard.
1727	William Heath.
1727	John Martyn.
1734	John Amyott.
1747	Christopher Predham.
1796	John Hicks.
1829	Death of John Hicks and end of the office of Provost Marshal-General.
	Provost Marshals were then appointed locally and no records are available until:
1861	Major T. Trout.
1881	Captain W. Silk.
1885	Major C. Broackes.
1895	Major J. L. Emerson.
1898	Major J. W. M. Wood, M.V.O.
1910	Major R. J. A. Terry, D.S.O., M.V.O.
1914	Colonel F. Darling.
1918	Brigadier-General A. H. C. James, D.S.O., M.V.O.
1919	Brigadier-General E. R. FitzPatrick, D.S.O.
1919	Colonel H. S. Rogers, C.M.G., D.S.O.
1924	Colonel C. V. Edwards, C.M.G., D.S.O.
1928	Colonel G. T. Brierley, C.M.G., D.S.O.
1930	Colonel J. de V. Bowles, D.S.O.

1934   Colonel W. B. Hayley, D.S.O.
1938   Colonel S. V. Kennedy, M.C.
1939   Colonel W. B. Hayley, D.S.O.
1940   Major-General Sir Percy Laurie, K.C.V.O., C.B.E., D.S.O., J.P.
1943   Major-General J. Seymour Mellor, C.B.E., M.C.
1945   Major-General I. D. Erskine, C.B., C.B.E., D.S.O.
1948   Brigadier L. F. E. Wieler, C.B., C.B.E.

OVERSEAS

1611   Provost Marshal appointed in Colony of Virginia, America.
1678   Thomas Lott, India.
1679   Tileman Holt, India.
1687   Provost Marshal appointed in St. Helena (name unknown).
1703   Wheatley Garthorn, India.
1707   Ephraim Goss, India.
1727   George Tipping, Gibraltar.

Appointed under Section 74 of the Army Act in Overseas Theatres

1885   Egypt   Lieut.-Colonel J. H. Sandwich
1899   South African War   Lord Byng of Vimy (then Major Byng).
1914–15 B.E.F., France   Colonel The Hon. Vesey Bunbury, V.C.
1915–18 B.E.F., France   Brigadier-General W. Horwood.
1918–19 B.E.F., France   Brigadier-General H. S. Rogers.

B.E.F., France (Second World War)

1939–40 Colonel S. V. Kennedy, M.C.

B.L.A.

1943–45 Brigadier Bassett F. G. Wilson, O.B.E., M.C.

B.A.O.R.

1945–46 Brigadier J. N. Cheney, O.B.E.
1946   Colonel L. C. East, D.S.O., O.B.E.
1946–47 Colonel H. V. McNally, O.B.E.
1948   Colonel R. A. Leeson, M.B.E.

M.E.F.

1940–44 Colonel F. C. Bryant, C.M.G., D.S.O., O.B.E.
1944–46 Colonel L. C. East, D.S.O., O.B.E.

M.E.L.F.

1946–47 Colonel D. W. L. Melville, O.B.E., M.C.
1948   Colonel G. A. C. Peter, O.B.E., M.C.

INDIA

1943–45 Brigadier A. R. Forbes.
1945–46 Brigadier N. C. M. Sykes, C.B.E., M.C.
1946   Colonel H. Shuker (Indian Army).
1947   Colonel R. M. Davies (Indian Army).

P.A.I.C.

1942–43 Colonel A. R. Forbes.
1943–45 Colonel R. E. L. Warburton, M.C.
1945   Colonel Lovell-Payne.

North Africa A.F.H.Q./C.M.F.

    1942–44   Colonel N. C. M. Sykes, C.B.E., M.C.
    1944–45   Colonel A. R. Rees-Reynolds, C.B.E.
    1945–46   Colonel H. V. McNally, O.B.E.

C.M.F.

    1946–47   Colonel N. M. Blair, O.B.E.

S.E.A.C.

    1944–45   Colonel P. D. J. Waters, M.C.

A.L.F.S.E.A., S.E.A.L.F., FARELF.

    1946–47   Brigadier R. A. Leeson, M.B.E.
    1948   Colonel P. Godfrey-Faussett, O.B.E.

West Africa

    1944–45   Major T. A. J. Bennett.
    1945–47   Major J. G. H. Griffiths.
    1948   Major R. Davenport.

Deputy Provost Marshals at the War Office

    1941–43   Colonel P. J. T. Pickthall, M.C.
    1943–44   Colonel B. D. Armstrong.
    1944–45   Colonel C. T. O'Callaghan, O.B.E., M C
    1945–47   Colonel P. Godfrey-Faussett, O.B.E.
    1947–50   Colonel H. V. McNally, O.B.E.

ROLL OF HONOUR, 1939–1945

The names of dead officers could not always be traced through the personnel branches of their parent arms. It is therefore regretted that this list may be incomplete.

OFFICERS OF THE PROVOST SERVICE

Major C. E. Campion ...	General List
Major A. P. Cunningham	General List
Major K. M. Munro ...	Loyal Regiment
Major E. G. Theophilus	Worcestershire Regiment
Major E. C. Knowles Weston	Royal Armoured Corps
Capt. N. Boyle ...	General List
Capt. T. N. Burdes	Royal Northumberland Fusiliers
Capt. T. A. V. Denton	Dorsetshire Regiment
Capt. W. B. Gray	King's Regiment
Capt. G. Hayton	Worcestershire Regiment
Capt. K. N. Ingram ...	Somersetshire Light Infantry
Capt. G. A. Mounsey ...	General List
Capt. E. M. Nash	Gloucestershire Regiment
Capt. O. P. Ormrod ...	Royal Artillery
Capt. A. J. Phillips	Royal Artillery
Capt. H. G. Stoner	General List
Capt. I. A. M. Brown ...	Grenadier Guards
Lieut. F. J. Clarke	Northamptonshire Regiment
Lieut. W. Kirkwood	East Lancashire Regiment
Lieut. A. C. Morrison ...	General List
Lieut. E. J. Mowl	General List
Lieut. T. W. Sanders ...	Green Howards
Lieut. G. L. Wilson	Royal Fusiliers

WARRANT OFFICERS, NON-COMMISSIONED OFFICERS AND MEN OF THE CORPS OF ROYAL MILITARY POLICE

L./Cpl. L. C. Acford
Sgt. H. W. Adams
L./Cpl. R. Adams
L./Cpl. C. C. Adams
Cpl. H. Adams
L./Cpl. C. Addy
Cpl. A. H. Adkin
L./Cpl. R. Agar
Cpl. R. Agnew
L./Cpl. A. Agnew
L./Cpl. F. K. Alderton
L./Cpl. W. Alexandria
Cpl. J. P. Allengame
Pte. N. F. Allsop
L./Cpl. G. N. Ambler

Pte. D. H. Amor
L./Cpl. S Anderson
L./Cpl. E. C. Andrews
L./Cpl. K. G. Armitage
Pte. J. W. Armstrong
L./Cpl. D. Armstrong
L./Cpl. J. Arnold
L./Cpl. H. Ashdown
L./Cpl. J. W. Atkinson
L./Cpl. R. M. Austin
Cpl. J. Avery
L./Cpl. R. E. J. Avery
L./Cpl. J. Aylward
Pte. N. H. Bache
Sgt. A. J. Bailey

L./Cpl. A. T. Bailey
L./Cpl. R. G. Bailey
Pte. A. W. Bailey
Sgt. W. G. O. Baker
L./Cpl. H. Baldwin
C.Q.M.S. F. J. Ball
Sgt. L. Ball
Cpl. L. J. Ball
L./Cpl. L. B. Bannister
L./Cpl. D. Barber
L./Cpl. S. J. Barclay
Pte. I. Barclay
L./Cpl. S. Barker
L./Cpl. E. R. Barker
L./Cpl. F. Barlow
L./Cpl. L. R. Barnes
L./Cpl. W. A. Baston
Cpl. L. H. Bath
L./Cpl. F. T. Beagley
L./Cpl. W. D. Beal
L./Cpl. A. E. Beales
Pte. C. H. Beardsworth
Cpl. B. Bedwell
L./Cpl. J. Bell
Pte. J. Bell
Pte. T. Bellas
L./Cpl. P. H. Benjafield
Sgt. D. F. H. Benn
Pte. J. J. Benson
L./Cpl. D. Bentley
Pte. J. Biddulph
Pte. J. Bilton
Pte. J. A. Bird
L./Cpl. M. Bish
L./Cpl. R. A. Black
L./Cpl. H. A. Black
Cpl. D. Blacker
L./Cpl. C. H. Blood
C.Q.M.S. H. Blower
L./Cpl. L. W. Blow
L./Cpl. E. Boardman
L./Cpl. J. C. Boddy
L./Cpl. H. Bolton
Sgt. L. G. N. Bond
L./Cpl. J. P. Boon
Sgt. T. Booth
Pte. S. Booth
Cpl. E. G. Borgino
Pte. J. H. Bott
L./Cpl. F. W. Bottrill
L./Cpl. J. Boucher
L./Cpl. C. C. Boyes
Cpl. W. Bradshaw
L./Cpl. J. Brennan
Pte. A. J. Brent

L./Cpl. A. C. Brickwood
L./Cpl. W. Briggs
L./Cpl. S. J. Bright
Cpl. D. H. Brodrick
L./Cpl. J. F. Brooks
Pte. G. D. Brooks
L./Cpl. G. A. Broughton
Sgt. H. Browitt
Cpl. C. Brown
Sgt. J. G. Brown
L./Cpl. H. Brumhill
L./Cpl. H. C. Bull
L./Cpl. H. Bullard
L./Cpl. E. Bunce
L./Cpl. J. R. Bunce
L./Cpl. C. G. Bunting
Pte. J. A. Bunyan
L./Cpl. W. T. Burbridge
Cpl. E. T. Burke
L./Cpl. H. Burrell
L./Cpl. M. Bussey
L./Cpl. J. Butcher
L./Cpl. G. K. Butcher
L./Cpl. R. E. Butler
Sgt. C. Button
L./Cpl. H. G. J. Cable
Sgt. H. L. Gallaway
L./Cpl. N. A. A. Calthorpe
L./Sgt. F. Campbell
L./Cpl. T. H. Cann
L./Cpl. A. Cannell
L./Cpl. L. Cannon
L./Cpl. H. A. Cardy
Pte. J. F. Carley
L./Cpl. H. Carmichael
Sgt. R. Carnegie
L./Cpl. J. P. Carrigan
C.S.M. T. Carruthers
L./Cpl. W. Carson
L./Cpl. F. T. Carter
L./Cpl. P. M. Casburn
Sgt. R. S. Cashmore
L./Cpl. R. W. Caspell
L./Cpl. G. S. Chadbourne
Pte. A. J. Chandler
L./Cpl. J. Chaplin
L./Cpl. F. Chiverton
L./Cpl. J. P. H. Church
L./Cpl. S. Clapham
Pte. S. Clark
Sgt. A. E. Clarke
Sgt. E. C. Clarke
L./Cpl. L. Clarke
L./Cpl. R. Clayton
L./Cpl. R. A. Clegg

L./Cpl. J. H. Clift
L./Cpl. C. Clyne
Pte. R. Coates
L./Cpl. L. R. Cobbett
L./Cpl. P. L. Cobbold
L./Cpl. C. Cockerham
Cpl. L. W. Cole
L./Cpl. P. Coleman
L./Cpl. W. J. Collett
Pte. R. Colley
Sgt. P. G. Collin
Sgt. E. Colwill
L./Cpl. W. H. Combridge
L./Cpl. A. Connolly
L./Cpl. B. G. Cook
L./Cpl. J. W. Cooke
L./Cpl. S. T. Cooke
L./Cpl. T. Cooke
Sgt. J. E. Cornish
L./Cpl. S. R. Cornwall
Pte. J. W. Cotter
Pte. R. Cousins
L./Cpl. J. Cowan
L./Cpl. G. Cowan
L./Cpl. H. C. Cox
L./Cpl. W. Coy
Cpl. C. G. Crabb
Cpl. S. R. Crabb
Pte. S. Crackett
R.S.M. R. Cretsor
L./Cpl. K. Crighton
L./Cpl. C. S. Crisp
Cpl. B. Croft
L./Cpl. C. Cronin
L./Cpl. G. S. Crowe
Sgt. L. M. Crowley
Sgt. W. Cunnah
C.S.M. R. Curry
Sgt. H. Curtis
L./Cpl. W. P. Dalby
L./Cpl. R. G. Dance
L./Cpl. W. Danvers
L./Cpl. C. H. Davey
Pte. L. G. Davey
Sgt. A. Davidson
Cpl. C. M. Davies
Pte. E. Dawkins
C.S.M. S. E. Dawson
L./Cpl. J. D. Davies
L./Cpl. J. Davies
L./Cpl. S. A. Davies
L./Cpl. C. H. Davis
L./Cpl. C. Davis
L./Cpl. S. Dawson
L./Cpl. W. R. Dawson

Pte. C. H. Dean
L./Cpl. R. H. Denman
Pte. W. Devine
Pte. F. H. Diggle
S./Sgt. F. E. Dixon
L./Cpl. S. R. Dixson
L./Cpl. E. Dobney
L./Cpl. W. Dodds
Pte. H. W. Dodman
L./Cpl. A. Dormer
Cpl. W. Douglas
Cpl. J. Douglas
L./Cpl. G. A. Downes
Cpl. R. J. Downey
L./Cpl. E. P. Downham
Pte. R. Draper
L./Cpl. A. Drummond
L/Cpl. T. Draper
Sgt. C. F. Drew
L./Cpl. C. Dubock
L./Cpl. W. A. Duff
C.S.M. L. Dugdal
L./Cpl. A. D. Duke
L./Cpl. C. Duke
L./Cpl. R. Dunkley
Cpl. R. Dunn
L./Cpl. G. E. Dutton
Sgt. J. R. Duxbury
L./Cpl. R. S. Eastman
Sgt. A. Eastoe
L./Cpl. G. A. Eden
L./Cpl. T. Edwards
L./Cpl. A. E. Ellis
L./Cpl. C. Evans
Pte. F. G. Evans
Pte. A. E. Falconer
Cpl. W. L. J. Falkner
Sgt. A. M. Farquharson
Sgt. G. A. Farquhar
Cpl. A. E. Featherstone
Cpl. D. H. Fenn
Sgt. L. Ferrie
L./Cpl. H. H. Fields
Pte. O. A. Finchman
Pte. J. H. Finn
L./Cpl. W. J. Fisher
Sgt. J. Fisher
Pte. T. Fishwick
Pte. J. J. Fitzsimons
Pte. F. T. Flitter
L./Cpl. F. E. Flude
C.Q.M.S. H. Foster
L./Cpl. G. A. Foster
L./Cpl. D. L. Foster
Pte. W. Fox

L./Cpl. R. W. Francis
L./Cpl. W. Freeman
Pte. S. Freeman
Cpl. V. F. Frost
Pte. T. S. Froud
L./Cpl. H. M. Froud
Pte. B. Furzer
Pte. J. W. Gadsby
Cpl. R. Gadsby
Sgt. W. J. Gadsden
Sgt. F. Gallagher
Pte. C. W. Gallop
L./Cpl. R. Garnett
L./Cpl. R. D. Garrett
L./Cpl. C. F. Garrity
L./Cpl. W. Gavin
L./Cpl. H. M. Geldart
Pte. J. C. Gessey
L./Cpl. W. S. Gibbard
Pte. W. Gillett
Pte. C. R. Gillingham
L./Cpl. T. S. Gilmour
L./Cpl. F. Gilmore
L./Cpl. P. Gilruth
L./Cpl. J. L. Gladding
L./Cpl. A. R. Godfrey
L./Cpl. S. A. Gooch
L./Cpl. S. E. Goodman
L./Cpl. J. Googan
L./Cpl. W. R. G. Gook
L./Cpl. A. G. J. Green
C.S.M. J. N. Green
L./Cpl. F. W. Green
L./Cpl. H. C. Gooding
Pte. J. G. Green
Cpl. L. W. Green
L./Cpl. R. E. Greenfield
Sgt. H. M. S. Greenham
L./Cpl. F. Greenstreet
L./Cpl. J. Griffin
L./Cpl. W. L. Griffin
L./Cpl. D. Griffin
L./Cpl. S. C. Griffin
L./Cpl. H. A. Griffin
L./Cpl. E. R. Griffiths
Cpl. T. Griffiths
L./Cpl. A. W. Griggs
L./Cpl. P. Grimley
L./Cpl. J. Grundy
Pte. J. Gudger
L./Cpl. J. Gulliver
Cpl. J. E. Guthrie
L./Cpl. J. Hackett
L./Cpl. A. E. Hadley
Cpl. R. R. C. Hager

L./Cpl. H. Halev
L./Cpl. A. E. Hall
L./Cpl. A. Ham
L./Cpl. W. V. Hambrook
L./Cpl. W. Hanley
L./Cpl. C. H. Hanson
L./Cpl. H. G. Harden
L./Cpl. B. Harland
L./Cpl. G. W. Harper
Pte. E. Harrington
L./Cpl. H. Harris
L./Cpl. J. Harris
L./Cpl. J. C. Harris
L./Cpl. G. E. Harrison
L./Cpl. T. Harrison
L./Cpl. J. Harrison
Pte. A. Hartland
Cpl. A. Hartman
Pte. J. T. Haugh
Pte. E. C. Havies
Pte. G. Hawker
L./Cpl. R. F. Hawkins
L./Cpl. J. M. Hawkins
Pte. L. Hayhurst
L./Cpl. W. C. Hayward
Pte. H. C. Havwood
Pte. F. N. Hazell
L./Cpl. J. E. Hazzard
L./Cpl. H. Heighway
L./Cpl. F. J. Hellier
Pte. J. Henderson
Cpl. T. J. Henderson
L./Cpl. G. M. Hesketh
Sgt. J. A. Heughan
L./Cpl. G. H. Hewes
Pte. C. F. Hewitt
L./Cpl. E. W. Higgs
L./Cpl. H. Higson
L./Cpl. R. J. Hill
L./Cpl. G. C. Hilliard
Sgt. J. Hindmarsh
L./Cpl. J. T. Hinds
C.S.M. H. H. Hirst
L./Cpl. A. A. Hiscoe
L./Cpl. W. Hockey
Pte. F. G. Hocking
L./Cpl. J. W. Hodge
L./Cpl. C. A. Hodges
Pte. J. S. Hodgson
Sgt. E. C. Hodgson
Pte. E. H. Hodgson
Sgt. C. A. S. Holden
Cpl. A. E. Holleley
Sgt. S. Holme
L./Cpl. L. Holmes

L./Cpl. P. Holt
L./Cpl. A. E. Hookham
L./Cpl. E. J. Hookway
L./Cpl. D. Hopkin
L./Cpl. A. Hopkinson
Cpl. L. Hopson
L./Cpl. W. P. Hornblow
Cpl. L. M. Horner
Cpl. J. H. Horning
Pte. W. J. Hughes
L./Cpl. J. Hughes
L./Cpl. E. Hulme
L./Cpl. H. H. Humphrey
L./Cpl. J. H. Humphreys
Sgt. R. G. Hunt
L./Cpl. R. G. Hunt
Pte. G. Hurst
L./Cpl. C. M. Hutson
L./Cpl. S. D. Hyde
Cpl. K. S. Hymas
Pte. J. Hynd
R.S.M. J. Innes
L./Cpl. E. E. Ivins
L./Cpl. C. W. Jackman
Cpl. J. H. Jackson
L./Cpl. H. H. Jackson
Pte. A. A. Jackson
L./Cpl. L. James
Sgt. T. A. James
L./Cpl. H. T. James
L./Cpl. J. Jarvis
Pte. J. H. Jay
L./Cpl. G. M. H. Johnston
L./Cpl. D. Johnston
L./Cpl. R. Jones
L./Cpl. F. Jones
L./Cpl. C. I. Jones
Pte. J. E. Jones
L./Cpl. R. F. Jones
L./Cpl. A. R. Jones
L./Cpl. R. Jones
R.S.M. A. J. Jones
Sgt. J. G. Jones
L./Cpl. B. K. Jones
L./Cpl. P. W. Jones
L./Cpl. R. Jukes
L./Cpl. J. Keelty
L./Cpl. C. H. Kehr
Pte. E. S. Kelsall
L./Cpl. F. Kendrick
L./Cpl. H. Kenny
Pte. G. Kenyon
L./Cpl. W. Kersley
L./Cpl. C. L. Kettlewell
Cpl. R. K. Killick

L./Cpl. M. E. Kinchin
Pte. J. King
L./Cpl. J. F. Kingscote
Pte. F. G. Kirby
L./Cpl. A. Kirk
Pte. C. Kirkland
L./Cpl. J. E. C. Knibb
L./Cpl. G. D. J. Knights
L./Cpl. J. R. Laird
L./Cpl. T. Laking
L./Cpl. R. Lamb
Sgt. S. R. Langford
L./Cpl. A. Langley
Pte. H. J. Langton
L./Cpl. W. Latham
L./Cpl. B. C. Laurence
L./Cpl. W. R. Laurence
L./Cpl. F. Lawther
L./Cpl. F. Laycock
Cpl. S. M. Leaver
Sgt. E. Ledgard
Pte. W. H. Lee
L./Cpl. F. G. Leppard
L./Cpl. S. G. Lewis
L./Cpl. R. Lewis
Cpl. D. R. Lloyd
L./Cpl. W. A. Longhurst
L./Cpl. A. E. Lovell
Cpl. F. Lowe
L./Cpl. T. Lowe
Pte. P. R. Lucas
Pte. N. Lundy
Pte. G. Lynch
L./Cpl. C. Macarthy
L./Cpl. W. S. MacKenzie
L./Cpl. W. MacKenzie
Pte. I. Macleod
L./Cpl. K. M. Macphedran
Cpl. A. Macqueen
Cpl. M. Maher
L./Cpl. P. R. Maile
L./Cpl. S. F. Mansell
L./Cpl. D. Mapps
Sgt. F. Mardall
L./Cpl. D. F. Margeram
L./Cpl. G. Marr
Cpl. W. J. Marshall
Pte. I. Marson
R.S.M. J. Marston
Cpl. T. Martin
L./Cpl. R. Matthews
Pte. E. A. Mattocks
L./Cpl. J. Matts
L./Cpl. C. A. Mawby
L./Cpl. W. E. Mawdsley

L./Cpl. W. G. McBride
L./Cpl. E. McCarthy
L./Cpl. P. McCormick
L./Cpl. L. McDonald
S./Sgt. W. B. McGeachie
Pte. J. McGowan
L./Cpl. R. C. McGregor
L./Cpl. A. McKenzie
L./Cpl. G. McLeod
Sgt. D. McLew
L./Cpl. R. O. McQuillan
Pte. W. J. Meade
L./Cpl. L. A. Melligan
L./Cpl. T. C. Mellows
L./Cpl. E. R. Melthorpe
Pte. W. H. Merrifield
Sgt. S. W. Merritt
L./Cpl. R. H. Merry
L./Cpl. H. Metcalfe
Pte. D. J. Mileham
Sgt. F. W. Miles
L./Cpl. H. E. Milford
Pte. W. L. Millar
Pte. V. Miller
L./Cpl. H. Miller
Pte. L. C. Miller
L./Cpl. A. W. Miller
L./Cpl. H. E. Mills
Sgt. J. Mills
L./Cpl. E. Mills
L./Cpl. L. N. Milne
L./Cpl. W. Miners
Cpl. L. C. Mitchell
Pte. A. J. Mitchell
Pte. J. Mitchell
L./Cpl. W. H. Mollett
L./Cpl. R. H. Monagham
L./Cpl. G. Monk
L./Cpl. P. Montgomery
L./Cpl. W. Moore
Pte. C. G. Moore
Cpl. G. A. Morgan
L./Cpl. F. C. A. Morris
Pte. F. C. Morris
L./Cpl. F. J. Morris
L./Cpl. W. J. Morris
Cpl. J. A. Mortimer
Pte. L. A. Mouncer
L./Cpl. A. Mountfield
L./Cpl. E. T. Mulcahy
L./Cpl. B. Mullin
L./Cpl. D. P. Murphy
L./Cpl. F. F. Murray
Pte. G. E. Muttick
L./Cpl. C. J. Muttock

S./Sgt. L. Nash
Pte. A. H. Negus
L./Cpl. L. S. J. Nellor
Pte. J. Nelson
L./Cpl. R. O. Newall
L./Cpl. J. T. F. Newby
Pte. F. C. Newman
L./Cpl. S. E. Newton
Cpl. F. W. Nichol
L./Cpl. W. Nichol
L./Cpl. T. B. Nimmo
L./Cpl. G. W. A. J. Nisbet
L./Cpl. F. H. Nixon
Pte. F. J. Nixon
L./Cpl. A. A. Nobbs
Cpl. D. W. Norman
Cpl. W. Norman
L./Cpl. G. E. Normington
Sgt. W. W. Norrie
Pte. F. J. North
Pte. R. R. T. North
L./Cpl. J. D. Notman
L./Cpl. C. W. Oakenfull
L./Cpl. E. E. Oakley
Pte. R. O'Brien
Sgt. T. P. O'Keeffe
L./Cpl. J. C. Oldham
L./Cpl. E. S. Oliver
L./Cpl. K. Olley
L./Cpl. H. J. Onslow
L./Cpl. A. M. Orman
Sgt. L. E. Osborne
L./Cpl. J. G. Owen
L./Cpl. W. J. Padgham
L./Cpl. W. H. Palmer
L./Cpl. J. Parker
Cpl. E. J. Parker
L./Cpl. W. H. Parsons
Pte. T. R. Partington
Cpl. A. W. Partridge
L./Cpl. A. A. Passfield
Pte. T. O. Pate
Pte. L. Patmore
Cpl. G. Patton
Cpl. S. F. Paxton
L./Cpl. C. V. Payne
L./Cpl. T. Payton
L./Cpl. A. A. Peacock
L./Cpl. L. F. Pearce
L./Cpl. R. H. Pearson
L./Cpl. T. Peddar
Cpl. P. G. B. Peeke
Cpl. H. E. Pegrum
Pte. F. R. Penfold
L./Cpl. N. Penson

L./Cpl. H. Perkins
L./Cpl. R. J. Perry
L./Cpl. F. Phillips
L./Cpl. R. A. Phillipo
L./Cpl. J. A. Phimister
L./Cpl. W. Pike
L./Cpl. E. Pinder
L./Cpl. H. E. Pipe
L./Cpl. J. L. Pitts
L./Cpl. C. W. H. Pollock
L./Cpl. A. Poole
L./Cpl. C. Porter
L./Cpl. W. R. Powell
L./Cpl. V. A. Powell
Sgt. J. L. Pratt
L./Cpl. W. Pratt
R.S.M. J. Prescott
Pte. D. A. Preston
L./Cpl. C. Price
L./Cpl. A. E. Prior
Pte. R. S. Pritchard
L./Cpl. C. R. Pugh
Pte. F. Pullen
Cpl. J. Queen
Sgt. A. S. Quested
L./Cpl. A. T. Radmall
L./Cpl. B. A. Ralph
L./Cpl. W. Ransom
L./Cpl. G. W. T. Read
L./Cpl. A. F. Reading
Sgt. A. C. R. Redford
L./Cpl. T. H. Redhead
L./Cpl. D. T. W. Reynolds
L./Cpl. G. W. S. Rice
Pte. J. Richards
Pte. C. Richardson
L./Cpl. A. W. Ridgewell
Pte. H. W. Ridge
L./Cpl. R. T. Riding
L./Cpl. D. Rieman
L./Cpl. G. Rigby
L./Cpl. J. W. Rigby
L./Cpl. R. S. Robbins
Pte. C. Robbins
L./Cpl. W. I. Roberts
Sgt. A. Roberts
L./Cpl. E. Roberts
L./Cpl. R. Roberts
Pte. J. C. F. Robertson
L./Cpl. C. Robertson
L./Cpl. M. Robinson
Pte. A. Roffe
L./Cpl. G. H. Rogers
L./Cpl. J. Rogers
Pte. J. Rogers

L./Cpl. S. A. Roper
L./Cpl. T. A. Rose
L./Cpl. T. A. Rossiter
L./Cpl. F. Rotherham
Sgt. G. W. Rowe
L./Cpl. A. Royle
L./Cpl. H. F. Russell
L./Cpl. J. Rust
Pte. J. Rutherford
Cpl. W. H. Sadler
L./Cpl. W. W. Sang
L./Cpl. A. H. Sangwin
L./Cpl. J. Saul
L./Cpl. B. J. Saunders
Pte. J. Saunderson
L./Cpl. E. J. Savage
L./Cpl. A. Saveall
L./Cpl. E. Schafer
Sgt. A. R. Scott
L./Cpl. W. Scott
Pte. H. B. Scowen
Pte. C. E. Seabrook
Pte. W. Seaton
L./Cpl. J. Semaine
L./Cpl. W. Semple
L./Cpl. M. H. Senior
L./Cpl. J. Senior
R.S.M. J. Seward
L./Cpl. A. E. Sharp
L./Cpl. B. Shaw
L./Cpl. H. Shaw
Cpl. S. Shaw
L./Cpl. J. E. Shearing
Pte. V. S. Shepherd
Cpl. J. J. Shiels
Pte. J. Shilton
L./Cpl. J. Shread
L./Cpl. H. R. Shrimpton
Sgt. S. Shuttler
L./Cpl. F. S. Simkiss
Sgt. H. Simmonds
Cpl. A. Simms
L./Cpl. E. W. Simons
L./Cpl. J. W. R. Simpson
Cpl. T. Simpson
L./Cpl. J. I. Sinclair
L./Cpl. T. Smallwood
Pte. J. Smethurst
Pte. A. G. Smith
Sgt. E. A. Smith
Pte. E. R. Smith
L./Cpl. E. G. Smith
L./Cpl. J. A. Smith
L./Cpl. James Smith
L./Cpl. Joseph Smith

Cpl. P. W. Smith
Cpl. R. G. Smith
L./Cpl. T. E. Smith
Cpl. W. Smith
L./Cpl. W. E. Smith
Pte. W. J. Smith
Pte. F. H. Soanes
Pte. F. L. Southwood
Sgt. E. R. Southcott
R.S.M. E. Southom
L./Cpl. L. Spedding
Sgt. L. Spencer
Sgt. F. H. Springham
Pte. W. E. Staite
C.Q.M.S. T. Stannage
Pte. H. Stanton
L./Cpl. C. F. H. Starke
L./Cpl. F. C. Starkey
L./Cpl. J. S. Staveley
L./Cpl. J. Stead
L./Cpl. J. Steele
L./Cpl. J. D. Steele
L./Cpl. V. F. Stemp
L./Cpl. S. F. Stephen
L./Cpl. M. Stephenson
L./Cpl. W. Stephens
Cpl. J. Stevenson
Pte. W. H. Steward
Pte. T. Stewart
L./Cpl. D. W. Stewart
Pte. G. B. Stewart
Cpl. A. J. Stocks
Pte. J. Stoddart
L./Cpl. F. E. Stone
L./Cpl. J. Storrar
L./Cpl. R. Stringer
L./Cpl. C. R. Stubbs
L./Cpl. T. H. Stump
L./Cpl. L. A. Sullivan
L./Cpl. C. E. Sullivan
Pte. J. Sunderland
L./Cpl. D. Swain
L./Cpl. L. O. Swanwick
Pte. J. Sweeney
L./Cpl. J. Sweeney
L./Cpl. H. G. Sweet
L./Cpl. J. J. Swindall
L./Cpl. A. W. Swinger
Pte. C. F. Symonds
Cpl. S. Tait
Sgt. A. Tait
Pte. T. Tanner
Pte. J. H. Taplin
L./Cpl. R. W. Tarn
L./Cpl. W. Tatlock

Pte. E. L. Taylor
Sgt. H. Taylor (4909043)
L./Cpl. T. H. Taylor
Cpl. G. J. Taylor
Sgt. H. Taylor (2613491)
L./Cpl. R. K. Taylor
Cpl. H. Taylor
L./Cpl. J. A. Taylor
L./Cpl. E. P. Taylor
L./Cpl. W. F. Taylor
L./Cpl. A. J. Tearle
L./Cpl. E. K. Tearle
Pte. F. C. Tedder
Cpl. W. Teggarty
L./Cpl. T. J. Temple
L./Cpl. D. Theabald
Cpl. I. Thomas
L./Cpl. A. J. Thomas
L./Cpl. I. Thomas
L./Cpl. N. Thompson
Cpl. S. E. Thompson
L./Cpl. J. Thompson
Cpl. R. F. Thompson
Pte. S. Thompson
Pte. J. Thomson
Pte. P. B. Thomson
L./Cpl. H. J. Thorne
L./Cpl. A. G. Thornton
L./Cpl. J. T. Thurmer
L./Cpl. F. A. Thursting
L./Cpl. F. Tilbury
L./Cpl. H. Tillotson
Sgt. M. W. K. Tisdall
L./Cpl. J. Toates
L./Cpl. G. E. Toleman
L./Cpl. J. F. Tollervey
L./Cpl. C. Tomlinson
L./Cpl. T. G. Toogood
L./Cpl. S. G. Tooke
Pte. W. Topping
L./Cpl. T. Topping
L./Cpl. G. H. Tovey
L./Cpl. J. R. Toyne
L./Cpl. J. Tregenza
L./Cpl. E. Trick
Sgt. E. C. Trow
L./Cpl. C. F. Turner
Pte. R. F. Turner
Sgt. H. Turner
Cpl. W. G. Turner
Sgt. G. S. Tusler
Cpl. W. Tweedale
L./Cpl. D. Tweedale
L./Cpl. F. Twining
L./Cpl. T. A. G. Tyler

L./Cpl. G. F. Tyrrell
L./Cpl. J. Tyson
L./Cpl. A. J. W. Upton
L./Cpl. A. W. C. Vanner
Cpl. S. Varley
L./Cpl. A. C. Veale
L./Cpl. R. G. Veale
L./Cpl. F. Vessey
L./Cpl. E. Vickery
L./Cpl. W. Vincent
L./Cpl. V. A. Vowles
L./Cpl. G. W. S. Wakeford
L./Cpl. J. Walker
L./Cpl. A. Walker
Pte. A. Walker
Sgt. R. C. Walker
L./Cpl. C. H. Waller
L./Cpl. J. S. Walsh
Cpl. C. H. Walton
L./Cpl. J. Warburton
S./Sgt. T. R. Ward
L./Cpl. W. E. Ward
L./Cpl. S. R. Ward
Pte. J. F. Ward
L./Cpl. P. F. Ward
Pte. B. Watkins
Cpl. I. Watkins
L./Cpl. C. H. Watson
L./Cpl. J. J. Watson
Sgt. E. Watson
L./Cpl. R. W. Watton
Sgt. G. G. Web
Pte. F. C. Webb
Pte. B. R. Webb
L./Cpl. S. Weir
L./Cpl. A. J. Wellstead
Cpl. N. A. Westcott
R.S.M. E. J. Whalley
R.S.M. F. White
L./Cpl. J. W. White
L./Cpl. W. H. White
Pte. P. J. White

L./Cpl. C. Whitmore
Sgt. S. J. Whitsey
L./Cpl. A. R. Whittle
Sgt. E. Whitton
Sgt. J. D. Wigley
L./Cpl. J. Wilkinson
L./Cpl. A. G. Wilkie
Pte. T. N. Williams
L./Cpl. D. L. Williams
L./Cpl. D. I. Williams
L./Cpl. S. H. Williams
L./Cpl. V. V. Williams
Pte. G. H. Williams
L./Cpl. E. Williams
Sgt. C. J. Wilmot
L./Cpl. F. Wilson
Sgt. S. W. Wilson
Pte. A. J. Wilson
L./Cpl. G. Wilson
L./Cpl. J. H. Wilson
L./Cpl. E. Winship
Pte. A. G. T. Witney
Pte. S. P. J. Wolfenden
L./Cpl. J. Wood
L./Cpl. G. J. Wood
L./Cpl. G. A. S. L. Wood
Sgt. H. W. C. Wood
L./Cpl. J. E. Woodhouse
L./Cpl. G. F. Woods
L./Cpl. R. S. Woolterton
L./Cpl. H. A. Wright
L./Cpl. C. J. F. Wright
Pte. S. C. Wright
L./Cpl. R. Wroath
Pte. A. J. Wyatt
L./Cpl. R. E. Wyatt
L./Cpl. F. Yates
Cpl. L. Yates
Pte. L. G. Yates
Sgt. F. Young
Cpl. S. J. Young
Sgt. J. Zachariades

HONOURS AND AWARDS

OFFICERS OF THE PROVOST SERVICE

[NOTE.—* indicates also Mentioned in Despatches]

Companion of the Order of the Bath

Major-General I. D. Erskine, C.B.E., D.S.O.
Brigadier L. F. E. Wieler, C.B.E.

Order of the British Empire

C.B.E.

Major-General I. D. Erskine, D.S.O.,
Colonel M. Sykes, M.C.
*Colonel A. R. Rees-Reynolds

O.B.E.

*Brigadier Bassett F. G. Wilson, M.C.
*Brigadier J. N. Cheney
Colonel C. T. O'Callaghan, M.C.
*Colonel P. Godfrey-Faussett
*Colonel F. C. Drake, M.C.
*Colonel F. A. Stanley
*Colonel H. V. McNally
*Colonel N. M. Blair
*Lieut.-Colonel P. H. Fitzgerald
*Lieut.-Colonel J. R. Archer-Burton
*Lieut.-Colonel G. W. Ball
*Lieut.-Colonel W. M. J. Carruthers
*Lieut.-Colonel J. Corbett
Lieut.-Colonel A. P. Green
*Lieut.-Colonel F. H. V. Keighley
Lieut.-Colonel C. H. A. Sturge
*Lieut.-Colonel G. C. White
Lieut.-Colonel F. Wright
Lieut.-Colonel J. Harper

M.B.E.

Lieut.-Colonel W. Heddon
*Lieut.-Colonel R. A. Leeson
Lieut.-Colonel H. Purston
Lieut.-Colonel W. G. Steward
Major J. D. L. Buist
Major R. W. Cairns
Major D. Clitherow-Smith
*Major C. B. E. Cowie
*Major S. F. Crozier

*Major R. S. L. B. Dobson
Major H. C. Forbes
*Major R. A. Guild
Major W. A. N. Jones
*Major H. M. Knee
Major W. G. Lloyd
Major W. F. Pearson
Major F. R. Pollard
Major G. D. Lockett

*Major G. T. Saunders
Major J. R. Stewart
*Major S. A. Ralli
Major A. Taylor
Major E. P. Wedlake-Lewis
Capt. J. F. W. Barker
*Capt. W. P. Clarke
Capt. W. H. Cooper
Capt. J. G. Ellis
Capt. M. A. Fitz-Gibbon

Capt. J. K. B. Ingram
Capt. W. T. Jones
Capt. P. Mulheir
Capt. C. Potter
Capt. C. Wood
Lieut. H. F. German
Lieut. R. H. L. Posgate
Lieut. P. C. B. Rowe
Lieut. F. M. Willetts

The Military Cross

Major M. C. Chittock
Major Pearson
*Capt. P. L. Birch
Capt. T. H. C. Lee

Capt. R. E. L. Warburton
Lieut. J. E. Clark
Lieut. T. W. H. Wilson

The Military Medal
Lieut. M. Corragher

British Empire Medal
Capt. G. Agass

Royal Victorian Medal
Lieut. M. McLoughlin

Efficiency Decoration
*Major L. O. M. Collingwood   *Capt. G. C. D. S. Lowe

Mentioned in Despatches

Colonel F. C. Bryant, C.M.G., O.B.E.,
    D.S.O.
Lieut.-Colonel J. Innes
Lieut.-Colonel T. C. Irvine, M.C.
Lieut.-Colonel N. Pascall
Lieut.-Colonel F. G. Powell
Lieut.-Colonel G. R. G. Hart, M.M.
Lieut.-Colonel Sharp
Lieut.-Colonel E. A. Swinden
Lieut.-Colonel W. G. D. Softly
Major B. O. Allen
Major H. M. A. Baker
Major W. C. Baglin
Major J. C. Birts
Major S. H. Bond, M.C.
Major J. A. Bowden
Major E. A. Clark
Major H. Dale Glossop
Major L. C. Cook
Major H. E. Elsmore
Major D. G. Evatt
Major M. F. Good
Major J. P. Huffam, V.C.

Major J. G. E. Hope
Major J. B. Harris
Major B. Howse
Major J. G. Jarvis
Major A. G. Joslin
Major A. Keay
Major J. R. Langford
Major J. F. Marr
Major E. J. Price
Major H. N. Raban
Major B. G. Raine
Major D. A. C. Rasch
Major M. O. V. Renshaw
Major G. E. Sharp
Major P. Simmons
Major H. Taylor
Major A. R. Watson
Major J. G. Wilby
Major E. J. W. Wickens
Major L. C. Wood
Major F. W. Woods
Major L. Wren
Major M. M. Yorke

Capt. J. A. T. Bower
Capt. U. J. Breeze
Capt. J. Brennan
Capt. N. Bentham
Capt. C. Bennett
Capt. W. J. Bilyard
Capt. J. B. Coe
Capt. A. B. Carter
Capt. R. Davies
Capt. B. C. Durbin
Capt. C. F. Gough
Capt. B. L. Goulding
Capt. C. J. Harper
Capt. S. Hallatt
Capt. H. Heathcote
Capt. F. A. G. Hort
Capt. G. F. D. Jones
Capt. P. F. J. Kent
Capt. D. R. B. Kaye
Capt. H. de M. Leathes
Capt. A. J. Lewin
Capt. W. J. Locke
Capt. A. P. Mitchell
Capt. A. Marriott
Capt. W. J. Newman
Capt. K. J. North
Capt. K. W. North
Capt. G. F. C. Papworth
Capt. J. A. Pike
Capt. C. W. C. Roper
Capt. C. G. Rochon
Capt. W. F. Small
Capt. J. W. H. Shaw
Capt. K. W. Slack
Capt. G. D. Simpson

Capt. C. L. Smith
Capt. C. M. Starling
Capt. C. G. Traherne
Capt. R. N. I. Taff
Capt. T. Turley
Capt. F. Tuplin
Capt. C. Venables
Capt. P. C. Wardle
Capt. H. N. Whitehead
Capt. N. R. Winwood
Capt. W. E. Wickes
Capt. G. F. Wiggington
Lieut. E. F. Berry
Lieut. R. R. M. Bacon
Lieut. J. Blenkharn
Lieut. F. A. Connett
Lieut. H. V. Chapman
Lieut. G. C. Dentish
Lieut. H. J. Dibbens
Lieut. A. H. Edney
Lieut. L. M. Fourney
Lieut. J. R. Green
Lieut. W. Gilling
Lieut. V. E. Griggs
Lieut. J. B. Heathcote
Lieut. A. A. Rennie
Lieut. G. W. Iredell
Lieut. A. R. Kendrick
Lieut. A. W. Knowles
Lieut. E. Lemeing
Lieut. E. J. Mowl
Lieut. G. E. W. B. Pierpoint
Lieut. W. F. Smithen
Lieut. T. Sanderson
Lieut. T. E. Williams

It is much regretted that the names of some officers who received a decoration while with the Provost Service may not appear in the above lists. This is because from some of the smaller and more distant theatres of war adequate information was not made available.

WARRANT OFFICERS, NON-COMMISSIONED OFFICERS AND MEN OF THE CORPS OF ROYAL MILITARY POLICE

Order of the British Empire

M.B.E.

R.S.M. J. R. Bamborough
C.S.M. L. R. N. Bell
R.Q.M.S. J. Bell
R.S.M. R. E. Beer
R.S.M. G. G. Booth

C.S.M. A. J. T. Brassett
R.S.M. R. A. Cooksey
R.S.M. G. A. Corney
R.S.M. W. Glasby
R.S.M. J. W. Gilman

R.S.M. T. E. Green
R.S.M. E. R. Hall
C.S.M. F. S. C. Hodker
C.S.M. G. Marshall
R.S.M. T. E. Morgan
R.S.M. H. McLeod
R.S.M. J. Morrison
R.S.M. S. B. Osborn

C.S.M. H. W. Procter
R.S.M. J. Ramsey
R.S.M. S. H. Slater
R.S.M. L. Tubby
R.S.M. E. Turbitt
R.S.M. W. R. Wakefield
R.S.M. H. T. Wright

British Empire Medal

Sgt. J. B. Armstrong
Sgt. G. Agass
Sgt. J. E. Austin
L./Cpl. W. H. Ayres
Sgt. E. C. Bailey
L./Cpl. W. Ball
C.Q.M.S. W. E. Bennett
L./Cpl. E. R. Brennan
C.S.M. A. J. Brown
Sgt. F. C. Banks
Cpl. D. Birch
L./Cpl. G. Broadley
Sgt. A. V. Burge
S./Sgt. J. R. Burgess
Cpl. J. G. Carr
Sgt. S. C. R. Carter
Sgt. J. Charnock
C.Q.M.S. J. Cook
Sgt. H. F. Croway
Sgt. H. J. Cox
Sgt. W. R. Ede
Sgt. T. H. Edwards
Sgt. C. V. Edmondson
Cpl. J. F. Formon
Sgt. F. Green
C.Q.M.S. A. W. Grehan
Sgt. W. P. Gallant
Sgt. E. Hart
Sgt. C. V. Hearn
Cpl. L. R. Hockaday
Sgt. R. H. Holmes
R.S.M. J. H. Howarth
Sgt. A. L. Houghting
W.O.I G. F. Jenkins
Sgt. R. Kennedy
R.S.M. A. E. Hardy

Sgt. A. T. C. Lanning
Sgt. J. Lindridge
Sgt. O. C. Little
Sgt. R. G. Lucas
Sgt. W. J. Lynn
C.S.M. P. W. Maccullum
Sgt. H. E. Manning
S./Sgt. R. Mackenzie
C.S.M. W. T. Marlow
Sgt. H. Meakin
L./Cpl. H. Mellor
L./Cpl. S. Metcalfe
Sgt. H. Milne
Cpl. W. H. Mitchell
Cpl. E. T. Marchant
Sgt. W. H. Marshallsay
Sgt. R. H. Muggeridge
Sgt. J. Newnham
L./Cpl. R. B. Nunn
C.S.M. E. F. Peagram
R.S.M. J. A. Pearce
C.S.M. J. Piggot
Havildar Piru Mall
Sgt. J. Pringle
Cpl. W. E. Rowlatt
Sgt. W. L. Sargent
L./Cpl. J. Simpson
Sgt. W. A. Slater
Sgt. G. A. Smith
Cpl. H. Stead
Cpl. W. S. Taylor
Cpl. E. C. Thompson
C.Q.M.S. H. J. Thomson
C.S.M. C. R. Witney
Sgt. G. M. McRae

The Distinguished Conduct Medal

Cpl. H. Adams
L./Cpl. J. S. Allan
L./Cpl. A. B. Corbett

L./Cpl. J. Eeles
R.S.M. W. Glenister
L./Cpl. S. Naish

The Military Medal

Sgt. R. Armstrong
C.Q.M.S. A. Avery
L./Cpl. D. Beckett
Sgt. G. E. Birch
L./Cpl. G. W. Boulton
Sgt. B. S. Bowley
Cpl. F. R. Bunting
Sgt. W. T. Bullen
L./Cpl. G. A. Bunce
Cpl. F. E. Bradbury
Sgt. G. W. Brown
Sgt. W. I. R. Charles
Cpl. V. H. Clare
L./Cpl. F. L. Clark
Cpl. R. D. Colman
Sgt. H. A. Cooper
Sgt. R. Cox
L./Cpl. D. H. Crane
L./Cpl. H. V. Crofts
Sgt. E. L. H. Day
Sgt. C. T. Domican
L./Cpl. P. Donaghy
Sgt. A. W. Evans
Sgt. E. Evans
Cpl. C. W. Ellis
Sgt. P. W. A. Fewings
Sgt. V. Fisher
Sgt. J. Ford
Sgt. W. J. Gadsden
Sgt. R. W. Gibson

L./Cpl. W. Guthrie
L./Cpl. H. Green
Sgt. R. Jacklin
Sgt. E. L. Joualt
L./Cpl. J. F. Kingscote
Cpl. T. Laing
Sgt. R. Macleod
Sgt. D. M. E. Macgillicuddy
L./Cpl. A. Murphy
L./Cpl. W. Nicholson
Sgt. C. H. Port
Cpl. H. J. Patterson
Cpl. D. Quinn
L./Cpl. J. Rayner
L./Cpl. A. Redford
L./Cpl. T. Redhead
L./Cpl. P. Rounce
Sgt. H. J. Simpson
L./Cpl. C. L. Sawyer
Cpl. W. Smalley
Sgt. F. H. Springham
Sgt. J. H. Thake
Sgt. V. V. Tozer
L./Cpl. W. R. Thomas
Sgt. W. L. Watts
C.Q.M.S. R. Watson
L./Cpl. J. Welsh
Sgt. H. Wilman (and Bar)
Cpl. E. F. Workman

Mentioned in Despatches

[NOTE.—* indicates Mentioned twice]

L./Cpl. J. H. Abrahams
Sgt. W. J. Axtell
C.S.M. G. Abel
L./Cpl. A. G. Alsop
Cpl. H. Antonlades
Sgt. E. R. Ashton
L./Cpl. E. Attkins
Cpl. G. W. Attwood
L./Cpl. W. G. Anderson
Cpl. M. C. Adams
Cpl. F. R. Anderson
R.S.M. E. Anderson
N.K. Abaji Shinde
R.S.M. C. V. Aitken
Sgt. F. Arundale
R.S.M. J. H. Albertson
Sgt. R. Allen
Sgt. T. R. Allen

C.S.M. L. J. Alton
Sgt. G. S. Atkins
Sgt. J. V. Aspden
L./Cpl. W. Bagot
Sgt. R. W. Balory
Sgt. E. D. Barker
L./Cpl. R. E. Bensley
Cpl. F. W. Ball
L./Cpl. R. Beck
R.S.M. A. J. Bird
Sgt. C. Bird
L./Cpl. A. E. Bourne
L./Cpl. G. Brookshaw
Sgt. W. T. Bullen
L./Cpl. L. C. Burfield
Sgt. H. T. Butler
Sgt. B. Bridge
Cpl. F. G. Brown

C.S.M. W. Broadfield
Sgt. H. P. Boswell
Sgt. S. H. Bexon
Sgt. A. W. Bricknell
L./Cpl. H. Bailey
Sgt. R. G. Bailey
Cpl. J. Bailey
L./Cpl. W. E. Baines
Sgt. W. J. Bardwell
L./Cpl. A. Barker
Cpl. W. Barringer
Sgt. L. W. Barrett
Sgt. W. Barratt
L./Cpl. W. Barwell
R.S.M. L. W. Bealey
C.S.M. J. J. F. M. Bearpark
R.Q.M.S. J. Bell
Cpl. N. Bennett
L./Cpl. E. Bloxan
Sgt. W. Boston
Cpl. J. W. Boulter
Sgt. R. W. Boulton
Sgt. W. Boyle
Sgt. J. Brechin
Sgt. T. A. Brennan
Cpl. R. Brewster
L./Cpl. E. Brocker
L./Cpl. L. Brockwell
Sgt. B. Brown
L./Cpl. T. Brown
C.Q.M.S. W. E. Bennett
Sgt. A. V. Burge
A./Cpl. J. P. Brogan
L./Cpl. F. R. Blackwell
L./Cpl. W. J. Bowwater
L./Cpl. W. M. Brophy
L./Cpl. R. R. Burns
Sgt. A. K. Batt
C.Q.M.S. H. M. Billups
C.Q.M.S. A. Beddow
Sgt. W. D. Brown
Cpl. G. A. Bucher
Cpl. C. Butterworth
L./Cpl. J. A. Barlow
Cpl. R. C. Butler
Sgt. J. R. Bartholomew
Cpl. B. W. Bull
Sgt. J. Bailey
Sgt. A. F. Borland
Sgt. T. W. Brighton
Sgt. R. Brown
Sgt. G. H. Bryant
Sgt. C. Beard
R.S.M. R. S. Beer
Sgt. T. Bowden

Sgt. J. A. Bradshaw
R.S.M. M. R. Bradshaw
C.S.M. H. Burden
C.S.M. N. Bursell
Sgt. W. A. Butcher
Cpl. E. H. Chaffer
Sgt. A. W. Chesney
Sgt. R. A. Churchill
Sgt. W. G. Cockle
L./Cpl. G. A. Coleman
Cpl. J. Cooper
L./Cpl. B. W. Courtney
Sgt. H. T. Coy
Sgt. F. Cranshaw
Sgt. F. J. Chant
Sgt. A. E. Clinton
Sgt. T. R. Collins
Cpl. S. Carlton
Cpl. W. J. Carter
Cpl. C. B. Connett
C.Q.M.S. L. Cusworth
L./Cpl. H. Calthorpe
L./Cpl. L. P. Carrison
Sgt. D. Carstairs
Cpl. E. Caswell
L./Cpl. W. Catt
Cpl. E. Chapman
L./Cpl. N. Chiesnall
Sgt. A. R. Clarke
L./Cpl. E. Clarke
Cpl. H. Clarke
Sgt. H. Clayton
Cpl. A. J. Cogram
Sgt. A. T. Coleman
Cpl. N. L. Collins
C.Q.M.S. J. Cook
Cpl. N. Cooper
Cpl. R. H. Copsey
S./Sgt. H. W. Cornes
Cpl. W. A. C. Crees
Sgt. G. Crawte
L./Cpl. J. J. Curran
Sgt. G. Cussons
Cpl. E. J. E. Coulson
L./Cpl. J. Comins
L./Cpl. S. S. Curd
L./Cpl. C. G. Crabb
Sgt. J. B. Cartner
L./Cpl. C. C. Case
Pte. Castleton
C.S.M. G. A. Cutts
C.Q.M.S. E. Y. Cleave
Sgt. H. Cogger
L./Cpl. R. Coulson
Sgt. T. L. Carless

Sgt. J. A. Crawford
Sgt. T. J. Chivers
R.S.M. C. W. G. Carrington
R.S.M. G. A. Corney
Sgt. R. G. Dandy
Sgt. R. S. Drinnan
Sgt. J. Drysdale
Sgt. C. Duncan
Sgt. W. Duff
L./Cpl. J. Dunlop
Sgt. L. D. Deal
Sgt. J. A. S. Durno
Cpl. C. Day
C.Q.M.S. G. Dalgliesh
R.S.M. T. L. A. Daniels
R.S.M. S. C. Darville
L.W.O.I. S. Daughtrey
Sgt. J. E. Davies
Sgt. M. B. Dawson
L./Cpl. T. Dixon
Cpl. A. Dooley
L./Cpl. A. Dunford
Cpl. F. G. Dunnett
Cpl. W. Dyer
Cpl. F. Derbyshire
A./Cpl. W. G. Dossett
L./Cpl. G. Davidson
L./Cpl. C. J. Dighton
L./Cpl. R. Dunsire
Pte. Dinsdale
R.S.M. R. Davies
Sgt. J. J. Davies
*Sgt. J. Dabbs
L./Cpl. F. Davis
Sgt. C. T. Domican
Sgt. G. H. F. Dunne
R.S.M. C. Dodd
Cpl. J. E. Easton
Pte. G. G. Edwards
Sgt. G. O. Evans
Sgt. J. Evins
C.Q.M.S. E. Eborn
C.Q.M.S. L. H. Eaton
Sgt. G. W. Edwards
C.Q.M.S. H. J. Edwards
R.S.M. E. G. Evans
Sgt. J. Eccles
C.Q.M.S. T. H. Eaton
Sgt. V. Fisher
L./Cpl. G. S. Fotheringham
L./Cpl. A. G. Fultcher
L./Cpl. R. L. Flint
Pte. E. Felton
Cpl. J. Faulkner
R.S.M. F. Fisher

C.Q.M.S. S. J. G. Fitzie
Pte. J. Forth
Cpl. J. L. Ferguson
Cpl. E. J. Ford
L./Cpl. C. Faulkner
L./Cpl. T. E. Frape
L./Cpl. R. French
Sgt. A. J. Foley
Sgt. W. V. Fox
Sgt. E. Farrar
L./Cpl. H. Feasby
L./Cpl. J. V. G. Ford
Cpl. J. Ford
Sgt. A. R. Gibbons
Cpl. E. H. Gilbert
Sgt. W. T. Gilbert
L./Cpl. E. C. Gooch
L./Cpl. F. Grimshaw
L./Cpl. E. Grimshaw
L./Cpl. M. Glen
S./Sgt. G. Gorman
L./Cpl. A. H. Gibbs
Sgt. E. F. Goldsmith
Sgt. J. Goodfellow
Cpl. T. Gothort
Cpl. J. Grant
R.S.M. T. E. Green
L./Cpl. G. F. Gregson
L./Cpl. G. A. Grohman
Sgt. T. J. Groves
C.S.M. H. Gillespie
Cpl. E. J. Green
C.S.M. T. A. Gibson
Sgt. W. P. Gallant
Sgt. J. F. Gallagher
L./Cpl. J. E. T. Guthrie
R.S.M. T. Gordan
Sgt. E. R. Goode
C.S.M. M. L. Guirard
R.S.M. R. Gungry
C.Q.M.S. H. J. Goddard
Sgt. F. H. Gardener
Sgt. C. Gaskell
Sgt. A. W. J. Godfrey
Sgt. J. Green
L./Cpl. A. Gaines
Sgt. R. W. Gibson
C.S.M. T. A. Gibson
L./Cpl. W. M. K. Gordon
C.S.M. G. C. Grigg
Cpl. F. J. T. Godley
Sgt. A. E. Harry
Sgt. A. Hiscock
L./Cpl. T. H. Hargood
L./Cpl. A. L. Harris

Sgt. L. Harrison
Sgt. F. V. Hill
L./Cpl. W. H. Holland
Sgt. W. R. Howard
Sgt. C. Howell
C.S.M. T. H. Hoggett
Sgt. A. Hacking
C.S.M. J. Hainsworth
Cpl. J. M. Hatcher
L./Cpl. A. Haxton
R.S.M. W. Hazlewood
Sgt. F. V. Hunwicks
Cpl. A. J. Hooksted
R.S.M. G. Heaps
Cpl. F. E. Hearn
L./Cpl. A. Hill
Cpl. P. C. Hillsdon
Cpl. J. F. Hind
Sgt. A. W. Hitchens
Cpl. L. F. Holgate
Cpl. A. Holleley
Sgt. R. T. Howard
R.S.M. J. Howarth
R.S.M. J. H. Howarth
Cpl. F. Howden
C.S.M. R. Huggins
Cpl. R. Hughes
L./Cpl. G. Humphreys
L./Cpl. C. A. Hurworth
Cpl. E. C. Huxtable
Cpl. L. J. Hoar
Cpl. W. Hutchinson
L./Cpl. H. L. Hearn
L./Cpl. G. Harper
Sgt. J. Howard
Sgt. A. C. Hardacre
R.S.M. A. E. Hardy
Sgt. C. A. Holden
Sgt. E. T. Horton
L./Cpl. A. E. Howell
Sgt. F. Hardy
R.S.M. F. E. Hartwell
C.S.M. R. R. Horne
Sgt. W. B. Hart
Sgt. C. High
Sgt. H. J. Hatcher
Sgt. F. H. Holmes
C.S.M. W. J. Houlton
L./Cpl. G. F. Harrington
Sgt. E. Hart
L./Cpl. A. Humphreys
Sgt. M. Herd
R.S.M. C. F. Holmes
Sgt. J. Hoult
Sgt. H. Howard

Sgt. B. G. D. Henshaw
L./Cpl. E. G. Haroy
Cpl. E. H. Hind
Cpl. F. G. Isted
Cpl. F. H. Jones
S./Sgt. J. R. Jones
Sgt. C. Jarvis
L./Cpl. C. Jeffreys
Cpl. F. T. Jenkins
R.S.M. G. F. Jenkins
C.Q.M.S. F. Jennings
L./Cpl. F. Jevons
Sgt. C. W. Jones
Pte. D. Jones
Cpl. E. R. Jones
R.S.M. E. R. Jones
Sgt. L. Jones
Cpl. J. Jones
Cpl. E. Johnson
L./Cpl. E. Jones
Sgt. C. M. Jumeau
C.Q.M.S. F. J. Jennings
Cpl. R. Jacklin
Cpl. E. Keitch
Sgt. R. Kennedy
C.S.M. H. H. King
Sgt. T. Kennedy
C.Q.M.S. C. A. Kenward
L./Cpl. S. Kearns
Cpl. F. E. N. Keen
Sgt. W. Kellett
Sgt. S. Kent
L./Cpl. J. King
Cpl. L. G. King
Havildar Kharke Thapa
L./Nk. Kushal Khan
R.S.M. P. King
Sgt. H. Knaggs
Sgt. M. Klopper
L./Cpl. E. Latham
Sgt. W. Lessells
L./Cpl. F. K. Lambourne
Cpl. G. E. Lawrence
Sgt. G. J. Lawson
R.S.M. H. J. Leaney
L./Cpl. S. Lee
L./Cpl. S. G. Lewis
L./Cpl. R. A. Lockwood
Cpl. A. W. Lake
L./Cpl. J. Laycock
Cpl. T. Leonard
Sgt. E. Leach
Sgt. A. H. Lee
L./Cpl. K. Leake
L./Cpl. E. Lewis

Cpl. J. Linbridge
R.S.M. H. Loveland
R.S.M. W. Miller
L./Cpl. A. Macdonald
Sgt. F. Martin
Pte. E. W. Mawson
Sgt. G. Mellor
L./Cpl. A. N. Millar
L./Cpl. T. Milner
L./Cpl. A. R. Morgan
L./Cpl. F. C. Morris
Sgt. C. Mortimer
Cpl. L. Morton
L./Cpl. A. E. Mawson
L./Cpl. T. R. Mabbott
Cpl. L. A. Males
L./Cpl. F. Mallery
Sgt. P. Marsh
Cpl. E. Marshall
Cpl. L. A. Mason
C.Q.M.S. W. McEvoy
C.Q.M.S. F. S. Morgan
Sgt. W. B. Morgan
Sgt. W. G. Morris
Sgt. N. Mounsey
Cpl. L. Murphy
L./Cpl. T. Mackenzie
L./Cpl. N. Murray
L./Cpl. W. Murray
Sgt. R. Malone
L./Cpl. R. Mann
C.Q.M.S. R. S. Marsden
L./Nk. Mehar Singh
L./Nk. Mohd Ajlam
Sgt. G. M. McRae
Sgt. A. McGaw
Sgt. G. Marshall
C.Q.M.S. S. Matthews
Cpl. C. W. Mitchell
Cpl. A. Moore
Sgt. N. Martlew
L./Cpl. J. Marsh
L./Cpl. W. H. Mackman
Cpl. R. W. Martin
Sgt. A. D. Matthews
L./Cpl. W. McAlpine
Sgt. H. J. McDonald
C.S.M. J. G. McDowell
R.S.M. T. McNair
C.S.M. J. E. Melton
C.S.M. E. E. Merralls
Sgt. F. Mooney
Sgt. J. Moore
Cpl. R. I. Morris
Sgt. V. A. J. Morris

L./Cpl. R. Mornmore
Sgt. A. R. Newall
L./Cpl. S. Newlands
L./Cpl. A. A. Nobbs
S./Sgt. J. Nelson
*W.O.I J. Natress
Cpl. A. J. Neilson
Sgt. S. A. Nicholson
Sgt. J. J. Nolan
Sgt. J. Nelson
Sgt. W. P. Nicholas
Sgt. A. F. North
Sgt. H. H. Osborn
R.S.M. S. Osborn
L./Cpl. P. C. Ovenden
Sgt. F. C. H. Owen
Cpl. W. Oliver
L./Cpl. L. F. Paling
L./Cpl. W. J. Parry
Pte. L. Patchett
Cpl. R. Paterson
Cpl. L. W. Phillips
Sgt. A. J. Pember
Sgt. A. H. Plow
Cpl. P. Percival
L./Cpl. R. Phillips
Cpl. W. J. Poole
L./Cpl. F. S. Pack
L./Cpl. F. G. Paice
L./Cpl. D. Pattison
Sgt. J. W. Peacock
Cpl. E. Pearce
R.S.M. J. A. Pearce
Pte. L. Pearson
L./Cpl. J. Pilcher
L./Cpl. R. W. Pinkney
L./Cpl. R. E. Pollard
L./Cpl. R. P. Pope
Sgt. A. W. Powell
L./Cpl. W. Porter
A./Sgt. J. D. Pirt
A./Sgt. G. S. G. Porter
L./Cpl. G. Petty
C.S.M. C. Pyke
C.Q.M.S. E. C. Pearce
Pte. L. T. Paradine
R.S.M. C. J. Parker
C.Q.M.S. R. E. Preece
L./Cpl. H. Prest
L./Cpl. J. Pringle
W.O.II C. C. Pudner
R.S.M. J. Piggott
Sgt. W. Paulson
C.S.M. W. Priestley
R.S.M. H. R. Peach

C.S.M. R. C. Povey
Sgt. J. E. Pritchard
Sgt. S. R. Quinton
L./Cpl. J. B. Robinson
L./Cpl. J. K. Reason
L./Cpl. J. L. Rigby
Cpl. H. G. Robinson
L./Cpl. D. Rudda
Sgt. R. W. Rogers
Cpl. R. E. Rushton
L./Cpl. C. Reeder
Pte. W. Reed
Sgt. H. G. S. Reed
Sgt. K. M. Ratcliffe
Sgt. P. T. Richards
Cpl. R. F. Rawlingson
L./Cpl. J. Roberts
L./Cpl. E. W. Robinson
Cpl. H. Richardson
Cpl. C. S. Runacres
R.S.M. C. W. Roper
L./Cpl. F. W. Rothwell
Cpl. H. R. Ryder
Cpl. G. J. Rogers
C.Q.M.S. R. G. Risbridger
Sgt. J. O'B. Riley
C.Q.M.S. H. R. Ryder
R.S.M. C. Rogers
R.S.M. C. Rogerson
Sgt. A. E. H. Rowley
*C.S.M. H. Rushton
Sgt. R. Salter
Cpl. L. G. Scott
L./Cpl. A. Shaw
L./Cpl. G. R. Spratt
A./W.O.I A. G. Steward
L./Cpl. K. C. Storry
A./Sgt. J. Swindells
Cpl. G. H. Smith
Cpl. J. E. Smith
L./Cpl. A. C. Silverthorne
L./Cpl. P. C. Stimpson
L./Cpl. A. Street
C.Q.M.S. R. C. Street
Sgt. M. W. Smallwood
Sgt. V. F. J. Smith
Sgt. C. Sonnino
Sgt. R. G. Stote
Sgt. H. Shaw
Pte. C. E. Salter
R.S.M. J. Simpson
A./C.Q.M.S. M. Somerfield
L./Cpl. H. Secconbe
C.S.M. A. D. Saunders
Subedar Sisram

R.S.M. H. Schumacher
*R.S.M. A. E. P. Secker
Sgt. E. N. Scovell
Cpl. A. Scullion
L./Cpl. E. G. Simpson
L./Cpl. G. R. Slade
Cpl. G. E. Smith
L./Cpl. A. Scorah
Sgt. W. J. Sharman
Cpl. J. Sharpe
Cpl. A. C. Shorrocks
L./Cpl. C. J. Shute
*Cpl. G. S. Simpson
L./Cpl. T. H. Skerry
Sgt. E. P. Slade
Cpl. A. A. E. Smith
Cpl. R. Smith
L./Cpl. W. H. S. Spencer
Sgt. L. Stacey
Cpl. L. R. Stevens
Sgt. J. H. Swift
S./Sgt. S. L. Smith
C.S.M. H. Smith
C.Q.M.S. S. Straw
W.O.I A. Swinburn
C.S.M. S. McC. Seddon
Cpl. R. L. W. Sach
*R.S.M. L. Sanderson
Cpl. W. B. Sandford
Sgt. V. A. L. Sergison
L./Cpl. J. A. Sheffield
L./Cpl. F. T. Singleton
*R.S.M. S. H. Slater
C.S.M. A. T. Smith
Sgt. F. H. Springham
C.Q.M.S. J. H. Stott
R.S.M. J. Sutcliffe
L./Cpl. L. E. Swancott
L./Cpl. J. C. Southall
Cpl. R. Taylor
Cpl. H. E. Townsend
Cpl. J. Treleaven
Cpl. C. T. Turvey
S./Sgt. W. Tate
Sgt. A. Taylure
C.Q.M.S. A. G. Tomlin
L./Cpl. E. Thompson
Sgt. H. T. Truscott
C.S.M. E. C. Tombs
L./Cpl. C. R. Teasdale
W.O.II T. G. V. Thompson
L./Cpl. J. Tomlinson
Cpl. G. E. Twyman
Cpl. J. R. Thompas
Cpl. J. R. Thomas

R.S.M. H. F. Tudgay
Cpl. S. Turner
L./Cpl. P. Talbot
C.Q.M.S. J. S. Tarling
*Cpl. J. C. Turvit
*R.S.M. R. A. J. Tickel
Sgt. G. Titmas
L./Cpl. A. Todd
L./Cpl. Trowbridge
L./Cpl. T. P. Turnbull
Sgt. E. Turner
C.S.M. J. Thomas
Sgt. J. S. Taylor
Sgt. S. Vaughan
Sgt. D. Vernon
Cpl. A. W. Vallens
L./Cpl. W. Vaughan
Sgt. O. Wilson
Sgt. E. Wyer
Cpl. L. W. Walton
Sgt. A. F. Ward
L./Cpl. G. Wigglesworth
Cpl. G. F. Wilson
Sgt. J. Wood
R.S.M. R. W. Ward
C.S.M. R. White
A./Sgt. D. S. Wheatley
A./Sgt. F. J. Ward
A./Sgt. G. B. Welford
L./Cpl. V. Williams
L./Cpl. S. Winskell
L./Cpl. H. A. Wilson
Cpl. T. Walsh

L./Cpl. F. Walton
Cpl. E. W. Welsby
Cpl. J. F. R. Whitie
R.S.M. H. T. Wright
L./Cpl. S. Woolley
Cpl. W. Whitehead
Cpl. H. A. Wilkins
Sgt. D. Wilkinson
L./Cpl. S. Williams
Sgt. H. Wilman
Cpl. W. K. Wilson
Sgt. A. Wood
R.S.M. G. E. B. Wood
Cpl. J. Wood
Cpl. H. J. Williams
Cpl. R. P. Williams
Sgt. J. Wright
Sgt. A. W. White
L./Cpl. A. Waller
L./Cpl. J. A. Wilesmith
Sgt. E. Williams
L./Cpl. H. Wilman
C.S.M. H. P. Watts
L./Cpl. W. L. Watts
Cpl. N. A. Wescote
Sgt. J. T. Williams
Sgt. J. J. Woledge
Cpl. T. W. Woodcock
C.S.M. F. H. Woods
Sgt. F. Wright
L./Cpl. J. Young
C.S.M. J. Zetner

INDEX